For my wife and our
beautiful daughters.

Acknowledgements

It is frequently said that writing a book is a lonely, solitary act. Perhaps that is true in some cases, but it certainly wasn't the case with this book. If this book is any good, it's because of all the hard work, patience and feedback provided by everyone who helped along the way.

I owe a huge thank you to…

Michael Nolan, who invited me to write a book in the first place. Thanks for being willing to gamble on me.

Margaret Anderson and Gretchen Dykstra for overlooking my horrible misuse of punctuation and for generally making it sound like I know how to write much better than I do.

Danielle Foster for making the book look so fantastic, and putting up with a few last minute adjustments. Also, to Rose Weisburd, Joy Dean Lee, Aren Straiger, Mimi Heft, Rebecca Winter, Glenn Bisignani and the rest of the team at New Riders for helping make this book come to life.

Ed Merritt, Brad Frost, Guy Podjarny, Henny Swan, Luke Wroblewski, Tom Maslen and Erik Runyon for their incredible contributions. By being willing to share their expertise and experiences, they've made this a much richer book than it would have otherwise been.

Jason Grigsby for making sure I wasn't making things up along the way and for providing valuable (and frequently hilarious) feedback and encouragement throughout. Not only is Jason one of the smartest people I know, but he's also one of the most helpful. I'm thankful to be able to call him a friend.

Aaron Gustafson for writing such a great foreword. I've been learning from Aaron since I first started working on the web—to say I'm humbled and honored that he agreed to write the foreword is an understatement.

Stephen Hay, Stephanie Rieger, Bryan Rieger, Brad Frost, Derek Pennycuff, Ethan Marcotte, Chris Robinson, Paul Thompson, Erik Wiedeman, Sara Wachter-Boettcher, Lyza Danger Gardner, Kristofer Layon, Zoe Gillenwater, Jeff Bruss, Bill Zoelle, James King, Michael Lehman, Mat Marquis, Nishant Kothary, Andy Clarke, Ronan Cremin, Denise Jacobs and Cennydd Bowles for the insights, feedback and encouragement they provided along the way. This book owes a great deal to their collective awesomeness.

IMPLEMENTING
RESPONSIVE
DESIGN

Building sites for an anywhere, everywhere web

Tim Kadlec

New Riders

VOICES THAT MATTER™

IMPLEMENTING RESPONSIVE DESIGN:
BUILDING SITES FOR AN ANYWHERE,
EVERYWHERE WEB
Tim Kadlec

NEW RIDERS
1249 Eighth Street
Berkeley, CA 94710
510/524-2178
510/524-2221 (fax)

Find us on the Web at: www.newriders.com
To report errors, please send a note to
errata@peachpit.com

New Riders is an imprint of Peachpit, a division of
Pearson Education.

Copyright © 2013 by Tim Kadlec

Project Editor: Michael J. Nolan
Development Editor: Margaret S. Anderson/
Stellarvisions
Technical Editor: Jason Grigsby
Production Editor: Rebecca Winter
Copyeditor: Gretchen Dykstra
Indexer: Joy Dean Lee
Proofreader: Rose Weisburd
Cover Designer: Aren Straiger
Interior Designer: Mimi Heft
Compositor: Danielle Foster

Find code and examples available at the companion
website, www.implementingresponsivedesign.com.

ISBN 13: 978-0-321-82168-3
ISBN 10: 0-321-82168-8

9 8 7 6 5 4 3 2 1

Printed and bound in the United States of America

To everyone whose conversations, both in person and online, inspired the discussion that takes place in this book. This is an awesome community we have going and I'm proud to be a part of it.

My mom and dad for their love and words of encouragement throughout.

My lovely daughters for reminding me it was ok to take a break every once in awhile to play and for filling each day with laughs, kisses and hugs.

And my incredible wife, Kate. This book, and anything else I do that is any good, is a direct result of her loving support and encouragement. There are no words powerful enough to express how thankful I am for her.

Foreword

By Aaron Gustafson

A few years back, photography legend Chase Jarvis smartly observed that "the best camera is the one that's with you." It was a mildly shocking assertion at the time, but it rings true: the perfect shot is rarely planned. Rather, it sneaks up on you.

Perhaps the light is perfectly accentuating the fall foliage on your late afternoon stroll. Or perhaps your infant daughter just pulled herself up on two legs for the first time. In moments like these, it doesn't matter that your Leica is sitting on a shelf in the other room or that you left your Rebel in the car—what matters is that you have a camera, however crude, in your pocket and can capture this serendipitous and ephemeral moment.

Riffing on Jarvis's idea, Stephanie Rieger has made the case that the best browser is the one you have with you. After all, life is unpredictable. Opportunities are fleeting. Inspiration strikes fast and hard.

Imagine yourself as a cancer researcher. You've been poring over a mountain of research for months, looking for a way to increase interferon-gamma production in an effort to boost the body's natural ability to inhibit the development of tumors. Your gut tells you that you're close to an answer, but it's just out of reach. Then one morning, while washing the exhaustion off in a nice hot shower, it hits you. Eureka! You think you've got it—you just need to refer back to that paper you read last week.

Dripping, you leap from the tub and land on the bath mat. Without even grabbing a towel, you pluck your mobile off the counter and head to the journal's site, only to find yourself re-routed to a "lite" version of the website that shows you only general information about the publication and prompts you to subscribe.

Your fingers leave wet streaks across the screen as you frantically scroll down the page to find the inevitable link to "View Full Site" and click it. As the screen loads, you find yourself hovering 30,000 feet above a patchwork quilt of a homepage that could only have been designed by committee.

Several minutes of pinching, zooming, and typing later, you finally find the article, only to discover it's a PDF and nearly impossible to read on your tiny screen. Dejected, you put down the phone and sulk back into the shower, hoping it will wash away your disappointment.

Sadly, browsing the web on mobile is all too often a frustrating (and occasionally dehumanizing) endeavor. But it doesn't have to be.

In the pages of this very book, my friend Tim clearly outlines the steps you can (and indeed should) take to ensure that the sites you help create offer each user a fantastic experience, tailored to the capabilities of her device and respectful of her time, patience, and data limits. Don't let his small town charm fool you: Tim knows this stuff inside and out. I learned a ton from this book and I know you will too.

Aaron Gustafson is the author *Adaptive Web Design: Crafting Rich Experiences with Progressive Enhancement* (Easy Readers, 2011)

Contributions

The discussion around responsive design moves fast. Very fast. This book is intended to be a synthesis of the incredible discussion that is taking place in our community about this topic. To that end, I asked several people if they would be willing to contribute short pieces based on their recent projects and research.

Here are the contributions you'll find, in order of their appearance in the book:

- Vertical Media Queries, by Ed Merritt, page 70
- Performance Implications of Responsive Design, by Guy Podjarny, page 102
- Small Phone, Big Expectations, by Tom Maslen, page 136
- Responsive Design and Accessibility, by Henny Swan, page 141
- Selling Responsive Design, by Brad Frost, page 159
- RESS in the Wild, by Erik Runyon, page 210
- Beyond Layout, by Luke Wroblewski, page 242

Each of the seven contributors featured are experimenting with the cutting edge of responsive design. They're implementing the techniques discussed in this book, and pushing the discussion forward. I'm incredibly honored to be able to include their contributions—contributions based on hard-earned experience—in this book.

Contents

CHAPTER 10: LOOKING FORWARD   255

CHAPTER 1

THE ANYWHERE, EVERYWHERE WEB

Only an arrogant man would believe he could plan a city; only an unimaginative man would want to.   —JOHN KAY

The Web is an incredibly unstable environment.

New operating systems emerge daily. Browsers are iterating faster than ever. On any given day we encounter larger devices, smaller devices, devices with incredibly powerful web browsing capabilities, devices with very limited browsers, devices with touch screen control, and devices with trackpads and keyboards.

While new devices emerge, older devices and browsers remain in use. Technology may be evolving at an incredibly rapid pace, but that doesn't mean that the neighbor down the road is intent on keeping up. A new device may be released, only to be cancelled a few months later.

There are few rocks to cling to. What's true one day may not be true the next. The result of all of this is chaos.

● *Form factor*
The size, configuration, and physical characteristics of a device.

But that's the fun part. Chaos breeds confusion, but it also breeds innovation and creativity. As new *form factors* hit the market and browsers continue to push the boundaries, the number of applications and situations we can build for grows exponentially.

The Web is universal. It is ubiquitous. Unlike any medium that has preceded it, the Web can adapt to any screen and any context. It is inherently flexible and malleable.

This chapter will discuss:

- The rapidly increasing diversity of connected devices
- Factors such as display size, network speeds, standards support, input methods and context
- The impulse to create a separate experience for each situation (a losing battle)
- The need for responsive design and what it means to be responsive
- What you can expect from the remainder of the book
- Who should read this book
- How code is formatted in this book

Where we went wrong

Watching my infant daughters was an enlightening experience. Whenever they were given a new toy, they'd try to play with it the same way they played with their old toys. They searched for familiar traits, links that tied the old with the new. Only after using the new toys in that manner for a while would they discover all the new things they could do.

This makes sense: the past is known, the future is unknown. We embrace familiar *mental models*. We opt for the safe and familiar over the risky and new. The problem is that *basing the future on past experiences limits the evolution of new ideas and media.*

The Web has been no exception.

As designers, we've tried to recreate our control of the printed page on the Web. This mindset is reflected in the way we've created websites for our clients. We've targeted a specific browser. We've optimized for a specific width. We've implemented hack after hack to ensure that we can create identical experiences cross-browser and cross-platform.

We've done everything we can to put ourselves in control, but the fact remains that we were *never* in control: on the Web, *users are in the driver's seat.*

Users choose the browser they want to use. They can zoom in and out to increase or reduce the font size. They can maximize the browser or view it at half the available width. They can opt for a top-of-the-line device or a three-year-old model that's sitting on the discount shelf. They can use the default browser on their device or install one of the many freely available alternatives. They can view a site while on the go or while relaxing in the comfort of their own home. They have control over where, and how, they access our content.

As designers, we're starting to figure this out, but our assertions that a site has to look the same in all situations are evidence that we haven't quite let go. Nothing has made this more obvious than the incredible explosion of new devices and platforms emerging onto the scene.

● *Mental model*
A person's thought process about how something works in the real world.

The devices are coming, the devices are coming

I'm a paranoid traveler. I don't fear flying, but I fear missing my flight. As a result, I often find myself sitting in the waiting area of a crowded airport with some time to kill.

So I people watch. More specifically, I look around to see what kinds of devices people are using. On a recent trip, I was flying out of a small, rural airport, the kind of airport where it takes you five minutes to check in your bags. There were maybe twenty-five people in the waiting area, but oh the gadgets! There were Android phones and iPhones and, yes, a few older feature phones. Someone was reading on a Nook. Nearest to me, a lady with a few strands of gray in her hair was reading the news on her iPad.

We boarded the plane. After the stewardess gave the OK to turn electronic devices on again, people started reaching into their bags. That same lady, now sitting two rows in front of me in an aisle seat, reached into her carry-on and pulled out a Kindle to do some reading. When we landed she deposited the Kindle back into the bag, and pulled out an iPhone.

This one lady, over the course of about five hours, interacted with content on three different devices. It was a small reminder of just how many non-PC devices have emerged on the scene in recent years.

As of the end of 2011, there were 5.9 billion mobile subscriptions world-wide—87 percent of the world's population at the time.[1] That number is poised to grow significantly: global shipments of smartphones surpassed that of PCs for the first time ever in the fourth quarter of 2010.[2]

Web browsing on mobile devices is escalating as well, due in part to the much improved web experience that a phone can now provide. Early on, the few phones that could access the Internet did so only in a rudimentary fashion. The hardware was very limited. Devices were incapable of understanding more than a very simplified version of XML called Wireless Markup Language (WML).

---

1   "The World in 2011: ICT Facts and Figures" at www.itu.int/ITU-D/ict/facts/2011/material/ICTFactsFigures2011.pdf

2   "Smartphone sales pass PC sales for the first time in history!" at www.smartonline.com/smarton-products/smarton-mobile/smartphones-pass-pc-sales-for-the-first-time-in-history/

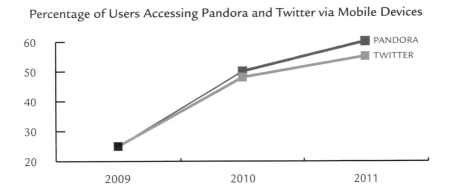

Percentage of Users Accessing Pandora and Twitter via Mobile Devices

Figure 1.1 Percentage of mobile traffic for Twitter and Pandora from 2009 to 2011.

Networks were brutally slow. Screen sizes were small and the methods of input were awkward and clumsy.

Mobile devices evolved though, as technology tends to do. A few more capable devices started coming out in the early 2000s, but it wasn't until the original iPhone was announced in 2007 that the game was completely changed. Suddenly, you could experience the "full Web" on your mobile device. The browsing experience of the iPhone and subsequent smartphones blew everything that came before it out of the water.

There's a funny thing about giving someone an experience that doesn't suck—they end up using it more often. Pandora, an online music-streaming site, received 60 percent of its traffic in 2011 from mobile devices; that number was 25 percent in 2009. In the same time frame, the social site Twitter has grown from 25 percent to 55 percent mobile (**Figure 1.1**).[3] In fact, traffic to mobile websites in general increased by a whopping 600 percent in 2010.[4]

Mobile phones may be at the head of the class, but they're far from being the only kind of device causing disruption. Tablets, currently led by Apple's iPad, are bridging the gap between phones and laptops. They offer the portability of a smartphone while sporting screen real estate akin to a small laptop. It is estimated that by 2015 sales of tablets will be in the neighborhood of $49 billion.[5]

---

3 "Mobile Devices Drive More Than Half of Traffic to Twitter and Pandora" at http://therealtimereport. com/2011/10/21/mobile-devices-drive-more-than-half-of-traffic-to-twitter-and-pandora/

4 "Smartphone market drives 600% growth in mobile web usage" at http://news.bango. com/2010/02/16/600-percent-growth-in-mobile-web-usage/

5 "Tablet Market May Surge to $49 Billion" at www.businessweek.com/technology/content/apr2011/ tc20110418_512247.htm

Internet-enabled TVs are still a relatively youthful market, but with major players such as Google and Apple tossing their hats into the ring, the potential is there for them to take off in the very near future. In the meantime, gaming devices such as the Microsoft Xbox 360 and Nintendo Wii come with built-in browsers, enabling users to view the Web right on their TV screens.

E-book readers, largely dominated by the family of Amazon Kindle devices and the Nook from Barnes and Noble, are also coming with built-in web browsers. The browsing experience is perhaps less refined and elegant than it is on a tablet, smartphone, or PC, but don't let that fool you into thinking people aren't using them. In this era of nearly ubiquitous connectivity, the best browser is the one you have with you.

Add all this up and it's easy to see that websites need to be usable on more devices than ever before. Each kind of device brings its own combination of constraints and capabilities.

Display size

Display size has always been variable, but at least we used to be able to antici-pate where we were headed. In 1984, the original Macintosh computer was released sporting a 512 × 342px resolution. As time went by, the resolution size steadily increased. Ten years later, in 1994, the Apple Multiple Scan 17" Dis-play was released, bringing with it a 1024 × 768px resolution.

Things were quickly shaken up though. Mobile devices that could connect to the Internet started to become available. When the iPhone brought a 320 × 480px resolution onto the scene in 2007, we could no longer guarantee that resolution sizes would become increasingly larger.

Looking over the landscape today, you'll find popular devices ranging from 280px wide to 1920px wide. The rug has been pulled out from underneath us—there is no standard resolution.

Network speeds

Latency
The delay in time as data is sent from one point to another.

The speed of the network in use can have a tremendous impact on users' web experience. Unfortunately, network speeds vary dramatically. One visitor might be on a very high-bandwidth wired connection; the next might be connecting on an EDGE mobile network with terribly low speeds and horrible *latency*.

Some devices and carriers let users create mobile hotspots with their phones so they can connect to a mobile network using a laptop. Smartphones are fully capable of connecting to Wi-Fi networks just as desktop computers do. The correlation between device and network has weakened. We can still make a guess, but it's far less accurate than it once was.

Standards support

Thanks to the increased number of platforms, browsers, and devices, competition is at an all-time high. New standards and features are being implemented at a faster rate than ever before.

This increased pace of evolution unfortunately causes as much chaos as it does stability. The word "support" is used very loosely. It's not a Boolean property—there are degrees. Many browsers support the same feature, but use a slightly different syntax. Others support only some parts of a standard. Still others, the worst culprits, manage to mix standards together with their own proprietary implementations, creating a muddled mess of syntax.

Further muddling the situation are the many cutting-edge devices that sport browsers with limited standards support. Consider the uber-popular Kindle. While the Kindle is primarily used as a reading device, it also comes with a built-in browser. The browser, as with the e-books on the device, is displayed using e-ink—so everything is grayscale.

While not quite as bad as say, Internet Explorer 6, the Kindle's browser isn't exactly what you'd call "top of the line" in terms of standards support. That does not mean that people don't use it. While it can be tempting to treat browsers with limited standards support as second-class citizens, that perspective is unacceptable because some devices that fall into that category are in fact brand new and of high quality.

Input method

For a long time, we enjoyed relative stability in the way people interacted with their computers. The keyboard has been around since the typewriter, and the mouse has been around since the Apple Macintosh came out in 1984. (Actually, the mouse has its origins as far back as the 1950s, but it was an obscure method of input until it came integrated with the Macintosh.)

It seems to be a recurring theme, but mobile shook that up a bit. Suddenly, input methods included scrollwheels, trackpads, and those horrible little arrow keys that are so difficult to press (or perhaps I just have fat fingers).

Touch rolled onto the scene, further complicating things. Touch devices warrant special consideration. Targets must be made larger to accommodate the human finger. Unlike devices with indirect manipulation, there is no hover state to rely on. While touch devices accommodate the JavaScript events familiar to mouse input, such as click, there's a noticeable delay when compared to native touch events. In addition, there's the potential for more natural interactions: swipe, pull to refresh, drag. All of this means that touch-enabled devices often need different scripts and styles than their counterparts.

Context

The physical and architectural characteristics of a device are not the only factors to consider. The context in which a device is used is another huge question mark.

Devices may be used in any number of situations: at home, on the road, at a bus stop, at night, during the day, around friends, or around strangers. This context can't be associated with a specific device type, either. Phones are used while on the go, but also while resting on the couch at home. Laptops can be used at a desk, but also while riding a busy train.

Context is a murky topic, but not one we can ignore. We'll come back to the context discussion in Chapter 9, "Responsive Experiences." For now, it's enough to know that understanding context is the key to moving from a Web that responds to devices to a Web that responds to people.

This incredible diversity of devices contributes to the chaos I mentioned earlier. But we are a species that, generally speaking, likes stability. So it should come as no surprise that the first way we tried to deal with this diversity was to silo user experiences into separate, optimized sites.

Figure 1.2 CNN has separate sites for its mobile and desktop experiences.

Separate sites

At the time of this writing, perhaps the most common approach to dealing with the diversity of devices is to create separate sites that serve specific kinds of devices (or, in some extremely misguided efforts, a specific device). Often this means having one site for mobile and another for desktop (**Figure 1.2**). Increasingly, however, it's not unusual for a company to have a desktop site, a tablet site, a site for mobile touch-enabled devices, and a simpler mobile site for devices without touch support—that's four different sites for one company.

This approach certainly has its merits. Creating a separate site for each kind of device makes it easier to tailor the experience significantly—both the content and the behavior. Whether this makes sense depends on the project, the business objectives, the users, the capabilities of the team, the budget, and all those other fun business considerations that come into play.

Unfortunately, it doesn't scale well: that's four sites that need to be updated, tested, and maintained. One site alone can often consume several developers—imagine the weight on each individual developer's shoulders when that project load is multiplied by four! Some suggest that custom content should be written for each site, which would take even more time and effort.

Divergence

Sometimes people ask if we'll start to see convergence, that is, if many of these complex issues will be resolved as the range of available devices and platforms narrows. To those people, I have one word to say: zombies.

In "The Coming Zombie Apocalypse," undoubtedly one of the best pieces of writing on the Web, Scott Jenson argues that this diversity will actually *increase*. He posits that it's not just the rate of change in technology that will continue to drive diversity, but also the reduction of cost:

> The commoditization of smartphone hardware is just the beginning. Plunging prices of integrated "system on a chip" devices, paired with free Linux clones like Android, have enabled not just cheap devices, but cheap cloud-based devices. This has applied to phone products like the Sony Ericsson LiveView, and also to home appliances like the Sonos home music system.
>
> These examples are just the initial, telltale signs of a huge new wave of cheap devices about to invade our lives—a zombie apocalypse of electronics, if you will.[6]

The market certainly seems to be shaping up to support his theory. Smartphones are becoming more and more affordable. Some versions of the iPhone, long one of the more costly models of mobile phones, can now be had for free with a contract.

As the cost of creating these devices goes down, it lowers the barrier for entry and opens the gates for more and more players to get involved with more systems and more devices. We're not looking at convergence at all: we're looking at a flood of new devices and form factors capable of experiencing the Web.

Even if we can keep up with the separate sites approach today, what about tomorrow? It's the tired example, but what happens when refrigerators are connected to the Internet? Will we then attempt to create a website targeted at refrigerators?

---

6   "The Coming Zombie Apocalypse" at http://designmind.frogdesign.com/blog/the-coming-zombie-apocalypse-small-cheap-devices-will-disrupt-our-old-school-ux-assumptions.htm

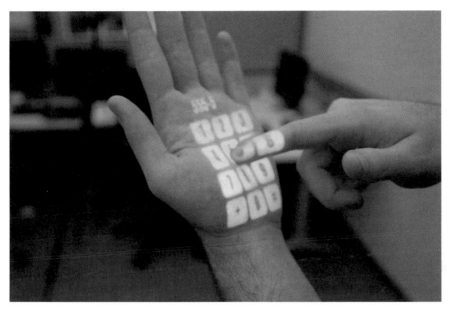

Figure 1.3 Microsoft's OmniTouch prototype turns any surface into a display—even your hand.

What happens when the screen can be anything? In 2011, Microsoft released a prototype of a device called OmniTouch, a clunky, ugly-looking device that sits on your shoulder. What it lacks in aesthetics, it makes up for in "wow." It projects its display onto anything—a wall, the floor, even your own hand (**Figure 1.3**). You can then interact with the projection. It removes any constraints inherent in a screen—the display could be anything. I wonder when we'll see the first website optimized for the human hand.

Building separate sites is not a future-friendly approach. In order to survive the upcoming swarm of devices, we must embrace the flexibility of the Web.

Becoming responsive

In May 2010, Ethan Marcotte wrote an article for A List Apart titled "Responsive Web Design." The approach he described was both simple and revolutionary. He used three existing tools (media queries, fluid grids, and scalable images) to create a site that displayed beautifully at multiple resolutions (**Figure 1.4**).

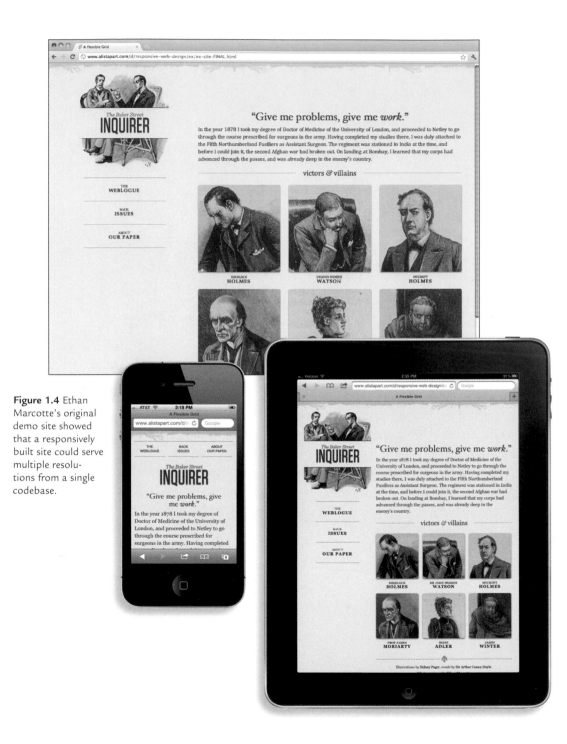

Figure 1.4 Ethan Marcotte's original demo site showed that a responsively built site could serve multiple resolutions from a single codebase.

In the article, he urged designers to take advantage of the Web's unique characteristics:

> This is our way forward. Rather than tailoring disconnected designs to each of an ever-increasing number of web devices, we can treat them as facets of the same experience. We can design for an optimal viewing experience, but embed standards-based technologies into our designs to make them not only more flexible, but more adaptive to the media that renders them.[7]

By and large, the article was praised, and rightfully so. Marcotte demonstrated that it was possible to deliver a great experience to a variety of devices, not by ignoring their differences and trying to impose control, but by letting go and embracing the fluidity of the Web.

Let's start by setting the record straight: a responsive site does not equal a mobile site. This point causes a lot of confusion and heated debate. Of course, much of the appeal of a responsive approach is that it can be part of a mobile strategy, but it's anything but a quick fix.

A responsive site is no more a mobile site than it is a desktop site, or a tablet site. Marcotte made this clear in his post, "Toffee-Nosed":

> When I'm speaking or writing about responsive design, I try to underline something with great, big, Sharpie-esque strokes: responsive design is not about "designing for mobile." But it's not about "designing for the desktop," either. Rather, it's about adopting a more flexible, device-agnostic approach to designing for the web.[8]

This *device-agnostic* concept is incredibly important. We can't know what devices people will use to access the Web. No other medium is accessible by such a wide spectrum of devices or by so many people. As designers, we need to capitalize on this.

● *Device-agnostic*
Anything (component, layout, etc) that is designed to be compatible across different device types and operating systems.

We're far from having it all figured out, but thanks to a lot of hard work and experimentation, the responsive approach is much improved from its first vision. The same three elements (media queries, fluid grids, and scalable images) remain at its core, but they are just the tip of the iceberg.

As it turns out, a successful responsive approach builds upon the very same principles laid down by *progressive enhancement*. It is, to be blunt, progressive enhancement on steroids.

---

7 "Responsive Web Design" at www.alistapart.com/articles/responsive-web-design/
8 "Toffee-Nosed" at http://unstoppablerobotninja.com/entry/toffee-nosed/

More on being future friendly

You'll see the phrase *future friendly* quite a few times in this book. Specifically, this refers to the Future Friendly manifesto.

Cooked up by a group of mobile developers, the Future Friendly manifesto is a set of principles to consider when choosing which web design solutions to implement. These principles are intentially high level. While specific techniques will fade in and out of relevancy over time, the values they are predicated on will remain constant. Keep these principles in mind when deciding which techniques to implement in your own projects.

Quoting from the manifesto at http://futurefriend.ly:

Laser Focus

We can't be all things on all devices. To manage in a world of ever-increasing device complexity, we need to focus on what matters most to our customers and businesses.

Orbit Around Data

An ecosystem of devices demands to be interoperable, and robust data exchange is the easiest way to get going. Be responsive to existing and emerging opportunities by defining your data in a way that: enables multiple (flexible) forms of access and notifications; uses standards to be interoperable; focuses on long-term integrity; includes meaningful and permanent references to all content; and supports both read and write operations.

Universal Content

Well-structured content is now an essential part of art direction. Consider how it can flow into a variety of containers by being mindful of their constraints and capabilities. Be bold and explore new possibilities but know that the future is likely to head in many directions.

Unknown Vessel, Identify

Reacting to every device variance makes inclusive design extremely challenging. A high-level, close-enough set of standards for device types can simplify the process of adaptation.

Command Your Fleet

Having a wide range of devices in our lives enables us to distribute tasks and information between them. When an experience is managed within a device collection, each device can tackle the interactions it does best. This negates the need to tailor all aspects of a service to every device and allows us to work within an ecosystem of device capabilities instead.

Progressive enhancement

For a long time, the web community advocated *graceful degradation*, a concept borrowed from other areas of computer science, such as networking. The idea was that when you created a site using all the newest features (for the most capable browsers) you made sure that older browsers wouldn't choke on the markup and could still access the content.

That might not sound entirely evil, but what it evolved into was a mindset that didn't put much, if any, thought into how these older browsers got to experience the content. As long as it was available in some form—no matter how painful the experience might be—you had successfully practiced graceful degradation.

The concept was not particularly future friendly. It showed a lack of respect for users of older browsers and ignored the increasing reality that there were new devices (mobile) that also featured less capable browsers.

In 2003, Steven Champeon and Nick Finck gave a presentation at South by Southwest (SXSW) in which they introduced a new concept that Steve named "progressive enhancement."[9]

Progressive enhancement essentially flips graceful degradation on its head. Instead of building for the latest and greatest browsers first and letting the less-capable browsers get by on what they can, you create a baseline experience first. This baseline experience uses semantic markup and structure and focuses on presenting the content in a clean, usable form.

You then start layering on the presentation and interactivity in a way that preserves that baseline experience, but provides a richer experience for more capable browsers.

Aaron Gustafson, a longtime advocate of the approach, compares progressive enhancement to a peanut M&M: the content is the peanut, the presentation (CSS) is the chocolate, and the interactivity (JavaScript) is the shell. The content can stand by itself, but as you layer functionality on top, it becomes a much more rich and complete experience (**Figure 1.5**).[10]

---

9 "Inclusive Web Design for the Future" at www.hesketh.com/thought-leadership/our-publications/inclusive-web-design-future

10 Aaron Gustafson, *Adaptive Web Design: Crafting Rich Experiences with Progressive Enhancement* (Easy Readers, 2011)

Figure 1.5 The three layers of a peanut M&M work as a nice analogy for progressive enhancement. The content is the peanut, the presentation is the chocolate and the interactivity is the shell.[11]

Responsive design uses the same kind of thinking to provide appropriate content and layout to a variety of devices. You start by creating a baseline experience and, with the use of techniques such as fluid grids and media queries, you enhance the experience for devices with more capabilities and larger screens (not always synonymous!).

Why another book on responsive design?

Make no mistake: Executing responsive design correctly is no simple feat. It requires a complete overhaul of the way we approach the Web. Our tools and processes were not created with our current challenges in mind. We need to step back and ask ourselves some questions:

- Does it make sense for the desktop to be the default experience?

- How do we adjust the work process to accommodate designing and prototyping for many different devices and screen sizes?

- How can we store content in a more structured manner?

---

11 Also from Aaron Gustafson, *Adaptive Web Design: Crafting Rich Experiences with Progressive Enhancement.* Photo used by permission.

- Are CMSs (content management systems) and WYSIWYG (What You See Is What You Get) editors inherently flawed?

- Should we reconsider our long-standing aversion to *user agent (UA) strings*?

- How do we make content more portable?

- How do we support the explosion of devices still to come in the future?

- Are current standards (HTML, CSS) built to withstand a Web this diverse?

- How can we embrace different contexts without losing a sense of coherence between experiences?

● **User agent strings**
A string passed by the user agent that identifies your browser as well as other information such as the operating system version.

Some of those questions are easily answered, some are difficult, and some are still being debated. When Marcotte wrote that article in May 2010, he did more than introduce a new technique: he kickstarted a much larger conversation involving the necessary maturation of our profession.

That's what this book is about—embracing the flexibility of the Web and practicing responsible responsive design. The upcoming chapters will guide you through the techniques you'll need to enhance your sites and create pleasant user experiences regardless of device. There will be answers, yes, but there will also be questions. Such is the nature of any medium that evolves as rapidly as the Web.

What's covered?

The book consists of nine chapters, including the introduction you're reading right now. The next three chapters introduce the three tenets of responsive design:

- **Fluid Layouts**

  This chapter discusses how to move away from fixed-width designs and start building fluid layouts and fluid typography.

- **Media Queries**

  This chapter provides an introduction to media queries: types of media queries, how to use them, and how to determine breakpoints.

- **Responsive Media**

  This chapter looks at fixed-width elements such as images, video, and advertising to see how they can be incorporated into a responsive layout.

With the three tenets firmly established, the rest of the book examines how responsive design impacts the rest of the web design process:

- **Planning**

  This chapter discusses the steps necessary for successfully planning a responsive site.

- **Design Workflow**

  This chapter examines how responsive design affects the design process. Specifically, it looks at the deliverables and steps in the responsive design process, and some of the changes we need to make.

- **Responsive Content**

  This chapter discusses how to plan for, create, and display content in a responsive layout.

- **RESS**

  This chapter covers how to combine the power of responsive design with detection methods such as client-side feature detection and server-side user agent detection to make more robust solutions.

- **Responsive Experiences**

  The final chapter looks at how to apply a responsive mindset to the entire web experience. Specifically, it shows you how to use context and unique device capabilities to create experiences that truly adapt to fit the needs of the user.

Who is this book for?

This book is intended for designers and developers who want to start creating sites that display and function well on a myriad of devices. You don't need any experience with responsive design—the first few chapters will get you up to speed.

You should, however, be comfortable with HTML and CSS and at least familiar with JavaScript. Chapter 8, "RESS," also uses some PHP code, but the concepts should be recognizable even without much knowledge of PHP.

Code examples

Throughout the book, various examples of code are included. These look like this:

```
1.    <html>
2.    <head>
3.        <title>Geolocation</title>
4.        <meta name="viewport" content="width=device-width" />
5.    </head>
6.    <body>
7.        <p>Testing the geolocation API.</p>
8.        <div id="results"></div>
9.    </body>
```

Changes in the code are `highlighted` so they can be easily identified.

In some cases, to conserve space, code that remains unchanged has been collapsed. This is signified by three dots like line 7 below:

```
1.    <html>
2.    <head>
3.        <title>Geolocation</title>
4.        <meta name="viewport" content="width=device-width" />
5.    </head>
6.    <body>
7.        ...
8.    </body>
```

The companion site

All the code in this book is available on the companion site at http://
implementingresponsivedesign.com. The companion site is also the place to
check for errata and additional resources about the topics discussed in this book.

Most code snippets in the book are used to build a single-page layout for a
fictional magazine called *Yet Another Sports Site*. While I do recommend working along with the text, it's certainly not necessary: this isn't a workbook in any
sense and the concepts and discussion can typically be followed without opening up a code editor.

Now that the housekeeping is done, let's get this party started, shall we?

A word about the JavaScript in this book

The average page online now weighs a ridiculous 1MB. Of that 1MB, 200KB comes from JavaScript, up 52.6 percent over the last year. This is a very troubling trend.[12]

A lot, though admittedly not all, of this JavaScript bloat can be attributed to the industry's increasing reliance on frameworks and plugins. It's quite tempting to reach for these pre-packaged solutions, because in many cases they're already well tested and documented. But they're not always necessary. Depending on the problems you're trying to solve, you can often get away with using only a fraction of the code.

In this book, all of the JavaScript is written without the help of any popular frameworks. To be clear, I'm not campaigning against frameworks. In fact, you'll encounter several helpful jQuery plugins in this book. What I'm arguing for is the careful consideration of what you include on your page. If you need a framework, use it. If you don't, then it may make sense to roll your own code and save some page weight.

---

12 Comparing the June 15, 2012 and June 15, 2011 runs at http://httparchive.org

CHAPTER 2
FLUID LAYOUTS

A very large Oak was uprooted
by the wind. . . .It fell among some Reeds,
which it thus addressed: "I wonder how you,
who are so light and weak, are not entirely
crushed by these strong winds." They replied,
"You fight and contend with the wind, and
consequently you are destroyed; while we on
the contrary bend before the least breath of air,
and therefore remain unbroken, and escape."
—"THE OAK AND THE REEDS," AESOP'S FABLES

In "The Oak and the Reeds," the large oak tree and the small reeds are blown this way and that by the wind. The oak tree tries to stand tall and rigid, resisting the powerful, scattering wind. Eventually, it falls, defeated.

The reeds, on the other hand, bend. It's not just that they're willing to bend, but that they're able. They don't fight the wind; they allow themselves to move with it. As a result, they bend and twist, but remain rooted.

For a long time, we've built our websites to be oak trees: rigid and fixed-width. They look fantastic, until they meet with the inevitable unpredictably of the Web. Instead of fighting this unpredictability, we need to embrace it.

That's the point that John Allsopp was making all the way back in 2000 when he wrote his seminal article for *A List Apart* entitled "A Dao of Web Design."[1] In an industry where what is best practice one day can be laughable the next, Allsopp's insights have proved to be incredibly prescient. He argued that the web community needed to embrace the flexibility of the Web and stop viewing the lack of control as a constraint:

> The Web's greatest strength, I believe, is often seen as a limitation, as a defect. It is the nature of the Web to be flexible, and it should be our role as designers and developers to embrace this flexibility, and produce pages that, by being flexible, are accessible to all.

Allsopp recognized that flexibility and unpredictability weren't things we should be struggling against. They are features, not bugs. They make the Web unique, and a much more powerful medium than print has ever been.

With the increasingly diverse landscape of devices, the inherent flexibility and unpredictability of the Web have become much harder to ignore. As a result, twelve years later the industry is finally catching up to the ideas Allsopp discussed in that article. The first, small step toward embracing this flexibility is to create fluid layouts for our sites, to be *responsive* to the dimensions of the device.

In this chapter, you'll learn:

- The four different types of layouts
- The different ways to size fonts, and which method to use
- How to create fluid grid layouts
- How to make fixed-width resources, like images, play nicely in a fluid layout
- How to combine fixed and fluid-width columns using `display:table`

---

1   A Dao of Web Design at www.alistapart.com/articles/dao/

Layout options

Understanding when a flexible layout might be the best choice requires that we review the other available options. Only by understanding what each offers can we make the right decision so our sites appear to the best advantage in a variety of environments.

In her excellent book, *Flexible Web Design*[2], Zoe Mickley Gillenwater defined four types of layouts: fixed-width, liquid (or fluid), elastic, and hybrid.

Each approach has its own strengths, constraints, and challenges.

Fixed-width

In fixed-width layouts the site width is constrained by a specific pixel measurement, 960px being the most commonly chosen width today. In 2006, Cameron Moll wrote a blog post entitled "Optimal width for 1024px resolution?" in which he dissected what the "optimal" width was to target for the increasingly popular 1024 resolution. After browser chrome was taken into consideration, that left somewhere between 974 and 984 pixels to play with. The number 960 was much friendlier for grid-based layouts (it's easily divisible by 3, 4, 5, 6, 8, 10, 12 and 15 and therefore offers a variety of grid options) and worked well with the Interactive Advertising Bureau's (IAB) standard ad sizes[3]. As a result, that measurement stuck.

Fixed-width layouts are the most common implementation on the Web. A fixed-width layout gives you the illusion of having a lot of control. Knowing exactly the width at which your site will display lets you create graphically intense designs that will look fairly consistent across different screens.

The biggest problem with fixed-width layouts is that you must operate under a lot of assumptions. When you determine how wide your site will be, you're making a guess as to what dimensions will best serve the largest percentage of visitors. This is a lot trickier than it seems. Even before the introduction of devices such as smartphones and tablets, there was a great deal of variability in the screen sizes used by visitors. That was just the start of it. Some people have

---

2 Zoe Mickley Gillenwater, *Flexible Web Design* (New Riders, 2008).

3 Optimal width for 1024px resolution at www.cameronmoll.com/archives/001220.html

browsers that are not maximized to the full width of their screens. Many others have plug-ins installed that display a sidebar in the browser, greatly reducing the actual real estate available for the site.

The "consistency" that a fixed-width design provides is also a bit misleading. If your site is 960px wide and a visitor has a smaller screen (let's say 800px wide), then she'll see only a portion of your site and an ugly horizontal scrollbar (**Figure 2.1**).

Figure 2.1 When the screen is narrower than the width of a fixed-width site, the visitor is greeted by the dreaded horizontal scrollbar.

Larger screens are not immune to issues either. If someone with a large monitor views your 960px-wide site, she'll be met with a large amount of unplanned white space. White space is good, as part of a design. An unanticipated overabundance of white space is beneficial to no one.

The rigidity of fixed-width layouts is even more of an issue in today's widely diverse ecosystem of devices. Many of the newest and most capable phones and tablets display sites zoomed out so they fit on the screen. These devices provide a pinch-to-zoom feature to drill down from there. While this experience is better than not being able to zoom in or access the site at all, it is still cumbersome and far from enjoyable.

Fluid layouts

In fluid layouts, dimensions are determined by percentages, not pixel measurements. As a result, they're much more malleable. So you may have a primary column that's sized at 60% of the width of the container, a right sidebar column sized at 30%, and a gutter of 10% in between. Using a layout defined in that manner means that it doesn't matter if the user is using a desktop computer with a browser width of 1024px, or a tablet sized at 768px wide: the widths of the elements in the page will adjust accordingly.

▶ **Note**
While Gillenwater used the term liquid in her categorization; in this book, these are considered fluid layouts.

A design built on a fluid layout avoids many of the problems that a fixed-width layout presents. Horizontal scrollbars can be prevented, for the most part. Since the site can adapt its width based on the width of the browser window, the design can adjust to better accommodate the available space, eliminating the unwanted white space that can occur with a fixed-width layout.

Implementing responsive strategies, such as media queries and styles for optimizing at different resolutions, is much easier with fluid layouts. (We'll discuss these strategies in later chapters.) There are fewer issues to fix, so you have fewer CSS rules to write. However, a fluid layout *by itself* is not enough to ensure that a design looks good on everything from a smartphone to a TV. Line lengths can become too wide on large displays, and too narrow on small displays. It's a start, but there's a reason why this isn't the only chapter in the book.

Elastic layouts

Elastic layouts are very similar to fluid layouts, except that their constraints are determined by the type size—typically using the em measurement. One em is the equivalent of the currently defined font-size. Say, for example, the body text is in a font-size of 16px. In that case, 1em equals 16px and 2em equals 32px.

Elastic layouts provide strong typographic control. A large body of research recommends a line length between 45 and 70 characters for ideal readability.[4] With an elastic layout, you can define the width of the container to be, say, 55em. This would ensure that the width of the container always maintains an appropriate line length.

Another benefit of elastic layouts is that as a visitor increases or decreases the font size, elements defined with elastic widths will scale in proportion to that font size. We'll talk more about this in the discussion of sizing fonts, later in this chapter.

Unfortunately, elastic layouts can bring back the dreaded horizontal scrollbar. If you have a font-size of 16px and you define the width of the container to be 55em, then any screen below 880px (16×55) will display a horizontal scroll-bar. The issue can be even more unpredictable than with fixed widths. If the visitor increases the font-size to say, 18px, the width of your container just got changed to 990px (18×55).

Hybrid layouts

The final layout option is to take a hybrid layout, which combines two or more of the preceding layouts.

For example, let's say you're using a 300px ad space. You might make the decision to have the sidebar column where the ad resides set to a fixed width of 300px, but use a percentage for the other columns. This ensures that the supplied graphics for the ads can be designed specifically for 300px. (Considering the rigidity of third-party ad services, this is a very important consideration.) However, the rest of the layout will expand to fill the remaining space in the browser.

---

4 The most frequently cited source is Robert Bringhurst's *The Elements of Typographic Style* (Hartley & Marks Publishers, 1992).

Using floats, this approach can get very messy, very quickly. If you set the side column to be 300px and the main column to be 70%, then you'll be right back to having a horizontal scroll bar when the screen size falls below 1,000 pixels. That's the measurement where the 300px sidebar exceeds the 30% of the *viewport* that it's allotted, leaving less than the 70% required for the main column. Thankfully, there's an alternative approach to creating hybrid layouts, which we'll discuss later in the chapter.

● *Viewport*
The browser's visible screen area.

If you managed to make it through that paragraph without sweating and having flashbacks to high school math class, I applaud you.

Which approach is the most responsive?

So which is the right method to be responsive to various devices and environments? Ultimately, it depends on your specific project. Each approach has its own benefits and limitations.

Most often, the right answer will be one of the more flexible layouts—fluid, elastic, or hybrid—because they are all much more future friendly than a fixed-width layout.

It is possible to switch between fixed-width layouts using *media queries*, but it's still a limited solution. A "switchy" approach would let you serve a few resolutions very well, but everything in between would suffer. The visitor is completely at the mercy of when you decide to change the layout. If her device doesn't fit the bill, her experience is little better than if you'd done nothing at all.

● *Media queries*
Media queries allow you to control which styles are applied based on device properties such as width, orientation and resolution.

So while a "switchy" approach is a step in the right direction, it's a little like taking up jogging only to follow each morning's run with 30 minutes on the couch eating ice cream. It's probably better than nothing, but you're not getting as much out of it as you could.

In contrast, using a fluid layout gets you at least part of the way there. Even without the aid of media queries, your design will be able to transition between different viewport sizes, even if there are some imperfections.

● *Breakpoint*
The point at which a new media query is applied. For example, a breakpoint at 980px would mean that a new media query kicks in when the browser width is above or below that number.

Once you introduce media queries, you eliminate the majority of the concerns that come with elastic or fluid layouts (see Chapter 3, "Media Queries"). The result is that your fluid layout does much of the work for you; you have fewer *breakpoints* to create and less CSS to write. With a strong, fluid layout, media queries become a way to adjust the design instead of completely rebuilding it.

Sizing fonts

Embracing the fluidity of the Web in your designs means starting by flexibly sizing your fonts. You can size fonts on the Web using any of a number of different units, but the primary options are: pixels, percentages, and ems.

Pixels

For quite some time, pixels were the preferred method for sizing fonts. The reason is simple: you have precise control over how a browser sizes the text. If you set the font-size to 18px, each browser will display that size at precisely 18px.

Unfortunately, this control comes at a cost. For starters, with pixel-sized fonts, there's no *cascade*—that is, the font size of the parent element has no effect on the font size of the child element. This means that you need to set a specific pixel size for each element where you want the text to display at a different size. This can be a pain for maintenance. If you decide you want the font size to increase across the board, you'll have to change each of those values.

More importantly, pixel-sized fonts are a potential accessibility concern. All major browsers allow the user to zoom in or out of a page. There are two ways a browser handles this. The first is to simply apply the zoom to everything on the page. So if a visitor zooms in, every element on a page will increase in size—not just the text. This method allows users to zoom regardless of how the font is sized (**Figure 2.2**).

The other method is to resize the text itself, but not the other elements on the page. This was a common behavior for a long time, and it is still implemented by some browsers.

Pixel-sized fonts, unfortunately, do not scale in Internet Explorer. This means that for anyone using a version of the browser prior to IE9, where font resizing was the default (or if they have turned font resizing on in the latest version), the size of the fonts on your page will not be adjustable.

The resizing issue also applies for many older, pre-touch devices. In some cases, nothing will scale. In other cases, parts of the page might, but the fonts would stay the same size, resulting in an unseemly site.

This ability to resize the text puts the user in control. In addition to being the considerate thing to do, this can also improve the accessibility of your site. Some visitors may have difficulty reading text below a certain size. Allowing them to increase the font size means that they can still enjoy your content.

Figure 2.2 On some newer browsers, the entire page is zoomed in, not just the fonts.

Sizing fonts in pixels is also not a very future-friendly approach. Different devices have different screen sizes and pixel densities. As a result, a pixel-sized font that looks good on one device may be too small, or too large, on another screen (for more on that, see "Default font sizes" later in this chapter). Using pixels to size fonts is one of the best examples of fighting against the flexibility of the Web.

Ems

A much more flexible, and increasingly popular, way of sizing fonts is to use the em unit instead. As discussed earlier, one em is equal to the current font size. If, for example, the body text is sized at 16px, then:

1em =16px

2em = 32px

Ems are resizable across browsers. They also cascade—which can be both a good thing and a bad thing. It's good in the sense that it eases maintenance. Sizing the fonts of your elements relatively means you need only adjust the initial baseline and the rest of the content will adjust automatically—proportions intact.

That ability to cascade can complicate things as well. For example, consider the following HTML:

```
<body>
    <div id="main">
        <h1>Question One <span>Please choose an answer from below.
            </span></h1>
    <p>In which book did H.G. Wells write: "Great and strange ideas
    transcending experience often have less effect upon men and women than
    smaller, more tangible considerations."</p>
        <ol>
            <li>The Invisible Man</li>
            <li>The War of the Worlds</li>
            <li>The World Set Free</li>
        </ol>
    </div>
    </body>
```

The HTML is styled with the following CSS:

```
body {
    font-size: 16px; /* base font size set in pixels */
}
h1 {
    font-size: 1.5em; /* 24px / 16px */
}
span {
    font-size: 1em; /* 16px / 16px */
}
```

In the example above, the base font-size is set to 16px. Our h1 element has a font size of 1.5em, the equivalent of 24px. We want our span to render at 16px, so we set it to 1em. The problem is that the context has changed. The base is no longer the 16px body font, it's the 24px font size attached to the h1 element. So, instead of our expected 16px font, our span will actually display at 24px.

Instead, we need to adjust the font-size of the span to bring it back down to size:

```
span {
    font-size: .666666667em; /* 16px / 24px */
}
```

Try to structure your CSS and HTML to keep font sizes predictable. For example, if you use your base font-size for the majority of your content, and only resize things such as header elements, you can avoid the issue entirely. Likewise, if your HTML is carefully crafted, you can sort out these issues very easily by the use of a *descendant selector*.

● *Descendant selector*
A CSS selector that matches any elements that are descendants of a specified element.

Percentages

Fonts sized in percentages, like ems, are also resizable and they cascade. Again, as with ems, if the base font-size is 16px, then 100% equals 16px and 200% equals 32px.

While theoretically there isn't a major difference between ems and percentages, it's slowly becoming more and more common that ems are the preferred unit of measurement for fonts on the Web. There really isn't a technical reason for this, it just makes sense to use ems when sizing text since the em unit is directly related to the size of the text.

However, courtesy of everyone's favorite browser, Internet Explorer, there is an issue with using the em unit to set the base font-size for your document. If the base font-size is defined using ems, Internet Explorer greatly exaggerates how small or large the font should be when resized. Let's say you define the base font-size to be 1em and you set the font-size for your h1 elements to be 2em. In most browsers, the h1 elements will behave exactly as you would expect: they will be approximately twice as large. In Internet Explorer, they'll be much larger, thanks to this little bug.

You can get around this issue by setting the base font-size on your body using a percentage.

```
body {
    font-size: 100%;
}
```

Remarkably, the default font-size is a relatively consistent 16px across most browsers and devices (see the sidebar for a little more information). By setting the size of the body font to 100%, you ensure that the content will be resizable, without exaggeration. From there, you can size the remainder of your type relatively using ems.

Default font sizes

For a while now it's been recognized that the default font-size on the body for desktop browsers is about 16px. So if you set the font-size on the body to 100%, you get a consistently sized font.

This behavior is not always true for other device types. For example, when I tested this on a BlackBerry running the Blackberry 6.0 operating system, the default font-size was 22px. The Kindle Touch is even more dramatic in its variance: it starts with a default size of 26px.

Before you start throwing things, there is a reason for this behavior. Many of these new devices have a high pixel density, so a 16px font would look quite small. The majority of devices get around this by reporting a different resolution to browsers. For example, the iPhone 4 has a resolution of 640x960 but reports a resolution of 320x480 to the browser.

Other devices, like the Kindle Touch, report their full resolution but increase the default font-size to compensate.

Ultimately, it is not the actual pixel size that's important: it's the readability of the font on the display that matters. Keep using 100% for the base font-size, but keep in mind that the pixel measurements of the fonts in use may not be 16px (this is a good case for using em units to define your media queries. We'll talk about this in the next chapter.)

Bonus round: rems

There's another flexible option for sizing fonts that has a lot of potential: the rem ("root em") unit. The rem unit behaves just as the em unit with one important difference: it sizes relative to the font-size of the root element—the HTML element.

Using rems, it would then be possible to avoid the cascading issues that occur with nested elements. Let's update the CSS so that the list items are styled using rems:

```
html {
    font-size: 100%; /* equates to ~16px */
```

```
}
h1 {
    font-size: 1.5em; /* 24px / 16px */
}
span {
    font-size: 1rem; /* 16px / 16px */
}
```

In the example above, the h1 element still uses a 24px font. However, the span element will now display at 16px. By using the root em unit, elements inherit their font size from the html element—not from the containing div.

The one caveat to rems is mobile browser support. In general, they are supported pretty well on the desktop: Internet Explorer 9+, Firefox 3.6+, Chrome 6.0+, Safari 5.0+, and Opera 11.6+. In addition, iOS 4.0+ and Android 2.1+ provide support. Unfortunately, at the time of this writing, other mobile platforms (including the popular Opera Mobile) do not support the rem unit.

To accommodate these cases, you would have to serve up a pixel-sized fallback option.

```
span {
    font-size: 16px;
    font-size: 1rem;
}
```

Using the above, browsers that support the rem unit will use that declaration, since it is declared last. Browsers without rem support will use the first declaration set in pixels, and ignore the rem declaration.

Which approach is the most responsive?

There are some trade-offs here to consider when deciding which approach to take. Using ems not only lets your type scale, but it can also make maintenance easier. If you decide to increase the font-size across your site, simply change the percentage applied to the body and you're all set. With rems, since you have to use a pixel fallback, you'll have to update any pixel-sized element throughout your code.

For the remainder of this book, we'll be using a percentage on the body and ems thereafter.

Tip
Many of the maintenance concerns can be alleviated by using a CSS preprocessor like SASS (http://sass-lang.com) or LESS (http://lesscss.org) and making use of variables.

Figure 2.3 The text sized in pixels: beautiful, but completely inflexible.

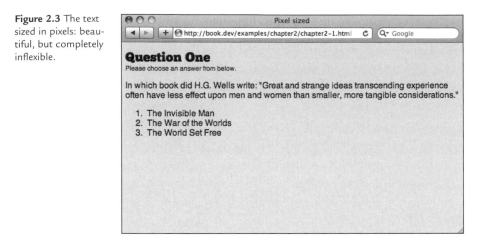

Converting from pixels

While it would be nice to believe that every project you work on will start fresh, thereby allowing you to design fluidly in the browser from the get-go, the reality is that's not very likely. Most projects will involve a transition, and in the meantime, you need to be able to convert those fixed sizes to something a bit more fluid.

Given that, let's take a look at that same snippet of text, completely sized in pixels (**Figure 2.3**).

```
body {
    font-size: 16px;
    font-family: Helvetica, sans-serif;
}
h1 {
    font-size: 24px;
}
span {
    font-size: 12px;
}
```

For starters, the body text is sized at 16px. The h1 element has a font-size of 24px, while our span has a font-size of 12px.

Converting this to a more flexible measurement is relatively simple. Start by setting the body text size:

```
body {
    font-size: 100%;
    font-family: Helvetica, serif;
}
```

Remember that setting the size as 100% means that, for most browsers, the base font-size will be 16px. It also gives us a flexible base to build on.

Converting the rest of the text to ems is simple, using a very basic formula. I know, I know—if you wanted to do math you would have bought a book on calculus. Thankfully you don't need to know the cosine of the square root of pi to be able to figure this out. The formula is simply:

target / context = result

For example, consider the h1 element. The target is 24px. The context is the font-size of the containing element—in this case, 16px on the body. So we divide 24 by the context of 16 to get 1.5em:

```
h1 {
    font-size: 1.5em; /* 24px / 16px */
}
```

Notice the comment following the declaration. As someone who frequently scratches his head when reviewing code I wrote the night before, let alone a month ago, I highly recommend using a comment to help you remember where that measurement came from.

Now we can apply that same formula to the span element. Since it's contained within the h1 element, the context has changed; it's now the h1 element. As a result, we need to set the span to have a font-size of .666666667em (16/24).

After we plug that in as well, the CSS looks like this:

```
1.   body {
2.       font-size: 100%;
3.       font-family: Helvetica, sans-serif;
4.   }
5.   h1 {
6.       font-size: 1.5em; /* 24px / 16px */
7.   }
8.   span{
9.       font-size: .5em; /* 12px / 24px */
10.  }
```

Figure 2.4 The
flexibly sized fonts
look identical to the
original fonts sized
in pixels. But now
when the font size
is increased, the
proportions remain
unchanged.

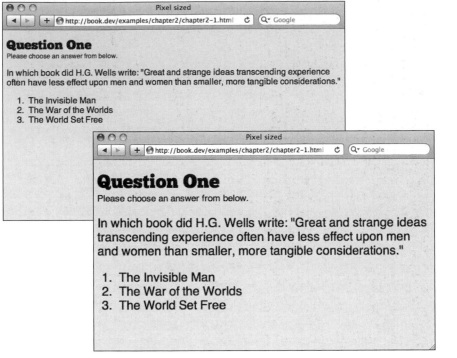

◆ **Tip**
Visit http://
implementing
responsivedesign.
com/ex/ch2/
ch2.1.html to see
this in action.

And there you have it—flexibly sized fonts. Now if we have to change the body font size, the proportions between the new size and the header elements will remain unchanged (**Figure 2.4**).

Grid layouts

▶ **Note**
For more detailed
information about
grids, read Khoi
Vinh's book, or get
a copy of Mark
Boulton's Designing
Grid Systems video
series.

Setting designs to a grid is an incredibly popular practice, one that predates the Web by many decades. Grids help to achieve balance, spacing, and organization on a site. A well-implemented grid system makes your site feel less cluttered and improves its readability and scanability.

In *Ordering Disorder: Grid Principles for Web Design*[5], Khoi Vinh highlights four major benefits of grid design, all of which add up to a design that feels more connected:

---

5   Khoi Vinh, *Ordering Disorder: Grid Principles for Web Design* (New Riders, 2010).

- Grids add order, creativity, and harmony to the presentation of information.

- Grids allow an audience to predict where to find information, which aids in the communication of that information.

- Grids make it easier to add new content in a manner consistent with the overall vision of the original presentation.

- Grids facilitate collaboration on the design of a single solution without compromising the overall vision of the solution.

A word about frameworks

There's no shortage of grid-based frameworks to be found online. These frameworks come with templates and CSS rules to help you quickly create pre-determined grid layouts. Some are flexible, some are not. Most have somewhere between 12 and 16 columns. It can be tempting to dust off your favorite framework with each new project, but we can be a bit more creative than that.

While there's nothing inherently wrong with a 12-column grid, using it for each and every site leads to a boring, predictable layout. To reap the full benefits of a grid-based approach, you need to consider it freshly for each project.

Don't be afraid to mix it up and implement a three- or five-column grid. Some of the most beautifully designed sites on the Web don't use anything as extensive as a 12-column layout. Sometimes, simpler really is better.

Content-out

The first thing to do when setting up a grid is determine the canvas. In graphic design, the canvas is your paper. Its dimensions determine the grid. You subdivide the canvas size into the number of columns you want (3, 5, 9, and yes, even 12) and work from there.

As we've already discussed, on the Web, you don't have these kinds of dimensions to work with. Instead, you have to work content-out: let the content define the grid.

Just to be clear, when I say "content" I'm not specifically talking about text. Content takes many forms: ads, videos, images, text. Each of these different types of content can determine your grid. For example, if you're a publishing company that makes its revenue largely from advertising, then it might be wise to determine your grid around one or two IAB ad sizes. Likewise, if you're redesigning a large site with a lot of legacy images, then it might make sense to create your grid around those dimensions.

Letting your content define the structure of your site is good design, but it's also practical. Instead of trying to shoehorn legacy images or ad spaces into a predefined grid, build your grid to support them from the very beginning. This leads to more cohesive design from page to page.

Enough chatter already, let's do some styling.

Setting the grid

◆ **Tip**
Visit http://
implementing
responsivedesign.
com/ex/ch2/
ch2-start.html to see
this code in action.

Let's kick things off by working for the fictional sports publication, *Yet Another Sports Site* (original, I know). Specifically, we're going to develop a grid for the article page. Some default styles are already in place for color and typography. (For demonstration purposes, we'll have to wait until the next chapter to include the header and footer.) Let's have a look at what we're working with:

```
1.   <body id="top">
2.       <div id="container">
3.           <article class="main" role="main">
4.               <h1>That guy has the ball</h1>
5.               <p class="summary">In what has to be considered a
                 development of the utmost importance, that man over
                 there now has the ball.</p>
6.               <p class="articleInfo">By Ricky Boucher |
                 <time>January 1, 2012</time></p>
7.               <section>
8.                   <img src="images/football.jpg" alt="Football" />
9.                   <p>...</p>
10.              </section>
11.          </article>
12.          <aside>
13.              <section class="related">
14.                  <h2>Related Headlines</h2>
15.                  <ul>
```

```
16.                    <li>
17.                        <a href="#">That Guy Knocked Out the Other
                           Guy</a>
18.                    </li>
19.                    ...
20.                </ul>
21.            </section>
22.            <section class="ad">
23.                <img src="images/ad.png" alt="Boombox ad unit" />
24.            </section>
25.            <section class="article-tags">
26.                <h2>Tagged</h2>
27.                <ul class="tags">
28.                    <li><a href="#">Football</a></li>
29.                    ...
30.                </ul>
31.            </section>
32.            <section class="soundbites">
33.                <h2>Sound Bites</h2>
34.                <blockquote>
35.                    ..this much is clear to me. If I were in his
                       shoes, I would have already won 5 Super Bowls.
36.                    <cite><a href="#">—Guy with big ego</a></cite>
37.                </blockquote>
38.            </section>
39.        </aside>
40.        <div class="more-stories">
41.            <h2>More in Football</h2>
42.            <ul class="slats">
43.                <li class="group">
44.                    <a href="#">
45.                        <img src="images/ball.jpg"
                           alt="Look, it's a ball!" />
46.                        <h3>Kicker connects on record 13 field
                           goals</h3>
47.                    </a>
48.                </li>
49.                ...
50.            </ul>
51.        </div>
52.    </div><!-- /#container -->
53. </body>
```

► **Note**

This page uses several HTML5 elements to provide more meaning, including the **aside** element styled below. For more information about HTML5, I highly recommend *HTML5 for Web Designers*, by Jeremy Keith (A Book Apart, 2010).

We're developers of the highest caliber (ahem), so we've already given a lot of thought to the content that will go on this page, and created a solid structure for it. We know there will be an article. Each article has a headline represented by an h1 element, a byline, and a quick summary, followed by the body text, which is wrapped in a section.

Each article page will also include a sidebar with the latest headlines in the form of an unordered list. Since *Yet Another Sports Site* doesn't charge for content, it'll have to make money somehow. As a result, each article page needs to have room for a 300px × 250px ad. This is the first constraint, and we can use this to help determine the grid.

Finally, the sidebar will also include a list of tags associated with the article and a few quotes. The tags will be in the form of an unordered list, and the quotes will be marked up using the blockquote element.

◆ **Tip**
Check out Robbie Manson's GitHub repository at https://github.com/ robbiemanson/ 960px-Grid-Templates for an assortment of grid templates for Photo-shop or Fireworks.

Let's start by creating the grid the old fashioned way—using pixel measurements.

Instead of just reaching for the nearest 12-column, 960px grid, let's try a nine-column grid. Each column will be 84 pixels wide, with a 24px gap in between for a total width of 948px. A 300px ad will fit very nicely in the last three columns of the grid, leaving us six to use for the article.

First, set the width of the containing element:

```
#container{
    width: 948px;
}
```

Next, float the article and aside elements, setting the width accordingly:

```
aside {
    float: right;
    width: 300px;
}
.main {
    float: left;
    width: 624px;
}
```

◆ **Tip**
Visit http:// implementing responsivedesign. com/ex/ch2/ ch2.2.html to see this in action.

At this point, the layout looks pretty darn lovely. The grid helps the design feel connected, and the article sports a friendly line length, making it easy to read.

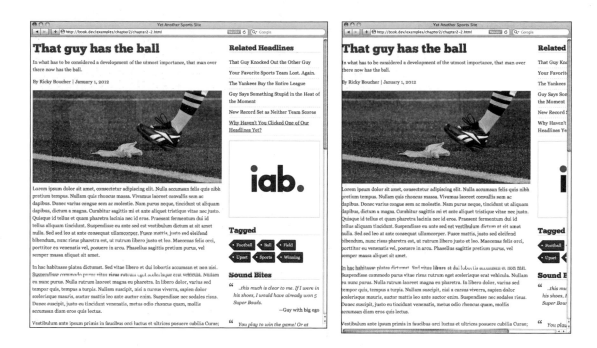

The problems show up very quickly if you bring the browser window size down: with anything 948px wide or lower, we get the dreaded horizontal scrollbar and all the content no longer shows on the screen (**Figure 2.5**).

We've designed to a grid, but the design is only appropriate for a small subset of our audience. Let's remedy that, shall we?

Figure 2.5 The page looks nice on a large screen, but problems arise as soon as the browser is resized.

MAKING IT FLEXIBLE

If you think back to the flexible font sizing, you can apply that same formula (target/context = result) to transform the layout into something a bit more flexible.

The context is the container: 948px. Using that measurement, transforming the layout into a fluid one is easy:

```
aside {
    float: right;
    width: 31.6455696%; /* 300/948 */
}
.main {
    float: left;
    width: 65.8227848%; /* 624/948 */
}
```

Box-sizing

If you've dug into the default styles that are in place, you've probably noticed the following three lines applied to, well, just about everything:

```
-moz-box-sizing: border-box;
-webkit-box-sizing: border-box;
box-sizing: border-box;
```

The default box model in CSS is a bit backwards. You define the width and any padding that you define adds to it. For example, if you create a column 300px wide and add 20px of padding to the left and right, that column is now 340px wide. This is particularly painful when trying to create a nice grid-based layout in a fluid site.

By using `box-sizing: border-box`, you're telling the browser to apply the padding *within* the defined width of the element. With that property applied, a 300px column with 20px of padding on either side will still be 300px wide; the padding is applied to the interior of the element. This makes things much simpler for planning a fluid layout.

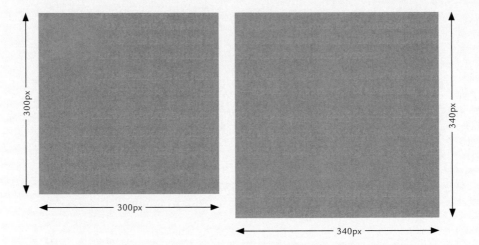

Without box-sizing applied (right), a 300px box with 20px of padding added will be 340px high and 340px wide. With box-sizing:border-box applied, the box will remain 300px high by 300px wide.

If you include the prefixed versions, then support is very good. The only major browser, desktop or mobile, that lacks support is Internet Explorer prior to version 8. In fact, support on most browsers has been around for a while. Chrome and Firefox, for example, have supported the prefixed syntax since their first versions.

Finally, let's fix the more stories section so that those too, are fluid.

```
.main {
    float: left;
    margin-right: 2.5316456%; /* 24px / 948px */
    width: 31.6455696%; /* 300/948 */
}
```

Now that both of the columns are set flexibly, we need to remove the fixed width that's currently set on the container. Instead of setting the width to be 948 pixels, let's set the width to be 95% of the screen, and add a little padding to provide some breathing room:

```
#container{
    width: 95%;
    padding: .625em 1.0548523% 1.5em; /* 10px/16px, 10px/948,
    24px/16px */
    margin: auto 0;
}
```

▶ **Note**

Why 95%? Honestly, there's no scientific reason. I tried a few different widths and 95% displayed pretty comfortably across different browser widths. Sometimes decisions made in design really are based on look and feel.

This example uses ems for the top and bottom padding, but percentages for the left and right. That's because of the context. The top and bottom padding values are determined by the font-size, so using ems makes sense.

FIXED WIDTH OBJECTS IN A FLUID WORLD

The next issue to address is the images. As you adjust the window size up and down, the fixed-width images stick out like sore thumbs. At larger widths, they take up only a fraction of the column. On smaller widths, they're far too wide. Thankfully, it's pretty easy to get them to play nicely.

The first thing to do is tell the images to fill the width of the aside, using the width declaration:

```
aside img,
.main img,
.slats img {
    width: 100%;
}
```

It's important to note that the img element in your HTML cannot have the height and width attributes set. If those values are set, the image will not scale proportionally. For fluid images to work, you need to control the dimensions through CSS alone.

The next thing is to use the `max-width` declaration. By setting the `max-width` to 100%, we're telling the browser to not let the size of the image exceed the size of its containing element (in this case, the sidebar). This way, as the screen is sized narrower, the image won't spill over or be cut off:

```
aside img,
.main img,
.slats img {
    width: 100%;
    max-width: 100%;
}
```

◆ **Tip**
Visit http://
implementing
responsivedesign.
com/ex/ch2/
ch2.3.html to see
this in action.

We now have a fluid layout—one that adjusts itself accordingly and is usable on a pretty large number of devices (**Figure 2.6**). There's more we can do with regard to images to improve the experience, but we'll save that discussion for Chapter 4, "Responsive Media."

Mixing fixed and fluid widths

The article is looking good, and it's fully flexible. Let's say we want to tighten up that right column though. There's nothing wrong with it now, but it might be nice if we could make that column remain at 300px and let the primary column stay fluid. This isn't a necessity at all, but given the advertising in the side column, it would be a nice touch.

Using floats, this is next to impossible. As we discussed earlier, the correct width for the primary column will vary depending on screen resolution. For example, if we go back to a fixed-width size for the right column and keep the primary column at its current 63.125% width, we'll run into issues whenever the size of the screen is under 960px.

There's a way around this though, and it involves using CSS tables.

Table layouts—the right way

Not so long ago, in a galaxy not so far away, most sites on the Web were laid out using tables. It was unsemantic, it was messy, and it made people cry, but it worked. Then along came the web standards movement with the idea of separation of content and presentation and stressing the importance of using semantic markup. A great battle ensued, and eventually standards came out on top.

Figure 2.6 The newly fluid layout looks great even when the screen size isn't exactly as planned.

The one thing that table layouts did better than CSS layouts was simplifying the idea of laying a site out in columns. You could mix fixed and fluid widths, rows and columns could line up—all of this could be done with relative ease. With CSS, it hasn't been so straightforward.

However, the display property of CSS actually lets you define a number of different table-related values to give you that same sort of control. In fact, there's a display property to make elements layout similar to each of the table-related HTML elements:

Table 2.1 Table-related display values

VALUE	CORRESPONDING ELEMENT	VALUE	CORRESPONDING ELEMENT
table	TABLE	table-column	COL
table-row	TR	table-column-group	COLGROUP
table-row-group	TBODY	table-cell	TD, TH
table-header-group	THEAD	table-caption	CAPTION
table-footer-group	TFOOT		

If the idea of using table values in CSS feels wrong to you, you can't be blamed. After all the table-based layout bashing that took place, you might quite understandably have a hard time looking at even kitchen tables without gagging a little. But using table values for CSS layout is a far cry from using HTML tables for layout. Table values for CSS define the visual presentation of your content, not the meaning of the content itself.

The table values of the display property haven't been widely used thus far. For that you can probably blame Internet Explorer. While Firefox, Safari, and Opera have all supported table values for a while now, it took until version 8 to bring support to Internet Explorer. At the time I'm writing this, the combined market share of Internet Explorer 6 and 7 has dipped below 5 percent, so I think it's about time to dust off CSS table layouts and start using them. Mobile support is also remarkably good.

If we apply the `table-cell` value to the display property of the columns, we can successfully mix fixed- and fluid-width columns:

```
.main {
    display:table-cell;
}
aside {
    display:table-cell;
    width: 300px;
}
```

Now, if the browser is resized, the right column remains a fixed 300px, while the width of the primary column fills the remaining space. We've lost the nice spacing between the two columns, but we can easily bring that back with a little padding:

```
.main {
    display:table-cell;
    padding-right: 2.5316456%; /* 24px / 948px */
}
```

Just like that we've combined fixed- and fluid-width columns, maintaining flexibility without having to deal with the chaos that a hybrid layout can cause when floats are involved (**Figure 2.7**). The main column can be a little unseemly at high resolutions, but we'll take care of that in the next chapter when we explore media queries.

SUPPORTING OLD VERSIONS OF INTERNET EXPLORER

For many sites, you may be able to stop here. Versions of Internet Explorer prior to version 8 are rapidly losing market share. Still, depending on your client, letting those versions of Internet Explorer render they way the currently do may not be enough. The content is all there, but that design might not pass. In those situations, you might need to serve some alternate styles.

To do that, you can use conditional comments. Conditional comments let you tell Internet Explorer to use another style sheet for certain versions of the browser. So let's say we create a style sheet called ie.css. To load it in Internet Explorer versions 7 and below, we use a conditional comment like the one below:

```
<!–[if lt IE 8]>
<link rel="stylesheet" href="/css/ie.css" media="all">
<![endif]-->
```

Now, any versions of Internet Explorer prior to version 8 will also load ie.css, allowing us to provide alternate styling for those browsers.

Figure 2.7 Using `display:table-cell`, the sidebar now stays a fixed 300px size while the main column adjusts to fill the remaining space.

Display:table caveat and a word about the future

Before you get too excited and start using `display:table` on everything in sight, there are a few potential gotchas to be aware of.

The first is that you can't absolutely position something contained within an element set to `display:table-cell`. If you need absolute positioning, you'll have to either insert another div within the table cell or bypass the `display:table` approach.

The other thing to remember is that tables are a bit more rigid. Sometimes the fluid nature of floats is desirable. For example, if something is too long, it can easily wrap underneath.

It won't be the last time you hear me say this: there's no silver bullet with web design. You must carefully consider your requirements before committing to any approach, and that includes `display:table`.

It's worth noting two specifications, CSS Grid Layout and Flexbox, that are designed to provide much greater control over layout. Support is very limited right now, which is why we're using `display:table`.

The only problem is that Windows Phone 7 also currently loads those styles. Considering that we'll be altering the styles for smaller screens using media queries in the next chapter, we don't want to override those styles with this IE-specific stylesheet. Thankfully, we can fix this with a simple change to our conditional comment (first documented by Jeremy Keith[6]):

```
<!--[if (lt IE 8) & (!IEMobile)]>
<link rel="stylesheet" href="/css/ie.css" media="all">
<![endif]-->
```

---

6 Windows mobile media queries at http://adactio.com/journal/4494/

Now that we can serve up alternate styles without affecting the experience we'll create for mobile phones, let's change the styles back to two fluid, floated columns in the ie.css file:

```
.main {
    float: left;
    width: 65.8227848%; /* 624/948 */
}
aside {
    float: right;
    width: 31.6455696%; /* 300/948 */
}
```

◆ **Tip**
Visit http://
implementing
responsivedesign.
com/ex/ch2/
ch2.4.html to see
this in action.

It's not the exact same layout as browsers with better standards support will receive, but it's close enough. Remember, sites don't have to look the same in every browser across every device. In fact, it's just not possible. Users of these older versions of Internet Explorer will still see a nice layout appropriate for their browsers.

Wrapping it up

Most of the time, fluid layouts (layouts built with percentages that can therefore adjust with the size of the screen) are your best option for laying out your site. You can create elastic layouts where the width is constrained in relation to the font size, or fluid layouts where the width is constrained by percentages.

Sizing your fonts in a flexible manner eases maintenance and improves accessibility. To accomplish this, stick to percentages or ems, though rems hold potential for the future.

Defining a grid helps to give your site structure and consistency. Instead of picking an arbitrary, predefined grid, try to build your grid from the content out. This can mean building a grid based on line length, images, ad sizes, or any number of other criteria.

Converting fixed units to flexible units is as simple as dividing the target size by the current context. You can use this formula for both widths and font sizing.

Using CSS tables will let you mix fixed and fluid width columns with ease. Support is excellent across modern desktop browsers, and you can easily feed an alternate design to Internet Explorer 7 and below using conditional comments.

The layout for the *Yet Another Sports Site* article is flexible and we're already accommodating more resolutions than we would have been had we laid our site out with a fixed layout. It isn't truly responsive yet, however. We still run into formatting issues if the screen becomes too narrow, and our design becomes untidy if the screen size is too wide.

In the next chapter, we'll tackle these issues using media queries, which let us target styles based on properties of the device in use. This powerful technique will take us well on our way to becoming truly responsive.

CHAPTER 3
MEDIA QUERIES

You must be shapeless, formless, like water.
When you pour water in a cup, it becomes
the cup. When you pour water in a bottle,
it becomes the bottle. When you pour water
in a teapot, it becomes the teapot. —BRUCE LEE

Have you ever had a peanut butter sandwich? Yes, that's right—a peanut butter sandwich. No jam. Just peanut butter spread between two pieces of bread.

It's perfectly edible. It's certainly better than eating two pieces of bread with nothing on them at all. Yet, it's not quite satisfying. You just know there's something missing: one ingredient that would make the whole thing much better.

You need the jam, of course.

In responsive design, media queries are the jam. (I'm envisioning strawberry, but feel free to imagine the flavor you prefer.)

Fluid layouts are a great start. They eliminate the constraints of a fixed-width layout and enable your site to display nicely on a larger number of screens. They can only take you so far, however.

Media queries let you define which styles should apply under specific circumstances by allowing you to query the values of features such as resolution, color depth, height, and width. By carefully applying media queries, you can iron out the remaining wrinkles in your layout.

When you're finished with this chapter, you'll be able to:

- Set the viewport of your site.
- Use media queries to adjust your site design.
- Organize and include media queries.
- Identify the needed breakpoints.
- Improve the navigation experience on small screens.

The last time we saw our article page, it was built with a fluid layout using the `display:table` properties. The sidebar was a fixed width, but the primary column and outer container were set in percentages so the width adjusted with the screen size.

▶ **Note**
Visit http://
implementing
responsivedesign.
com/ex/ch3/
ch3.1.html to see the
current version of
the page.

While you were turning the page, the header and footer magically appeared, giving the site a bit more form and structure. The article page currently looks as shown in **Figure 3.1**.

For some widths, this works out nicely. Upon closer inspection, however, some issues become apparent.

If we resize the window to be very wide, the line length increases. The wider we go, the further the line length of the article gets from the ideal. Other than that, however, the situation isn't all that bad; the layout holds up pretty well.

Figure 3.1 The *Yet Another Sports Site* page sports a stylish header and footer.

Figure 3.2 Making the browser window narrower causes the layout to look a little worse for wear.

But as we resize the window to be narrower, our lovely layout begins to look like it was hit repeatedly with a big stick. The window doesn't have to get very narrow before the first navigation item falls under the rest of the links (**Figure 3.2**). This isn't particularly elegant, but it's not necessarily a deal-breaker. The line length of the primary column also gets a bit too short. Remember, ideally we want that line length to fall somewhere between 45 and 70 characters. Anything under or above those numbers can have a negative impact on the reading experience.

As the window gets narrower, the issues get worse. By 360px or so, the navigation is a complete mess. The primary column can barely fit three words per line, and even the sidebar is cramped for space. Clearly we have some work to do.

Figure 3.3 When viewed on a smartphone, the site appears zoomed out.

You might think that this narrow window represents what your site visitors will see on a mobile device, because it seems about that width, but you'd be mistaken (**Figure 3.3**).

If you look at the article page on most smartphones, you won't see the issues caused by resizing the browser. Instead, the page maintains its original layout, but it's zoomed out so that the text and site appear quite small. To understand why this happens we need to take a closer look at the little squares on the screen: the pixels.

Viewports

The concept of a viewport is a simple one in terms of desktop browsers: the viewport is the visible area of the browser, the browser width. It's so simple, in fact, that no one really bothers to even think about it. But that all changes with phones. Despite having much smaller screens, they attempt to display the "full" site in order to provide a full web experience. Suddenly things get a little more complicated.

A pixel is a pixel, unless it isn't

When it comes to browsers, there are two kinds of pixels: device pixels and CSS pixels. Device pixels behave the way you would expect a pixel to behave. If you have a screen that's 1024px wide, then you can fit two 512px elements side-by-side in it.

CSS pixels are a bit less stable. CSS pixels deal not with the screen, but with the visible area within the browser window. This means that CSS pixels may not line up exactly with device pixels. While on many devices, one CSS pixel is the same as one device pixel, on a high-resolution display such as the Retina display of the iPhone, one CSS pixel is actually equal to two device pixels. Just wait … it's about to get even more fun!

Any time a user zooms in or out of a page, the CSS pixels change. For example, if a user zooms to 300%, then the pixels stretch to three times the height and three times the width they were set at originally. If the user zooms to 50%, then the pixels are reduced to half the height and half the width. The entire time, the device pixel count doesn't change—the screen is, after all, the same width. The CSS pixel count, however, does. The number of pixels that can be viewed within the browser window changes.

This comes into play in considering the viewport. Once again, you have two different viewports to consider: the visual viewport and the layout viewport.

The layout viewport is similar to device pixels in that its measurements are always the same, regardless of orientation or zoom level. The visual viewport, however, varies. This is the part of the page that's actually shown on the screen at any given point. **Figure 3.4** illustrates this.

On a mobile device, this can complicate things. To allow for a "full web" experience, many mobile devices return high layout viewport dimensions. For example, the iPhone has a layout viewport width of 980px, Opera Mobile returns 850px, and Android WebKit returns 800px. This means that if you create a 320px element on the iPhone, it will fill up only about a third of the screen real estate.

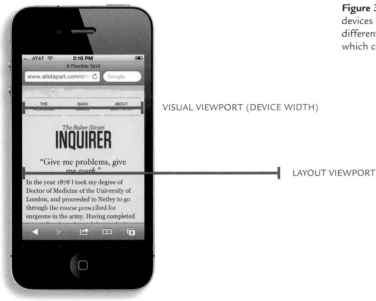

VISUAL VIEWPORT (DEVICE WIDTH)

LAYOUT VIEWPORT

Figure 3.4 Mobile devices have two different viewports which can vary greatly.

Viewport tag and properties

Thankfully WebKit gave us an out for this, and many other *rendering engines* have since followed suit. The viewport meta tag lets us control the scaling and layout viewport of many devices.

The format of the viewport tag is simple: just specify it as a viewport meta tag and list a set of directives:

```
<meta name="viewport" content="directive,directive" />
```

Meta tags are placed in the head of your HTML:

```
<head>
    <meta name="viewport" content="directive,directive" />
</head>
```

Let's take a walk through the viewport properties to see what's available.

● *Rendering engine* The component of a browser that takes markup (HTML, XML, etc) and styling information (CSS, XSLT, etc) and displays it on the screen as formatted content.

Figure 3.5
On the left, the width has been set to device-width, using the full 320 pixels that the iPhone offers. When set to a specific width that doesn't match the device (right) everything gets scaled.

WIDTH

The `width` directive lets you set the viewport to a specific width, or to the width of the device:

```
<meta name="viewport" content="width=device-width" />
```

Using `device-width` is the best solution. This way, your screen's layout viewport will equal the screen of the device—in device pixels.

If you use a specific width instead, such as 240px, most devices that don't have a width of 240px will scale to match. So, if your device has a screen width of 320px, everything will be scaled up by a factor of 1.33 (320/240) in an attempt to display the page neatly (**Figure 3.5**).

For this reason, you'll almost never use the `width` directive with an absolute value. Instead, you'll pass it `device-width`.

HEIGHT

The counterpart to width, height lets you specify a particular height:

```
<meta name="viewport" content="height=468px" />
```

This sets the viewport height to 468px. Again, as with the width declarative, a more foolproof method is to set the height equal to device-height:

```
<meta name="viewport" content="height=device-height" />
```

This sets the layout viewport equal to the height of the screen. In practice, you probably won't use height very much. The only time it's handy is if you don't want to let the page scroll vertically, which doesn't happen that often.

USER-SCALABLE

The user-scalable directive tells the browser whether or not the user can zoom in and out on the page:

```
<meta name="viewport" content="user-scalable=no" />
```

You'll often find pages that set user-scalable to no, typically to ensure the "pixel-perfect" display of a design. This is counter to the nature of the Web, and detrimental to users with accessibility needs. If you don't set the user-scalable directive, it will default to yes. As a result, it's best to stay clear of this one.

The iOS orientation bug

One common reason why developers use the user-scalable or maximum-scale properties is a persistent bug in iOS.

If you set the viewport to any value that lets the user scale the page, changing the device's orientation to landscape will result in the page scaling past 1.0. This forces the user to double-tap to get the page to zoom correctly and avoid the page being cropped.

If you disable scaling, using either the maximum-scale or the user-scalable feature, the issue goes away. The unfortunate, and major, downside is that your page becomes less accessible.

Fortunately for us, the issue has finally been resolved in iOS6. For older versions of iOS, Scott Jehl of the Filament Group put together a fix. His fix uses the device's accelerometer to determine when an orientation change occurs. When it does, it disables user zooming temporarily until the orientation change is complete. Once it's done, zooming is restored.

This clever fix is freely available at https://github.com/scottjehl/iOS-Orientationchange-Fix on GitHub.

Figure 3.6 A 320px-wide device will display normally if the initial-scale is set to 1 (left). With the initial-scale set to .5 (right), the page will appear zoomed out.

INITIAL-SCALE

Given a number between 0.1 (10%) and 10.0 (1000%), the initial-scale declarative sets the initial zoom level of the page. Take the following declaration:

```
<meta name="viewport" content="initial-scale=1, width=device-width />
```

Using the above declaration, if the width of the device is 320px, the page will display at 320px. If the width is 200px, the page will display at 200px.

Let's look at one more example:

```
<meta name="viewport" content="initial-scale=.5, width=device-width" />
```

In the example above, the width attribute is set to the width of the device and the initial-scale is set to .5 (50%). This means that the browser will display everything zoomed out. On a 320px-wide device, the page will display at 640px (**Figure 3.6**). On a 200px-wide device, it will display at 400px.

MAXIMUM-SCALE

The maximum-scale declarative tells the browser how far the user can zoom in on a page. In mobile Safari, the default is 1.6 (160%), but you can pass any number between 0.1 (10%) and 10.0 (1000%).

As with user-scalable, if you set the maximum-scale declarative to 1.0, you disable the user's ability to zoom in and thereby limit the accessibility of your site.

MINIMUM-SCALE

The `minimum-scale` declarative tells the browser how much the user can zoom out on a page. In mobile Safari, the default is 0.25 (25%). As with `maximum-scale`, you can pass any number between 0.1 (10%) and 10.0 (1000%).

If you set the `minimum-scale` declarative to 1.0 (100%), you disable to the ability to zoom out. As you've already seen, this limits accessibility and should be avoided.

FIXING THE VIEWPORT ISSUE

Armed with the knowledge of the viewport meta tag and its declaratives, you can get rid of the "zoomed out" look on your page and make mobile devices use the width of the device as the constraint. To do this, set the `width` declarative equal to `device-width`:

```
<meta name="viewport" content="width=device-width" />
```

CSS device adaptation

As it turns out, the meta viewport element is actually non-normative. In plain English, it's not a definitive standard. In fact, a close look at the W3C documents reveals that the only reason it's still included in the specification is to provide a road map for browsers to migrate to the new `@viewport` syntax.

The `@viewport` rule lets you specify any of the descriptors used in the meta viewport element (width, zoom, orientation, resolution, and so on) directly in the CSS. For example, to set the viewport equal to the device width, you would insert the following into the CSS:

```
@viewport {
    width: device-width;
}
```

Support is currently limited to prefixed implementations in Opera and Internet Explorer 10. However, given the stance on the meta viewport element, it is reasonable to expect that at some point support for the meta viewport element will be removed from browsers as they migrate to supporting the `@viewport` rule instead.

Figure 3.7 With the viewport set, the site displays just as it did on the desktop, only zoomed out.

Now when we load the page on a mobile device, it behaves just as it did when we resized our browser window on the desktop. That's because the phone is now using its own width as the visual viewport. We won't use any of the other declaratives because they're not necessary for what we're doing, and we don't want to fall into the trap of trying to control the environment at the risk of reducing accessibility.

It doesn't take a keen eye to tell that by setting the viewport, we've actually just made the situation worse (**Figure 3.7**)! Now, our site looks equally beaten by the stick on the phone and the desktop. It's time to call on our friend, the media query, for help.

Media query structure

Media queries let you question the browser to determine if certain expressions are true. If they are, you can load a specific block of styles intended for that situation and tailor the display.

The general form of a media query is:

```
@media [not|only] type [and] (expr) {
    rules
}
```

A media query has four basic components:

- Media types: specify the type of device to target
- Media expressions: test against a feature and evaluate to either true or false
- Logical keywords: keywords (such as and, or, not, or only) that let you create more complex expressions
- Rules: basic styles that adjust the display

Let's take a closer look at each one.

Media types

One of the wonderful features of the Web is its ability to serve content to a variety of media. The Web extends far beyond the screen. Information can be printed or accessed via Braille tactile feedback devices, speech synthesizers, projectors, televisions, and any number of other platforms.

Media types were developed to bring order to this chaos. The most basic approach is to use a media type on its own, without writing a full media query. Indeed, if you've ever created a print stylesheet, then you've already used media types.

Each media type tells the user agent (such as a browser) whether or not to load that stylesheet for a given type of media. For example, if you use the screen media type, the user agent will load your styles as long as you're using a computer screen of some sort. If you use the print media type, then those styles will load only when printing or in print preview.

CSS defines ten different media types:

Table 3.1 Media types

TYPE	TARGET DEVICES
all	All devices (default)
braille	Braille tactile feedback devices
embossed	Paged braille printers
handheld	Handheld devices (typically small screen and possibly monochrome)
print	Printing or print preview
projection	Projected presentations
screen	Color computer screen
speech	Speech synthesizers
tty	Media using a fixed-pitch character grid (terminals or teletypes)
tv	Television devices

In a stylesheet the query would be:

```
@media print {
}
```

or externally, using the media attribute on a link element, it would be:

```
<link rel="stylesheet" href="print.css" media="print" />
```

In either case above, the CSS referenced would be applied only when printing a page, or when viewing a page in print preview.

Every media query must include a media type. If you don't set one, it should default to all, but the actual behavior varies from browser to browser.

In practice, you will find yourself using all, screen and print almost exclusively. Unfortunately, a long history of developers using screen instead of say, handheld or tv, has resulted in most devices deciding to support screen instead of their specific media type. It's not really their fault: had they not made that decision most sites wouldn't even display on their devices.

By themselves, media types only let you target a wide range of devices. To make detailed enhancements to the page, you need to narrow the field. That's where media expressions come into play.

Media expressions

The power of media queries is their ability to test against different features of a device using expressions that evaluate to either true or false. A simple example would be to determine whether the width of the viewport is greater than 320px:

```
@media screen and (min-width: 320px) {
}
```

That media block checks two things. First, it tells you whether the media type is a screen. Second, it tests the width of the viewport—that's the expression. Specifically, the min- prefix ensures that the width is at least 320px. **Table 3.2** lists the different features you can test against, as well as whether or not the feature can be used with the min- and max- prefixes.

Primarily, you'll stick to using width, height, orientation, resolution and perhaps aspect-ratio. Browser support for color, color-index, and device-aspect-ratio is subpar. Monochrome, scan, and grid don't really apply to most devices at the moment.

Logical keywords

In addition to media types and media expressions, you can use a number of optional keywords to make your media queries more powerful.

AND

You can use and to test against more than one expression:

```
@media screen and (color)
```

The above example tests to make sure the device has a color screen.

NOT

The not keyword negates the result of the entire expression, not just a portion of it. Consider the following:

```
@media not screen and (color) {...} //equates to not (screen and (color))
```

For the media query above, the query returns false for any device that has a color screen. It's also worth noting that you can't use the not keyword to negate a single test—it must precede the rest of the query.

Table 3.2 Media features

FEATURE	DEFINITION	VALUE	MIN/MAX
width	Describes the width of the display area of the device	<length> (e.g., 320)	yes
height	Describes the height of the display area of the device	<length> (e.g., 600)	yes
device-width	Describes the width of the rendering surface of the device	<length> (e.g., 320)	yes
device-height	Describes the height of the rendering surface of the device	<length> (e.g., 600)	yes
orientation	Indicates if the device is in portrait (height greater than width), or landscape (width greater than height)	portrait|landscape	no
aspect-ratio	Ratio of the value of the width feature to the value of the height feature	<ratio> (e.g., 16/9)	yes
device-aspect-ratio	Ratio of the value of the device-width feature to the value of the device-height feature	<ratio> (e.g., 16/9)	yes
color	Number of bits per color component of the device (returns zero if the device is not a color device)	<integer> (e.g., 1)	yes
color-index	Number of entries in the color look-up table for the device	<integer> (e.g., 256)	yes
monochrome	Number of bits per pixel on a monochrome device (returns zero if the device is not monochrome)	<integer> (e.g., 8)	yes
resolution	Resolution (pixel-density) of the device (resolution may be expressed in dots per inch [dpi] or dots per centimeter [dpcm])	<resolution> (e.g., 118dpcm)	yes
scan	Scanning process of "tv" devices	progressive | interlace	no
grid	Returns whether the device is a grid device (1) or a bitmap device (0)	<integer> (e.g., 1)	no

Media queries level 4

There is some work being done to standardize additional features to query. At the time of writing this there are three features being added: script, pointer and hover.

The script media feature will query to see if ECMAscript is supported, and if that support is active (if it hasn't been disabled). This value of the script feature will either be 1 (scripting is supported) or 0 (scripting is not supported).

The pointer media feature will query about the accuracy of the pointing device (such as a mouse or finger). If there are multiple input methods, the device should return the results for the primary input mechanism.

The value of the pointer feature will either be none (no pointing device included), coarse (limited accuracy—like a finger on a touch-based screen) or fine (such as a mouse or stylus).

Finally, the hover media feature will query whether or not the primary pointing method can hover. If the device has many pointing methods, it should report the results for the primary method. A device that is primarily touch-based would return a value of 0 to signify hovering is not an option, even if a device like a mouse (which supports hover) could be connected and used.

None of these things are set in stone, so it's possible that the specifics will change. Still, it's interesting to see what is on the horizon.

Ed Merritt

VERTICAL MEDIA QUERIES

Ed Merritt is a designer, front-end developer, amateur baker and real ale lover who has been using pixels, fonts, and the occasional div to craft interfaces for the Web since 2001. Ed works with some lovely, talented people at Headscape.co.uk and is the founder of TenByTwenty.com, a little studio producing fonts, icons & Wordpress themes. Ed lives by the beach in Bournemouth, on the south coast of the UK.

THE PROJECT

In mid-2010, while designing a new website for the Environmental Defense Fund, I happened to read Ethan Marcotte's article "Responsive Web Design." I loved the thought of adapting the layout to the viewing environment. The idea was still very new and the design was already underway (proposing a fully responsive approach at that point would have been outside the scope of the project), but I was keen to include at least some elements of the approach.

THE PROBLEM

The homepage featured a carousel front and center, with the rest of the page following below. This worked very effectively, but we discovered that on a 1024px × 768px screen (visitors' second most common resolution, according to the organization's stats), with the most common setup (browser window fully expanded, with no additional toolbars), the viewable area ended just after the carousel. In testing we learned that because users weren't seeing any content cut off at the bottom of the viewable area, they were falsely assuming this was the end of the page and very few scrolled at all.

These days, concerns about the fold are behind us for the most part, as users are happy to scroll, but as our testing showed, in some cases the layout of the page can actually misguide users into thinking they've already reached the bottom of the page. In their browser, there's a definite point at which the visible area ends and if the content appears to end too, why would they scroll further? The challenge was to show them that there was more to see.

THE SOLUTION

I'd already settled on creating two fixed widths for the site: a "full" layout (for viewports of 1024px wide and above) and a "narrow" layout (for widths from 800px to 1024px). This solution wasn't fully responsive by any means, but it was a step in the right direction for my first project making use of media queries.

With the vertical media query in place, more content would appear on shorter screens helping users understand that there was more to see.

I realized that by using a vertical media query I could alter the layout for devices with a vertical resolution below 768px. The narrow version already reduced the width of the page to three-quarters of its original width, reducing the height of the carousel proportionally. All I had to do was induce the narrow version for shorter screens too (see illustration).

Obviously in windows with short but still wide viewable areas there was horizontal space that was now going to waste. Fortunately, below the carousel the page was split into a main column of three-quarter width and a right column of one-quarter width. Resizing the carousel to three-quarter width created space alongside it for the right column to move into.

THE END RESULT

This approach appeased the client and made users aware that there was more content on the page to be seen. It also made more effective use of the available space, a nice bonus. (I'd rarely want a carousel to fill the entire viewable area anyway.) And all of this was accomplished by simply adding a media query for short but wide viewports.

This was a solution to a specific issue, but the principle was one that I could apply elsewhere. In subsequent projects, I've always taken a moment to sit back and ask myself, are there any circumstances (be it heights or widths) where the viewport would adversely affect the presentation of this content? And if so, is there anything I can do about it?

OR

There is no 'or' keyword for media queries, but the comma acts as one.
This lets you load a set of styles if any one of a series of specified expressions
evaluates to true:

```
@media screen and (color), projection and (color)
```

In the example above, the query evaluates as true if the device is either a color
screen device, or a color projection device.

ONLY

Many older browsers support media types, but not media queries. This sometimes results in the browser attempting to download styles that you don't want
the user to see. The only keyword can be used to hide media queries from
older browsers, as they won't recognize it. Browsers that do support the only
keyword process the media query as if the only keyword wasn't present. This
is generally a very good idea.

```
@media only screen and (color)
```

If a device doesn't support media queries, it ignores the query above entirely.
If it does support them, it evaluates the query the same way it would evaluate
the following:

```
@media screen and (color)
```

Rules

The last piece in the media query puzzle is the actual style rules you want to
apply. These are basic CSS rules. The only special thing about them is that
they're included within a media query:

```
@media only screen and (min-width: 320px) {
    a{
        color: blue;
    }
}
```

Embedded versus external

Media queries can be embedded in the main stylesheet or placed in the media attribute of a link element to include an external stylesheet.

You can embed media queries in a stylesheet like this:

```
a{
    text-decoration:none;
}
@media screen and (min-width: 1300px) {
    a{
        text-decoration: underline;
    }
}
```

In this case, links are underlined only when the screen is 1300px or wider.

External media queries are placed directly within the link element that loads each custom stylesheet. So, in the head element of the HTML you would have:

```
<link href="style.css" media="only screen and (min-width: 1300px)" />
```

The route you choose depends largely on the project at hand; each has its benefits and pitfalls.

For media queries that are embedded in a single stylesheet, all styles are downloaded regardless of whether or not they're needed, but the benefit is that you have to make only one HTTP request. This is an important consideration for performance, particularly if the device is being used on a mobile network. Mobile networks suffer from high latency, that is, the time it takes for the server to receive and process a request from the browser. Every time an HTTP request is made on a mobile network, it could be taking as much as four or five times as long as it would take on a typical wired Internet connection. The downside, of course, is that this one CSS file can get to be very large. So while you've saved a few requests, you've created a heavy file that can be difficult to maintain.

You might be surprised to learn that external media queries still result in all the styles being downloaded, even if they're not applicable. The rationale for this is that if the browser window size or orientation is changed, those styles are ready and waiting. Unfortunately, this results in several HTTP requests instead of just one. (The exception to that rule is devices that do not support media queries at all. If you preface your media queries with the only keyword, those devices will ignore these extra styles.)

◆ **Tip**

For a clever workaround to the issue of unnecessary CSS loading, be sure to check out eCSSential, created by Scott Jehl at https://github.com/scottjehl/eCSSential.

The advantage of external media queries is that the files will be smaller, helping to make them easier to maintain. You can also serve up a low-weight, simplified stylesheet to devices that don't support media queries and again, thanks to the only keyword, you don't have to worry about them applying styles they won't need.

Of course it depends on the project at hand, but more often than not I recommend one stylesheet with the media queries embedded. Additional HTTP requests are a surefire way to bring a site to a crawl, and performance is just too important to dismiss so casually.

Media query order

The next thing to consider when structuring your CSS is how to build a responsive site: from the desktop down or from mobile up.

Desktop down

Responsive design, as it was first taught and is still most commonly implemented, is built from the desktop down. The default layout is what you typically see on the screen of a browser on a laptop or desktop computer. Then, using a series of media queries (typically max-width), the layout is simplified and adjusted for smaller screens. A stylesheet structured in this way might look like the following:

▶ **Note**
In the sample code, ... represents the style rules. Refer to the introduction for more information about the coding conventions in the book.

```
/* base styles */
@media all and (max-width: 768px) {
  ...
}
@media all and (max-width: 320px) {
  ...
}
```

Unfortunately, building from the desktop down results in some serious issues. Media query support on mobile devices, while improving, is still somewhat sketchy. BlackBerry (pre-version 6.0), Windows Phone 7, and NetFront (which powers pre-third generation Kindle devices) all lack media query support.

While it's fun to imagine that every user has the latest and greatest technology running on the latest and greatest device, that is not the case. At the time of writing this, Android 4 is the latest version of that operating system, but just under 92 percent of the Android devices in use are running 2.3.x or earlier.[1] Older BlackBerry devices are incredibly common as well. Currently, 66 percent of BlackBerry users are running a version of the operating system that lacks media query support.[2]

The reality is that not everyone wants to keep up with rapidly evolving technology, and others may not be able to afford to.

Mobile up

If you flip things around and build the mobile experience first, and then use media queries to adjust the layout as the screen size gets larger, you can largely circumvent the support issue. Building the mobile experience first will ensure that mobile devices that do not support media queries will still be served an appropriate layout. The only desktop browser that you'll need to contend with is Internet Explorer. Prior to version 9, Internet Explorer does not support media queries, but as you'll see later in this chapter, it's pretty easy to account for that.

A stylesheet built from mobile up might have a structure like this:

```
/* base styles, for the small-screen experience, go here */
@media all and (min-width: 320px) {
...
}
@media all and (min-width: 768px) {
...
}
```

Support is not the only advantage of building mobile up. Creating the mobile experience first can help reduce the complexity of your CSS as well. Consider the aside from the *Yet Another Sports Site* article page. On the large screen, it's set to `display:table-cell` and given a width of 300px. On a small screen, it probably makes more sense to have the aside displayed linearly, that is, stacked underneath the article itself. If the page were built from the desktop down, the styles would look like this:

---

1 Platform Versions at http://developer.android.com/resources/dashboard/platform-versions.html
2 See "Choosing a Target Device OS" at http://us.blackberry.com/developers/choosingtargetos.jsp.

```
aside{
    display:table-cell;
    width: 300px;
}
@media all and (max-width: 320px) {
    aside{
        display:block;
        width: 100%;
    }
}
```

Building from mobile up, the styles would look like this:

```
@media all and (min-width: 320px) {
    aside{
        display:table-cell;
        width: 300px;
    }
}
```

Using the simpler layout first lets the browser defaults serve as a base to build on. As a result, the CSS required is simpler and cleaner.

Create your core experience

▶ **Note**
It's not exactly layout, but the line that sets the width of the ad to 100% is removed as well. Depending on the deal you have with advertisers, resizing it may not be an option. We'll talk more about this topic in Chapter 4, "Responsive Media."

Ideally, every project would begin with a core experience that's simple, streamlined, and usable by as wide a range of devices as possible. The breadth of reach is one of the greatest strengths of the Internet—try to maximize it whenever possible.

Keeping this in mind, we'll start our core experience with a simple, one-column layout. We can move any layout-related CSS to the bottom of the stylesheet and leave it commented out for now.

After combing through the stylesheet for any floats that have to do with the layout, or any `display:table` properties, the collection of commented out styles at the bottom of the CSS looks like this:

```
1.    /*
2.    .main {
3.        display: table-cell;
4.        padding-right: 2.5316456%;
5.    }
6.    aside {
7.        display: table-cell;
8.        width: 300px;
9.    }
10.   .slats li {
11.       float: left;
12.       margin-right: 2.5316456%;
13.       width: 31.6455696%;
14.   }
15.   .slats li:last-child {
16.       margin-right: 0;
17.   }
18.   nav[role="navigation"] li {
19.       float: left;
20.   }
21.   nav[role="navigation"] a {
22.       float: left;
23.   }
24.   footer[role="contentinfo"] .top {
25.       float: right;
26.   }
37.   */
```

With all this code commented out, the page looks like **Figure 3.8**.

There's not much going on here in terms of complexity, which is great. It means the core will be accessible by a wide range of devices. The navigation items could use a little separation though—a border might help there (**Figure 3.9**):

```
nav[role="navigation"] li {
    padding: .625em 2em .625em 0;
    border-top: 1px solid #333;
}
```

With the layout out of the way and this minor adjustment in place, the core experience is ready to go. It's time to start adding in media queries to improve the layout as it scales up.

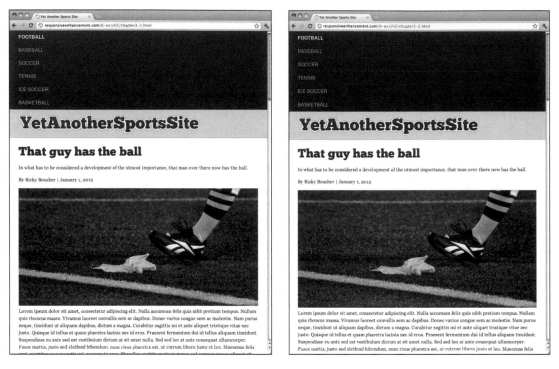

Figure 3.8 With the styles commented out, the page now has a simple, accessible one-column layout.

Figure 3.9 With a 1px border added to the navigational items, things are starting to look pretty sharp.

Determining breakpoints

The conventional method of determining breakpoints is to use some fairly standard widths: 320px (where the iPhone and several other mobile devices land on the spectrum), 768px (iPad), and 1024px. There's a problem with relying on these "default" breakpoints, however.

When you start to define breakpoints entirely by the resolutions of common devices, you run the risk of developing specifically for those widths and ignoring the in-between (case in point, rotate the iPhone to landscape and you've just introduced a 480px width). It's also not a particularly future-friendly approach. What's popular today may not be popular tomorrow. When the next hot device emerges, you'll be forced to add another breakpoint just to keep up. It's a losing battle.

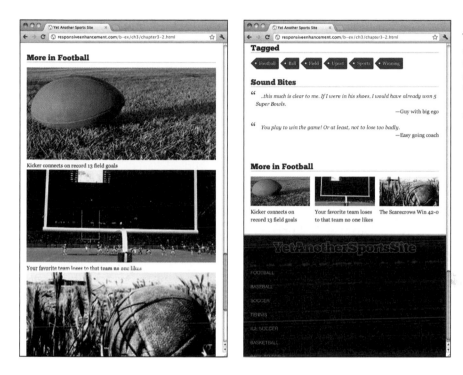

Figure 3.10
The images start to dominate the screen around 600px (left), so it makes sense to add a breakpoint here and adjust the design (right).

Follow the content

A better approach is to let the content dictate where your breakpoints occur, and how many of them you need. Start resizing your browser window and see where there's room for improvement.

By allowing the content to guide you, you're further decoupling your layout from a specific resolution. You're letting the flow of the page dictate when the layout needs adjusting—a wise and future-friendly move.

To identify your breakpoints, you can reduce the window of your browser to around 300px (assuming your browser lets you go that far) and then slowly bring up the size of the window until things start to look like they need a touch up.

By around 600px, the images in the "More in Football" section start to get a little obnoxious. Introducing a media query here to float those stories to the side, as they were in Chapter 2, "Fluid Layouts," probably makes sense (**Figure 3.10**):

▶ **Note**

The mediaQuery bookmarklet (http://seesparkbox.com/foundry/media_query_bookmarklet) is a handy tool for seeing just what size your screen is as you resize, as well as what media queries are currently applied.

▶ **Note**

In case you're follow-
ing along you should
still be working in
the file located at
http://implementing
responsivedesign.
com/ex/ch3/
ch3.1.html.

```
1.   @media all and (min-width: 600px) {
2.       .slats li {
3.           float: left;
4.           margin-right: 2.5316456%; /* 24px / 948px */
5.           width: 31.6455696%; /* 300 / 948 */
6.       }
7.       .slats li:last-child {
8.           margin-right: 0;
9.       }
10.  }
```

▶ **Note**

Why 860px? There's
no hard rule. If you
think the layout can
be improved by
adding a breakpoint
earlier, go ahead and
do it. Just remember
that each breakpoint
adds a little complex-
ity, so try to find a
nice balance.

Around 860px, all the aside content starts to feel spaced out. The window is still too narrow to put the aside off to the right, so instead, float the aside sections so they line up in rows of two (**Figure 3.11**):

```
1.   @media all and (min-width: 860px) {
2.       aside{
3.           display: block;
4.           margin-bottom: 1em;
5.           padding: 0 1%;
6.           width: auto;
7.       }
8.       aside section{
9.           float: left;
10.          margin-right: 2%;
```

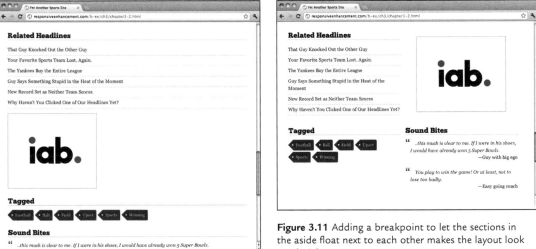

Figure 3.11 Adding a breakpoint to let the sections in the aside float next to each other makes the layout look much tighter.

```
11.          width: 48%;
12.      }
13.      .article-tags{
14.          clear: both;
15.      }
16.      .ad{
17.          text-align: center;
18.          padding-top: 2.5em;
19.      }
16.  }
```

At this breakpoint, it looks like the navigation items could be floated once again, instead of being stacked on top of each other (**Figure 3.12**). These styles are in the commented out CSS, so we'll grab them and place them in the media query. We'll also remove the border on the navigation items:

```
1.   @media all and (min-width: 860px) {
2.       ...
3.       nav[role="navigation"] li {
4.           float: left;
5.           border-top: 0;
6.       }
7.       nav[role="navigation"] a {
8.           float: left;
9.       }
10.      footer[role="contentinfo"] .top {
11.          float: right;
12.      }
13.  }
```

Figure 3.12 There's enough room to float the navigation now, bring the content further up the page.

Finally, it looks like the aside can be brought back up and to the right around 940px. The sections in the aside will also need to be told to not float, and to take up the full width once again:

```
1.    @media all and (min-width: 940px) {
2.        .main {
3.            display: table-cell;
4.            padding-right: 2.5316456%; /* 24px / 948px */
5.        }
6.        aside {
7.            display: table-cell;
8.            width: 300px;
9.        }
10.       aside img {
11.           max-width: 100%;
12.       }
13.       aside section {
14.           float: none;
15.           width: 100%;
16.       }
17.   }
```

At this point, the layout at 940px or wider looks a lot like it did at the end of Chapter 2, "Fluid Layouts" (**Figure 3.13**).

Figure 3.13 With one more breakpoint, the layout on a screen at least 940px wide looks a lot like it did before we started.

Figure 3.14
For wider screens, splitting the article in two columns helps to maintain a reader-friendly line length.

Enhancing for larger screens

Making the browser window even wider reveals that it's not long before the line length for the article starts to be hard to read. Many sites implement a max-width here to limit just how far the browser window can be resized, or bump the font size to improve the line length.

Instead of capping the width of the page just yet, let's make use of CSS3 multi-column layouts.

The multi-column layout module lets you tell the browser to display the content in several columns as needed (**Figure 3.14**). Support isn't too bad: Opera, Firefox, and WebKit all support it. Just be sure to use the correct prefixes in the case of Firefox, Internet Explorer 10, and WebKit. No prefix is necessary for Opera or Internet Explorer. Since this is a nice feature to have, but not essential to the site, we can progressively enhance the experience for these browsers:

```
1.  @media all and (min-width: 1300px) {
2.      .main section {
3.          -moz-column-count: 2; /* Firefox */
4.          -webkit-column-count: 2; /* Safari, Chrome */
5.          column-count: 2;
6.          -moz-column-gap: 1.5em; /* Firefox */
7.          -webkit-column-gap: 1.5em; /* Safari, Chrome */
8.          column-gap: 1.5em;
9.          -moz-column-rule: 1px dotted #ccc; /* Firefox */
10.         -webkit-column-rule: 1px dotted #ccc; /* Safari, Chrome */
```

```
11.         column-rule: 1px dotted #ccc;
12.       }
13.   }
```

Lines 3–5 tell the browser how many columns it should use to display the article. Lines 6–7 tell the browser to insert a 1.5em gap (24px) between the columns. Finally, lines 9–11 tell the browser to include a 1px, light gray dotted line in that gap to provide a little more visual separation (**Figure 3.15**).

The line length is now much better, but the page could still benefit from some separation between the article and the author information. The picture could use a little more distance from the content as well:

```
1.   @media all and (min-width: 1300px) {
2.       .main section img{
3.           margin-bottom: 1em;
4.           border: 3px solid #dbdbdb;
5.       }
6.       .main .articleInfo{
7.           border-bottom: 2px solid #dbdbdb;
8.       }
9.       ...
10.  }
```

With the border in place around the image and above the section, and the addition of the extra padding, the design is once again looking pretty sharp.

Figure 3.15
The addition of some spacing and a border help to separate the image from the text that follows.

That guy has the ball

In what has to be considered a development of the utmost importance, that man over there now has the ball.

By Ricky Boucher | January 1, 2012

Lorem ipsum dolor sit amet, consectetur adipiscing elit. Nulla accumsan felis quis nibh pretium tempus. Nullam quis rhoncus massa. Vivamus laoreet convallis sem ac dapibus. Donec varius congue sem ac molestie. Nam purus neque, tincidunt ut aliquam dapibus, dictum a magna. Curabitur sagittis mi et ante aliquet tristique vitae nec

viverra non, sodales eget augue. In hac habitasse platea dictumst. Class aptent taciti sociosqu ad litora torquent per conubia nostra, per inceptos himenaeos. Praesent nec neque quis odio hendrerit auctor nec vel erat. In ullamcorper nulla sed ipsum elementum varius. Morbi et sapien ac nisl suscipit tincidunt. Sed lacus nisl, tempus vel ultrices vel, vulputate a nunc. Suspendisse in diam vitae nulla tempor vulputate quis ac nunc.

Nam in dui eget augue malesuada adipiscing ac at massa. In sed auctor libero. Quisque egestas mollis lobortis. Vivamus lacinia metus at quam posuere condimentum. Vestibulum ante ipsum primis in faucibus orci luctus et ultrices posuere cubilia Curae; Etiam ipsum mauris, facilisis ut pharetra ut, lacinia vitae velit. Pellentesque habitant morbi tristique senectus et netus et malesuada fames ac turpis egestas.

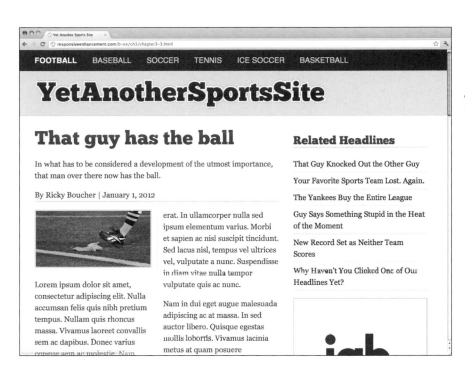

Figure 3.16 With pixel-based break-points if the visitor is browsing zoomed in, our carefully crafted layout goes to shambles.

Using ems for more flexible media queries

People browse the Web with their browsers set to different zoom factors. Some-one who has difficulty seeing may find that the majority of sites have a font size that is difficult to read, so he may set his preferences to zoom in by default.

When people use different zoom factors, the font size increases (or decreases). In Firefox and Opera, this isn't an issue; pixel-based media queries are recalcu-lated and applied according to the zoom factor. On other browsers, however, our perfectly placed pixel breakpoints fail us. Suddenly things start to float in awkward ways and our ideal line length is mercilessly thrown out the window (**Figure 3.16**). This same issue arises when, as we discussed in Chapter 2, "Fluid Layouts," a device uses a different default font size. For example, the Kindle's 26px sized fonts will wreck havoc on pixel-based media queries. We can combat these issues and make our site even more flexible by converting the breakpoints to ems.

As we also discussed in Chapter 2, converting pixel-based measurements to ems is as simple as dividing the target (the breakpoint) by the context (in this case, 16px, the body font size):

```
1.    /* 600px/16px = 37.5em */
2.    @media all and (min-width: 37.5em) {
3.    ...
4.    }
5.    /* 860px/16px = 53.75em */
6.    @media all and (min-width: 53.75em) {
7.    ...
8.    }
9.    /* 940px/16px = 58.75em */
10.   @media all and (min-width: 58.75em) {
11.   ...
12.   }
13.   /* 1300px/16px = 81.25em */
14.   @media all and (min-width: 81.25em) {
15.   ...
16.   }
```

▶ **Note**

If you zoomed in after loading the page, you may need to hit refresh to see it update. Most people using this feature have their zoom level set ahead of time, so this isn't typically an issue.

With the media queries now set using ems, even if the site is zoomed in a few levels, the media queries will kick in, ensuring that the layout remains optimized (**Figure 3.17**).

Using media queries based on em units is another way of embracing the flexibility and unpredictability of the Web. It puts the user in control of the experience, and allows the content to dictate the layout.

Figure 3.17 By setting breakpoints in em units, you ensure that the visitor will get an appropriate layout no matter their zoom factor.

Figure 3.18 When you view the page on a phone, the content is buried beneath a long list of navigational items.

Navigation

There's one last issue to be addressed before we wrap up our introduction to media queries: site navigation. All the excellent content in the world won't keep a visitor on your site if he can't figure out how to move around. Your navigation needs to be accessible and easy to use, no matter the screen size.

The navigation in our example is not mobile friendly at the moment. Stacking the navigational items on top of one another does make everything look tidy, but the article—the reason the visitor came to the page in the first place—gets buried (**Figure 3.18**).

What we want is navigation that adheres to the following criteria:

- It shouldn't take up precious screen real estate.

- It should be intuitive so the user doesn't feel disoriented or confused.

- It should be usable by a wide variety of devices (though the experience may vary depending on the capabilities of a given device).

▶ **Note**
Read Brad Frost's
post at http://
bradfrostweb.com/
blog/web/responsive-
nav-patterns/ for
a detailed list of
responsive naviga-
tion approaches, as
well as the benefits
and disadvantages
of each.

Let's run through a few quick options.

- **Don't do anything.** That's what the page essentially does right now. It's intuitive and the solution works on a variety of devices, but it consumes a lot of screen real estate.

- **Convert to select menu.** We could convert the navigation to a select menu. This would conserve screen space, be usable by most devices, and fall back nicely on those devices that can't handle the necessary JavaScript. However, select menus are familiar to users as being part of a form. They might be a little thrown off to see it used for navigation. We can't style it either, as most browsers don't allow for that.

- **Toggle the menu.** On small screens, we could use JavaScript to hide the navigation initially and offer the user a button to click to make the navigation display. This method passes all three tests: it conserves screen real estate, the solution is intuitive to the user, and it can be implemented on a wide variety of devices and falls back nicely on devices where JavaScript is not supported.

Since the toggle menu passes all three tests, let's use that approach for the *Yet Another Sports Site*.

Toggling

▶ **Note**
To improve the
solution, generate
the collapse button
dynamically using
JavaScript. There's no
reason for it to exist
when the JavaScript
isn't being applied.

You can implement a simple toggle with just a few lines of CSS and JavaScript.

First, add a link to your HTML that can be used to toggle the navigation. You can place the link right above the navigation list.

```
<a href="#nav" class="nav-collapse" id="nav-collapse">Menu</a>
<ul class="nav" id="nav">
```

TOGGLE CSS

Now, in the CSS, create a few rules to style the collapse button, and hide it initially.

```
1.    #nav-collapse{
2.        display: none;
3.        color: #fff;
4.        text-align: right;
5.        width: 100%;
6.        padding: .625em 0 .625em 0;
7.    }
```

```
8.    #nav-collapse.active {
9.        display: block;
10.   }
```

Lines 1–7 set a few basic styles on the collapse button, and hide it initially. Remember, if the browser doesn't support JavaScript, the navigation appears right away and the button is no longer necessary.

Lines 8–10 display the button if a class of "active" is applied. The JavaScript applies this class.

Using these styles, nothing changes in the browser without any JavaScript applied. This is what we want. If a browser doesn't support the necessary JavaScript, the navigation will be completely useful. Ideal, no. Useful, yes.

TOGGLE JAVASCRIPT

The JavaScript, too, is simple. Create a file called yass.js and include the script in your HTML, just before the closing body tag.

```
<script type="text/javascript" src="yass.js"></script>
```

Now, drop the following Javascript into yass.js.

```
1.    window.onload = function() {
2.        var collapse - document.getElementById('nav-collapse');
3.        var nav = document.getElementById('nav');
4.        //toggle class utility function
5.        function classToggle( element, tclass ) {
6.            var classes = element.className,
7.                pattern = new RegExp( tclass );
8.            var hasClass = pattern.test( classes );
9.            //toggle the class
10.           classes = hasClass ? classes.replace( pattern, '' ) :
              classes + ' ' + tclass;
11.           element.className = classes.trim();
12.       };
13.       classToggle(nav, 'hide');
14.       classToggle(collapse, 'active');
15.       collapse.onclick = function() {
16.           classToggle(nav, 'hide');
17.           return false;
18.       }
19.   }
```

When the page loads (line 1), it runs the JavaScript above. Lines 2–3 grab the navigation element and the collapse button so the script can refer to them later.

Lines 5–12 create a simple `toggleClass` function. This function takes an element, and checks to see if a specified class is applied. If it is, it removes it. If not, it applies it.

Lines 13–14 apply the `hide` class to the navigation and the `active` class to the button.

Finally, lines 15–18 define a function that is called anytime the collapse button is clicked. When called, the function toggles the `hide` class currently applied to the navigation. The result is that the button now controls the display of the navigation.

Right now, this code is run no matter what. Obviously, we don't want this. Instead, the code should run only when the navigation is displayed as a stacked list. It would be easy enough to check the width of the screen, but that would mean the breakpoint would be hard-coded in two locations: the CSS and the JavaScript.

If the script instead checks to see if the navigation is being floated and runs based on that, the breakpoint is kept in one place, making it easier to change later. While we're making that change, we can also pull the `classToggle` function out and put it into a utility object that we can build on later.

```
1.    var Utils = {
2.        classToggle : function(element, tclass) {
3.            ...
4,        }
5.    }
6.    window.onload = function() {
7.        var nav = document.getElementById('nav');
8.        var navItem = nav.getElementsByTagName('li');
9.
10.       //is it floated?
11.       var floated = navItem[0].currentStyle ? el.currentStyle['float'] :
          document.defaultView.getComputedStyle(navItem[0],null).
          getPropertyValue('float');
12.
13.       if (floated != 'left') {
14.           var collapse = document.getElementById('nav-collapse');
```

```
15.
16.            Utils.classToggle(nav, 'hide');
17.            Utils.classToggle(collapse, 'active');
18.
19.            collapse.onclick = function() {
20.                Utils.classToggle(nav, 'hide');
21.                return false;
22.            }
23.        }
24.    }
```

Let's break this down a bit.

Lines 8–11 grab a navigation item and check to see if it's floated. Line 11 might look a little intimidating, but all it's really doing is checking to see which way it should request the current style information. Internet Explorer doesn't play along very well, so if that's the browser being used, it checks a different property.

Armed with the value of the float property, the rest of the JavaScript can now be run only if the navigation items are floated. If we apply this and refresh the browser on a large screen, nothing happens. On a small-screen display, however, the collapse button appears on page load, allowing the navigation display to be toggled (**Figure 3.19**).

▶ **Note**

It's beyond the scope of this book, but if you want to boost your JavaScript skills, pick up a copy of *Professional JavaScript for Web Developers*, by Nicholas C. Zakas (Wrox, 2009).

Figure 3.19 With the toggling functionality in place, the navigation stays out of the way until the visitor needs it.

Supporting Internet Explorer

We're not in the clear quite yet. Everyone's favorite desktop browser, Internet Explorer, is giving us some headaches.

Only Internet Explorer versions 9 and later support media queries. This means that, if you've built mobile first, users with earlier versions will be presented with a layout intended for small screens.

This can quickly be fixed by using conditional comments to load the appropriate styles for Internet Explorer. Since we already have an ie.css stylesheet in place from Chapter 2, "Fluid Layouts," this should be pretty simple.

First, we'll change the conditional comment to apply to all versions of Internet Explorer prior to version 9. This means that version 9, which supports display:table, will use floats instead, but that minor trade off is worth it to avoid the added complexity of another Internet Explorer–specific stylesheet:

```
<!--[if (lt IE 9) & (!IEMobile)]>
<link rel="stylesheet" href=""/css/ie.css" media="all">
<![endif]-->
```

Now, we'll add the styles that were included only in the media queries and drop them into the Internet Explorer stylesheet:

```
1.   .main {
2.       float: left;
3.       width: 65.8227848%; /* 624 / 948 */
4.   }
5.   .slats li {
6.       float: left;
7.       margin-right: 2.5316456%; /* 24px / 948px */
8.       width: 31.6455696%; /* 300 / 948 */
9.   }
10.  .slats li:last-child {
11.      margin-right: 0;
12.  }
13.  aside{
14.      display: block;
15.      margin-bottom: 1em;
16.      padding: 0 1%;
```

```
17.        float: right;
18.        width: 31.6455696%; /* 300 / 948 */
19.    }
20.    nav[role="navigation"] li {
21.        float: left;
22.        border-top: 0;
23.    }
24.    nav[role="navigation"] a {
25.        float: left;
26.    }
27.    footer[role="contentinfo"] .top {
28.        float: right;
29.    }
30.    aside img {
31.        max-width: 100%;
32.    }
```

Internet Explorer should now be good to go. It's not responsive, but at least it serves up a fluid layout that displays pretty well at most screen sizes.

Wrapping it up

Fluid layouts are a start, but they can only take us so far. At some point, we need to adjust the layout, sometimes dramatically, to better accommodate different devices.

Smartphones try to let us experience the full Web. If the meta viewport element isn't being used, most smartphones display a zoomed version of the site.

Media queries let us test for features like width and height and adjust the CSS we apply to our design accordingly. They can be used both externally and internally. Each method has benefits and limitations, so it's important to choose the approach that best meets the project requirements.

While it's common to pick specific device widths for breakpoints, a better approach is to let the content dictate where you need to include a media query.

Responsive sites can be made even more flexible and accessible using ems, instead of pixels, for media queries.

Be sure to test on real devices. Doing so will alert you to things like navigation that may require adjustment for different displays.

In the next chapter, we'll look at the different approaches you can take to serve images that are sized appropriately, greatly improving the performance of your site in the process.

CHAPTER 4

RESPONSIVE MEDIA

Look! We've figured it seventeen different ways, and every time we figured it, it was no good, because no matter how we figured it, somebody don't like the way we figured it.

—BUDDY HACKETT AS BENJY BENJAMIN IN
IT'S A MAD MAD MAD MAD WORLD

When it comes to rich experiences online, we have a love/hate relationship. On one hand, beautiful images and interesting videos help to provide a deeper, more pleasant experience. On the other hand, including many images and videos on a page results in a slow loading time, which can be very frustrating. It takes careful consideration and planning to give our users the best of both worlds: a beautiful experience that loads as quickly as possible.

Using the methods outlined in the first three chapters, we've built ourselves a responsive site. It looks good on desktops, on tablet devices, and on smartphones. Users can resize the browser window to their hearts' content, and the layout will adjust accordingly. If delivering a responsive approach were this easy, this book would be short indeed. There's still plenty of room to tidy things up. The images, in particular, are an issue.

In this chapter, we'll discuss:

- Why performance matters
- How to conditionally load images
- What responsive image solutions are available, and their limitations
- How to swap out background images without downloading multiple images
- How to conditionally load web fonts
- What's ahead for responsive images
- How to make embedded video scale while maintaining its aspect ratio
- What to do with responsive advertising

What's the problem?

Once we hit the final breakpoint (1300px), the images associated with the "More in Football" section look a little worse for wear. Other than that, the images appear sharp and crisp.

We could probably improve the lead-in photograph for small screens. If the small version of the image were more tightly cropped, the image would maintain its initial impact, even when scaled down on the small screen. As it is, the flag and foot start to get lost at such a small size (**Figure 4.1**).

Figure 4.1 On small-screens, the flag and foot in the main image start to lose their impact.

The main problem though is not in how the images look, but in how much they *weigh*, how much demand they place on performance. Currently, the same images are being loaded regardless of the device in use. That means, for example, the 624px lead-in image is being downloaded even on small screens where a 350px image is all that's needed. The page performance is suffering, and that's a big deal to people visiting the site.

Performance

Unfortunately, performance is treated as an afterthought on many projects. A quick look at the data reveals that it should be anything but.

Most of us working with the Web have faster connections than the average Internet user. As a result, we experience the Web differently. Our users, however, are keenly aware of how painful it is to use a poorly performing site.

In 2009, the major shopping comparison site Shopzilla improved its page load time from 4 to 6 seconds to 1.5 seconds. The results were stunning. The site's conversion rate increased by 7 to 12 percent and page views jumped a whopping 25 percent.[1]

---

1 "Shopzilla Site Redesign–We get what we measure" at www.scribd.com/doc/16877317/Shopzillas-Site-Redo-You-Get-What-You-Measure

Mozilla found similar results when it trimmed page load time by 2.2 seconds: download conversions went up by 15.4 percent, which translated into an estimated 10.28 million additional downloads of Firefox per year![2]

The situation is much more dire for mobile phones. Networks are slower, hardware is less capable, and you have to deal with the messy world of data limitations and transcoding methods. In spite of all this, user expectations remain the same. In fact, 71 percent of mobile users expect sites to load on their phones as quickly as or faster than on their home computers.[3]

This is bad news for our site as it currently stands. Both the logo and article lead-in photo are very large. The article lead-in photo is 624px wide and weighs around 50KB. The small-screen layout could get away with using a much smaller image (somewhere around 300px), but we're still passing along the large desktop image instead of something more appropriate. Removing the amount of data sent down the pipe is an important consideration, and one we can't afford to ignore.

A quick assessment of the page reveals the following images that could be optimized:

- **The images for the "More in Football" section.** Each of these is only 300px, but they're really not needed on the small screen. In fact, they take up a lot of screen real estate and look out of proportion with the content (**Figure 4.2**). On the small screen, users have a better experience if only the headlines are displayed—not the images.

- **The article lead-in image.** The lead-in image is a whopping 624px and weighs in at just under 50KB. On small screens, an image half the size would work just as well. In addition, if the small-screen version of the image was more tightly cropped, the visual focus on the flag would be stronger.

- **The logo.** The logo weighs in at 10KB, so it's much lighter than the lead-in article. It is, again, about twice as big as it needs to be.

---

2   "Firefox & Page Load Speed–Part II" at http://blog.mozilla.org/metrics/2010/04/05/ firefox-page-load-speed---part-ii/

3   "What Users Want from Mobile" at www.gomez.com/resources/whitepapers/ survey-report-what-users-want-from-mobile/

Figure 4.2 The images in the "More Football" section take up a lot of precious screen real estate on small-screen devices.

Selectively serving images to mobile

Let's start by removing the images in the "More in Football" section from the core experience. It might be tempting to just use display:none and call it a day, but that doesn't fix the problem, it only hides it.

An image set to display:none will still be requested and downloaded by the browser. So while the image won't show up on the screen, the issue of the extra request and weight is still there. Instead, as usual, the correct approach is to start with mobile first and then progressively enhance the experience.

Begin by removing the images from the HTML entirely:

```
1.  <ul class="slats">
2.      <li class="group">
3.          <a href="#">
4.              <h3>Kicker connects on record 13 field goals</h3>
5.          </a>
6.      </li>
```

```
7.        <li class="group">
8.            <a href="#">
9.                <h3>Your favorite team loses to that team no one likes</h3>
10.           </a>
11.       </li>
12.       <li class="group">
13.           <a href="#">
14.               <h3>The Scarecrows Win 42-0</h3>
15.           </a>
16.       </li>
17.   </ul>
```

**● Custom data
attributes**
Preceded by a
data- prefix, these at-
tributes store custom
data private to the
page, often for script-
ing purposes.

Obviously, the images will not load with this HTML. On the small-screen
display, that's the way it'll stay. For the larger sizes, a little JavaScript will bring
the images back. Using the HTML5 data-* attributes as hooks, it's easy to tell
the JavaScript which images to load:

```
1.    <ul class="slats">
2.        <li data-src="images/ball.jpg" class="group">
3.            <a href="#">
4.                <h3>Kicker connects on record 13 field goals</h3>
5.            </a>
6.        </li>
7.        <li data-src="images/goal_post.jpg" class="group">
8.            <a href="#">
9.                <h3>Your favorite team loses to that team no one likes</h3>
10.           </a>
11.       </li>
12.       <li data-src="images/ball_field.jpg" class="group">
13.           <a href="#">
14.               <h3>The Scarecrows Win 42-0</h3>
15.           </a>
16.       </li>
17.   </ul>
```

JavaScript

The first thing to add is a quick utility function to help select elements. It's not
necessary, but it's definitely useful to have around:

```
1.    q : function(query) {
2.        if (document.querySelectorAll) {
```

```
3.              var res = document.querySelectorAll(query);
4.          } else {
5.              var d = document,
6.              a = d.styleSheets[0] || d.createStyleSheet();
7.              a.addRule(query,'f:b');
8.              for(var l=d.all,b=0,c=[],f=l.length;b<f;b++) {
9.                  l[b].currentStyle.f && c.push(l[b]);
10.                 a.removeRule(0);
11.                 var res = c;
12.             }
13.             return res;
14.         }
15.     }
```

If you're unfamiliar with native JavaScript, that might look a bit messy. That's OK. All the function does is take a selector, and return the elements that match it. If you can grasp the code, that's great. If not, as long as you understand what it accomplishes, that's enough for our purposes.

Armed with that function, the part that actually loads the images is pretty straightforward:

```
1.  //load in the images
2.  var lazy = Utils.q('[data-src]');
3.  for (var i = 0; i < lazy.length; i++) {
4.      var source = lazy[i].getAttribute('data-src');
5.      //create the image
6.      var img = new Image();
7.      img.src = source;
8.      //insert it inside of the link
9.      lazy[i].insertBefore(img, lazy[i].firstChild);
10. };
```

Line 2 grabs any elements with a data-src attribute applied. Then, in line 3 the script loops through those elements. In lines 4–7, the script creates a new image for each element using the value of the data-src attribute. The script then inserts the new image (line 9) as the first element within the link.

With this JavaScript applied, the images aren't requested right away. Instead, they're loaded after the page has finished loading, which is what we want. Now, we just have to tell the script not to load for small screens.

Guy Podjarny

PERFORMANCE IMPLICATIONS OF RESPONSIVE DESIGN

Guy Podjarny, or Guypo for short, is a web performance researcher and evangelist, constantly chasing the elusive instant web. He focuses heavily on mobile web performance, and regularly digs into the guts of mobile browsers. He is also the author of Mobitest, a free mobile measurement tool, and contributes to various open source tools. Guypo was previously the co-founder and CTO of Blaze.io, later acquired by Akamai, where he now works as a Chief Product Architect.

Responsive Web Design (RWD) tackles many problems, and it's easy to get lost in questions around how maintainable, future-friendly, or cool your responsive website will be. In the midst of all of these, it's important to not lose sight of how *fast* will it be. Performance is a critical component in your user's experience, and many case studies demonstrate how it affects your users' satisfaction and your bottom line.

Today, smartphone browsers are often redirected to dedicated mobile websites, known as *mdot* sites, which tend to be significantly lighter in content and visuals than their desktop counterparts. This translates to having fewer images, scripts and stylesheets to download, which helps make those websites faster. The equation is simple—downloading fewer bytes with fewer requests is faster than having more of both.

Responsive websites, however, don't follow this pattern. I recently ran a performance test on 347 responsive websites (All the websites listed on http://mediaqueri.es/ in March, 2012). I loaded the homepage of each in a Google Chrome browser window resized to 4 different sizes, ranging from 320x480 to 1600x1200. Each page was loaded multiple

times using www.webpagetest.org, a web performance measurement tool.

The results were depressing. Despite changing their look across window sizes, the weight and load time of the website hardly changed. 86% of the websites weighed roughly the same when loaded in the smallest window, compared to the largest one. In other words, despite the fact the websites *look* like an mdot site when loaded on a small screen, they are still downloading the full website content, and are thus painfully slow.

While every website is different, three causes for this over-downloading repeated across practically all websites.

- Download and Hide
- Download and Shrink
- Excess DOM

Download and Hide is by far the top reason for this bloat. Responsive websites usually return a single HTML to any client. Even on "Mobile First" websites, this HTML contains or references all that's needed to provide the richest experience on the biggest display. On a smaller screen, sections that shouldn't be shown are hidden using the display:none style rule.

Unfortunately, `display:none` doesn't help performance one bit, and resources referenced in a hidden part of the page are downloaded just the same. Scripts within hidden sections still run. DOM elements are still created. As a result, even when hiding the majority of your page's content, the browser will still evaluate the page in resources and download all the resources it can find.

Download and Shrink is a conceptually similar problem. RWD uses fluid images to better match the different screen sizes. While visually appealing, this means the desktop-grade image is downloaded every time, even when loaded on a much smaller screen. Users cannot appreciate the high quality image on the smaller screen, making the excess bytes a complete waste.

Excess DOM is the third episode of the same story. RWD websites return the same HTML to all clients. Browsers parse and process hidden areas of the DOM despite being hidden. As a result, loading a responsive website on a small screen results in a DOM that is far more complicated than what the user experience demands. A more complicated DOM leads to higher memory consumption, expensive reflows, and a generally slower website.

These problems are not simple to solve, since they're the result of how RWD and browsers work today. However, there are a few practices that can help you keep your performance under control:

- Use Responsive Images
- Build Mobile First
- Measure

Responsive Images are already discussed in this book at length, and help address the "Download and Shrink" problem. Since images are the bulk of the bytes on each page, this is the easiest way to significantly reduce your page's weight. Note that CSS images should be responsive as well, and can be replaced using media queries.

Build Mobile First means going a step beyond designing a Mobile First website, and actually coding a dedicated website for the lowest resolution you care about. Once implemented, this website should perform as well as other mdot sites, and be reasonably lightweight. From that point on, only enhance the page using JavaScript or CSS, to avoid over-downloading. Clients that have no JavaScript support will get your basic experience, which should be good enough for these edge cases. Note that enhancing with JavaScript and keeping performance high isn't simple, and best practices for it are not fully established yet—which brings me to my next point.

Measure. Treat performance as a core part of your website's quality, and don't ship without understanding and accepting its performance. If you know your mobile website weighs over 1 MB, you're likely to delay its launch until you do something about it. Measurement tools vary, but I would recommend Mobitest for testing on real devices (http://akamai.com/mobitest) and WebPageTest for testing on desktop browsers (www.webpagetest.org), resized them using the `setviewportsize` command.

In summary, Responsive Web Design is a powerful and forward thinking technique, but it also carries with it significant performance implications. Make sure you understand these challenges and design to avoid them, so that users won't abandon your website before they got to experience your amazing visuals and content.

Introducing matchMedia

In Chapter 3, "Media Queries," the script we built to toggle the display of the navigation on small screens checked to see if the list items in the navigation were floated. If they were, the collapse feature was created. This time, let's use the handy matchMedia() method.

The matchMedia() method is a native JavaScript method that lets you pass in a CSS media query and receive information about whether or not the media query is a match.

To be specific, the function returns a MediaQueryList object. That object has two properties: matches and media. The matches property returns either true (if the media query matches) or false (if it doesn't). The media property returns the media query you just passed in. For example, the media property for window.matchMedia("(min-width: 200px)") would return "(min-width: 200px)".

matchMedia() is supported natively by Chrome, Safari 5.1+, Firefox 9, Android 3+, and iOS5+. Paul Irish has created a handy polyfill for browsers that don't support the method.

With the matchMedia polyfill in place, telling the browser to insert only the images above the first breakpoint simply requires wrapping the code inside a matchMedia check:

▶ **Note**
Irish's polyfill is available on GitHub at https://github.com/paulirish/matchMedia.js or in the example files on the companion site at http://www.implementingresponsivedesign.com.

● *Polyfill*
A snippet of code that provides support for a feature the browser does not yet support natively.

```
1.  if (window.matchMedia("(min-width: 37.5em)").matches) {
2.      //load in the images
3.      var lazy = Utils.q('[data-src]');
4.      for (var i = 0; i < lazy.length; i++) {
5.          var source = lazy[i].getAttribute('data-src');
6.          //create the image
7.          var img = new Image();
8.          img.src = source;
9.          //insert it inside of the link
10.         lazy[i].insertBefore(img, lazy[i].firstChild);
11.     };
12.  }
```

Now when the page is loaded on a phone, or the screen is sized down, the images are no longer requested (**Figure 4.3**). This is a big win for performance on small screens. There are now three fewer HTTP requests, and the size of the page has been reduced by about 60KB (the size of those three images combined). Best of all, the headlines are still there and the links are completely functional. The experience doesn't suffer at all.

Figure 4.3 On small screens, the images in the "More in Football" section won't be requested, greatly improving the performance of the page.

With those images out of the way, we can focus on the lead-in image and the logo. We want those images, the logo in particular, to show up no matter the resolution. So, instead of conditionally loading them, we'll load them every time, but sized appropriately. This is where things get hairy.

Responsive image strategies

They say there are only seven stories in the world, they just get told in different ways. In the same way, there are currently only three strategies for handling responsive images: fighting the browser, resignation, or going to the server.

Fighting the browser

Most front-end solutions attempt to fight the browser. They try their best to switch which image is loaded before the browser can download the wrong one.

This is an increasingly difficult task. Browsers want pages to load quickly, so they go to extreme lengths to download images as quickly as possible. Of course, this is a good thing—you want your site to load as quickly as possible. It's really only annoying when you want to beat them to it.

Resignation

A few strategies out there basically admit defeat to the browser. Typically the approach is to load the small-screen image first, by default. Then, if necessary, load the larger image for larger screens as well.

Obviously this is not ideal. Larger screen devices will be making two requests where only one is needed. That's something to avoid if possible. Performance is important on large-screen devices, too.

Going to the server

Finally, a few methods use the server and some form of detection to determine which image to load. This method doesn't have to race the browser, because all the logic is executed before the browser ever sees the HTML.

However, going to the server is also not particularly future friendly. Maintaining information about every device that might request your content will become increasingly difficult as they proliferate (thanks to the decrease in the cost of manufacturing computing devices). Information about devices will also be less reliable as more and more devices allow content to be viewed in different ways: projections, embedded webviews, or on another screen entirely.

Responsive image options

There are limitations to every approach to responsive images currently available. To illustrate this, let's look at a couple different techniques for setting responsive images, and evaluate whether they're right for the *Yet Another Sports Site* page.

Sencha.io Src

Sencha.io Src is as close as you're going to get to a plug-and-play solution for responsive images. The service, originally created by James Pearce, takes an image that you pass and returns it resized. To use it, you simply preface your image source with the Sencha.io Src address like so:

```
http://src.sencha.io/http://mysite.com/images/football.jpg
```

Sencha.io Src uses the user agent string of the device making the request to figure out what size the device is and then resizes your image accordingly. By default, it resizes the image to 100% of the screen width (though it will never size up).

A great deal of customization is possible. For instance, if you want the service to resize your image to a specific width, you can pass that along as another parameter. For example, the following line of code resizes the image to 320px wide:

```
http://src.sencha.io/320/http://mysite.com/images/football.jpg
```

▶ **Note**
You can find detailed documentation for Sencha.io Src at http://docs.sencha.io/0.3.3/index.html#!/guide/src

Sencha.io Src is also smart enough to cache the requests, so the image isn't generated each and every time the page loads.

Unfortunately, this probably isn't the best solution for *Yet Another Sports Site.* Sizing the images to 100% of the screen size only helps on small screens. On a large display, when the article spans two columns, the image remains its original size because Sencha.io Src looks at the screen width, not the width of the containing element. While it's possible to tell Sencha.io Src to use that width, it involves using the service's experimental client-side measurements feature and doing a bit of JavaScript hackery.

While the current version of the page doesn't run into the issue, Sencha.io Src is also limiting if you want to do more than just resize an image, for instance, if you want to recrop the image. Perhaps the "More in Football" images could become square thumbnails at some point. If they did, a simple resize wouldn't work. Some art direction capability is needed, and Sencha.io Src doesn't allow for that.

You might also be a bit uncomfortable using a third-party solution for this. If the company changes its policy or goes out of business, you could very well be out in the cold and looking for another solution entirely.

Adaptive Images

Another solution bordering on plug-and-play is Adaptive Images, created by Matt Wilcox. It determines the screen size and then creates, and caches, a resized version of your image.

▶ **Note**
The code for Adaptive Images can be found at http://adaptive-images.com

It's an excellent solution for an existing site where you may not have time to restructure your markup or code. Getting it up and running is a simple three-step process:

1. Place the .htaccess and adaptive-images.php files that are included in the download into your root folder.

2. Create an ai-cache folder and grant it write permissions.

3. Add the following line of JavaScript to the head of your document:

```
<script>document.cookie='resolution='+Math.max(screen.width,
screen.height)+'; path=/';</script>
```

That line grabs the resolution of the screen and stores it in a cookie for future reference.

While there are many options you can configure in the adaptive-images.php, much of the time you'll be able to get away with just setting the $resolutions variable to include your breakpoints:

```
$resolutions = array(860, 600, 320); // the resolution breakpoints to
use (screen widths, in pixels)
```

If you're paying close attention, you'll notice that the breakpoints are slightly off from the CSS of the *Yet Another Sports Site* page. There's no 320px break-point in the CSS, and the highest two breakpoints, 1300px and 940px, are not included in the $resolutions array. This is because of the way the script works.

The smallest breakpoint, in this case 320px, is the size at which the image will be created for any screen that does not exceed that width. So, for example, a 300px screen will receive a 320px image because it's the lowest size defined in the $resolutions array. A 321px screen, since it exceeds the 320px value de-fined in the array, will receive the next size image—in this case, 600px. If we left 600px as our first breakpoint, any device with a screen size below 600px would have received a 600px image.

We also don't need the two highest breakpoints, because again, the script will try to resize an image to the breakpoint size. It will never size the image larger than it already is, so really, anything above 624px (the physical dimension of the image) doesn't matter much—the script won't resize the image.

Once created, the images are stored in the ai-cache folder (you can change the name) so they don't have to be regenerated. There's also a configuration setting to control how long the browser should cache the image.

The installation is simple, and again, it's a great solution for existing sites that need to get something in place, but it's not without its faults. Unfortunately, no opportunity for art direction exists since the images are dynamically resized.

Art direction and responsive images

Much of the conversation about responsive images revolves around file size. While that's an important consideration, it isn't the only one. Sometimes, resizing an image for smaller screens can reduce its impact.

Consider this example photo of a football helmet.

The photo looks nice at its original size, and is well balanced. If we make the image smaller, suddenly the helmet is almost too small to be recognized.

This is an instance where art direction is necessary. Resizing the image alone causes it to lose its impact and recognizability. By tightening the crop instead, we keep the focus on the helmet despite the small image size.

The script also doesn't help you if the image is actually smaller at a large resolution. For the *Yet Another Sports Site* page, that's a problem. When the screen is above 1300px, the article goes to two columns and the image is placed inside one of them, reducing its size. Using the Adaptive Images script, the largest version of the image will still be downloaded.

○ *Content Delivery Network*
A collection of servers deployed in multiple locations to help deliver content more efficiently to users.

The other concern with this approach is that the URL stays the same, regardless of the size of the image being requested. This could cause issues with *Content Delivery Networks (CDNs)*. The first time a URL is requested, the CDN may cache it to improve the speed the next time that same resource is requested. If multiple requests for the same URL are made via the same CDN, the CDN may serve up the cached image, which may not be the size you actually want served.

What's ahead for responsive images?

Just to be clear: relying on a combination of server-side detection and JavaScript cookies is entirely a stopgap method. If there were something more permanent out there, I'd advocate it. Unfortunately every responsive image method available today is essentially a hack, a temporary solution to cover up the problem.

More long-term solutions, such as a new element, new attribute or new image format, have been discussed. In fact, if you're feeling a bit frisky, there's a fully functioning polyfill for one such as-yet non-existent element available on GitHub at https://github.com/scottjehl/picturefill. Unfortunately, the problem is far from being solved because the answer isn't as simple as "what is easy for developers to use."

In a blog post discussing the conflict of opinions between two popular proposed solutions, Jason Grigsby hit the problem on the head.[4] To improve performance, browsers want to be able to download images as soon as possible, before the layout of the page is known. Developers, on the other hand, rely on knowledge about the page layout to be able to determine which image to load. It's a difficult nut to crack.

I am confident that with time, a proper solution will emerge. In the meantime, as already mentioned, the best approach will vary depending on the project at hand.

---

4 Read more about the real conflict behind <picture> and @srcset at http://blog.cloudfour.com/the-real-conflict-behind-picture-and-srcset/

Wait, what's the answer here?

Ultimately, no definitive solution currently exists for responsive images. Each method has advantages and disadvantages. The approach you take will depend on the project you're working on.

Of the two approaches we've discussed, settling on Adaptive Images is probably the best route to take since it doesn't require any reliance on a third-party source.

Background images

The folks over at *Yet Another Sports Site* are pretty happy with the site, but they'd like to see a visual indication in the header that helps visitors identify which section of the site they're in.

After 30 seconds of exhausting Photoshop work, we provide them with two silhouettes of footballs as shown in **Figure 4.4**.

They're happy with the way this looks on the large screen, but on anything smaller than the 53.75em breakpoint, where the logo starts to overlap, they'd like the background image to go away.

This is another area where building mobile up is helpful. Let's consider what would happen if we built the site desktop down using media queries.

Your base styles would be the place to include the background image and you would have to override it in a later media query. It would looked something like this:

```
1.    /* base styles */
2.    header[role="banner"] .inner{
3.        background: url('../images/football_bg.png') bottom right
      no-repeat;
4.    }
5.    ....
6.    @media all and (max-width: 53.75em) {
7.        header[role="banner"] .inner {
8.            background-image: none;
9.        }
10.  }
```

Figure 4.4
The header sporting its spiffy new background image.

On paper, this seems fine. But in reality, for many browsers, this would result in downloading the image even on a small screen device where it wouldn't be used. Most notable among these is the default browser on Android 2.x. Remember, while version 4 is current at the time of this writing, about 95 percent of Android devices are running an earlier version. This means that almost all Android traffic on mobile devices would be downloading the image without needing it.

To avoid this penalty, a better method would be to declare the background image within a media query like so:

```
1.   /* base styles */
2.   @media all and (min-width: 53.75em) {
3.       header[role="banner"] .inner{
4.           background: url('../images/football_bg.png') bottom right
                 no-repeat;
5.       }
6.   }
7.   ....
8.   @media all and (max-width: 53.75em) {
9.       header[role="banner"] .inner {
10.          background-image: none;
11.      }
12.  }
```

Doing that would be enough to get Android to play along nicely.

Since we built the page mobile up, the whole process is much simpler. The base experience doesn't need the background image, so we can introduce it in a media query later on:

```
1.   /* base styles */
2.   @media all and (min-width: 53.75em) {
3.       header[role=banner] .inner{
4.           background: url('../images/football_bg.png') bottom right
         no-repeat;
5.       }
6.   }
```

► **Note**
If you want the juicy details about a variety of methods for replacing and hiding background images, take a look at http://timkadlec.com/2012/04/media-query-asset-downloading-results/ to see the tables of results from tests I've been running.

Using this approach means that only browsers that need to display the background image will request it—performance problem solved!

Of course, once again, building mobile up means that Internet Explorer 8 and below won't see this background image by default. However, we already have an IE-specific stylesheet in place thanks to conditional comments. We can just add this declaration in there and we're good to go.

While we're at it

Currently, we're using web fonts to load the ChunkFive font that is being used in the header elements. The style declaration looks like this:

```
1.   @font-face {
2.       font-family: 'ChunkFiveRegular';
3.       src: url('Chunkfive-webfont.eot');
4.       src: url('Chunkfive-webfont.eot?#iefix') format
         ('embedded-opentype'),
5.           url('Chunkfive-webfont.woff') format('woff'),
6.           url('Chunkfive-webfont.ttf') format('truetype'),
7.           url('Chunkfive-webfont.svg#ChunkFiveRegular') format('svg');
8.       font-weight: normal;
9.       font-style: normal;
10.  }
```

▶ **Note**
Why all the different font files? You have browser differences to thank for that. While browser support is pretty good, they can't seem to agree on one format.

That declaration works nicely. The browser grabs the file it needs and renders the font. The sizes of the files aren't even that bad. There's a downside though. Currently, WebKit-based browsers won't display text styled with a web font until that web font has been downloaded. This means that if a user comes along on an Android, BlackBerry, or iPhone over a slow connection (or uses a laptop through a tethered connection for that matter), the header elements will take some time to actually display. This is a confusing experience for users and should be avoided.

We can't determine bandwidth (yet—check out Chapter 9, "Responsive Experiences," for a preview of what's to come), but we know the likelihood of a slow network is highest with a mobile device. It would be nice to save the user the trouble and load the fonts for larger screens only.

The approach we used to conditionally load background images works for fonts as well. So, let's move the @font-face declaration inside of a media query. Doing so ensures that devices below that breakpoint will not attempt to grab the fonts:

```
1.   @media all and (min-width: 37.5em) {
2.       ...
3.       @font-face {
4.           font-family: 'ChunkFiveRegular';
5.           src: url('Chunkfive-webfont.eot');
6.           src: url('Chunkfive-webfont.eot?#iefix')
             format('embedded-opentype'),
7.             url('Chunkfive-webfont.woff') format('woff'),
8.              url('Chunkfive-webfont.ttf') format('truetype'),
9.              url('Chunkfive-webfont.svg#ChunkFiveRegular')
     format('svg');
10.          font-weight: normal;
11.          font-style: normal;
12.      }
13.   }
```

With that small tweak in place, the web font will load only on screens larger than 37.5em (~600px). While it's still possible for a user with a slow connection to get stuck with the WebKit delayed loading bug, by removing the fonts from small-screen displays we've also removed the most likely victim: people using mobile devices (**Figure 4.5**).

Figure 4.5
Web fonts will no longer be loaded on small screens to improve performance.

High-resolution displays

Just in case you thought swapping images out based on screen size wasn't difficult enough, it turns out there is at least one more situation that might require different images: high-resolution displays. The problem really started with the Retina display on the iPhone 4, but it's been exacerbated by the iPad 3 and the latest versions of the MacBook Pro both supporting a Retina display.

The Retina display sports a whopping 326ppi (pixels per inch) pixel density, compared to 163ppi for the iPhone 3 display. This high density means that images can appear to be incredibly detailed and sharp—if they're optimized for the display. If they're not, they will appear grainy and blurry.

● *Pixel density*
The number of pixels within a specified space. For example, 326ppi means there are 326 pixels within every inch of a display.

Creating images for high-resolution displays means creating larger images, which in turn means larger file sizes. Therein lies the rub. You don't want to pass these larger images to screens that don't need them. Currently, there isn't a great way to do that with content images: it's the same sort of problem we discussed previously when trying to load images appropriate for different screen widths.

For CSS images, you can use the `min-resolution` media query for all browsers except those running on WebKit. For WebKit-based browsers, you must use the `-webkit-min-device-pixel-ratio` media query.

The `-webkit-min-device-pixel-ratio` media query takes a decimal value representing the pixel ratio. To target the Retina display on the iPhone, iPad, or new MacBook Pro you need a value of at least 2.

The `min-resolution` media query takes one of two values. The first is the screen resolution in either dots per inch or dots per centimeter. Doing this requires a little math, and some of the early implementations were inaccurate. As a result, I recommend using the new dots per pixel (dppx) unit. Not only does it remove the need for any math (it lines up perfectly with the ratio value accepted by the `-webkit-min-device-pixel-ratio` media query), but it also avoids the older, incorrect implementations. Support for the dots per pixel unit is still a little sketchy, but since displaying Retina-ready images is a nice enhancement rather than an essential feature, I'm pretty comfortable using it.

```
1.  header[role="banner"] .inner {
2.      background: url('../images/football_bg_lowres.png') bottom right
        no-repeat;
3.  }
4.  @media only screen and (-webkit-min-device-pixel-ratio: 2),
5.      only screen and (min-resolution: 2dppx) {
6.          header[role="banner"] .inner {
7.              background: url('../images/football_bg_highres.png')
                bottom right no-repeat;
8.          }
9.  }
```

The above media query targets any device with a pixel ratio of at least 2. Lines 1–3 set the background image for low resolutions. Lines 4 and 5 target devices with a pixel ratio of at least 2. If the pixel ratio is at least 2, then lines 8–10 apply a higher-resolution image for the background.

SVG

One solution for both high-resolution displays and images that scale across screen sizes is Scalable Vector Graphics (SVG). SVG images are vector images whose behavior is defined in XML. This means they can scale well without actually increasing file size. It also means they can be programmatically altered and adjusted.

One great example of how SVG can improve an experience is the work Yiibu, a mobile company in Edinburgh, did for the Royal Observatory at Greenwich. The company was working on a project that involved a responsive site featuring images of constellation patterns that needed to scale down. When using regular images and scaling, the small-screen images lost much of their detail. Using SVG and some smart scaling, Yiibu was able to adjust the images for small screens so the detail was retained (**Figure 4.6**).

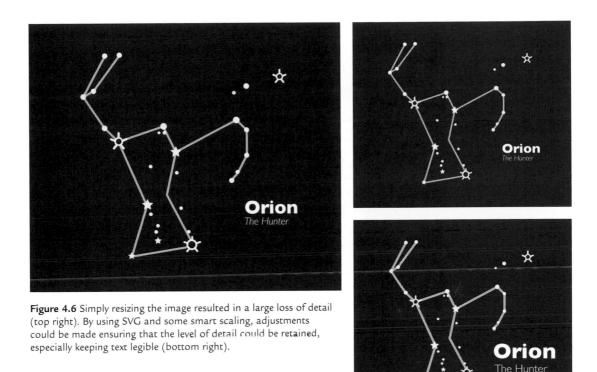

Figure 4.6 Simply resizing the image resulted in a large loss of detail (top right). By using SVG and some smart scaling, adjustments could be made ensuring that the level of detail could be retained, especially keeping text legible (bottom right).

There are two real issues standing in the way of SVG: browser support and lack of tools. As usual, Internet Explorer 8 and under don't play along. More importantly, neither does the default browser on Android 2.x—the most popular version of that platform. Those browsers that *do* support SVG images vary in their level, and quality, of support.

The most popular tools for image creation and manipulation, such as Photoshop, are not built with vector formats like SVG in mind. If you want to create SVG images, you need to find another tool to do it in.

As tools and browsers start to catch up, SVG images may become a very common tool in a web developer's toolbox.

Other fixed-width assets

Images aren't the only asset that present some problems for responsive sites. Let's look at two in particular: video and advertising.

Video

Embedding videos in a responsive site is, perhaps surprisingly, a little more complicated than it first appears. If you're using HTML5 video, it's simple. You can use the same max-width technique we discussed for making images fluid:

```
1.    video{
2.        max-width: 100%;
3.        height: auto;
4.    }
```

Most sites, however, pull their videos from a third party (YouTube or Vimeo, for example) using an iFrame. If you apply the same trick, the width scales but the height retains its original value, breaking the aspect ratio (**Figure 4.7**).

Figure 4.7 Unfortunately, using max-width: 100% and height: auto on video embeds will result in the video breaking the aspect ratio.

That guy has the ball

In what has to be considered a development of the utmost importance, that man over there now has the ball.

By Ricky Boucher | January 1, 2012

Goofy - How to Play Football (1944)   Share ⬇ More info

Lorem ipsum dolor sit amet, consectetur adipiscing elit. Nullam tristique elit eget erat placerat non sagittis augue pharetra. Cras quam arcu, elementum quis tincidunt sed, interdum id elit. Aenean ullamcorper bibendum odio a rutrum. Vestibulum ante ipsum primis in faucibus orci luctus et ultrices posuere cubilia Curae; Donec at ullamcorper neque. Proin

The trick is something Thierry Koblentz called "intrinsic ratios."[5] The basic idea is that the box that contains the video should have the proper aspect ratio of the video (4:3, 16:9, and so on). Then, the video needs to fit the dimensions of the box. That way, when the width of the containing box changes, it maintains the aspect ratio and forces the video to adjust with it.

The first thing to do is create a wrapping element:

```
1.    <div class="vid-wrapper">
2.         <iframe></iframe>
3.    </div>
```

▶ **Note**
If you prefer, there's a helpful jQuery plug-in called FitVids that automates the process of making videos respond. Visit GitHub at https://github.com/davatron5000/FitVids.js to download it.

The wrapper serves as the containing box so it needs to maintain the proper aspect ratio. In this situation, the aspect ratio is 16:9. The video itself is positioned absolutely, so the wrapper needs an adequate amount of padding applied to maintain the ratio. To maintain the 16:9 ratio, divide 9 by 16, which gives you 56.25%.

```
1.    .vid-wrapper{
2.         width: 100%;
3.         position: relative;
4.         padding-bottom: 56.25%';
5.         height: 0;
6.    }
7.    .vid-wrapper iframe{
8.         position: absolute;
9.         top: 0;
10.        left: 0;
11.        width: 100%;
12.        height: 100%;
13.   }
```

The styles above also position the iFrame absolutely within the wrapper and set the height and width to 100% so it stretches to fill (lines 11–12). The wrapper itself is set to 100% of the article's width (line 2) so it adjusts as the screen size adjusts.

With these styles in place, the video responds to different screen sizes while maintaining its original aspect ratio.

---

5 "Creating Intrinsic Ratios for Video" at www.alistapart.com/articles/creating-intrinsic-ratios-for-video/

ENHANCING THE EXPERIENCE

As always, it's worth taking a step back and considering how the experience can be enhanced. At the moment, the video is being downloaded on all devices. That might not be the best approach for the base experience. To speed up the core experience, it would be nice to display only a link to the video. Then, for larger screens, the video embed could be included.

To do this, start with a simple link:

```
<a id="video" href="http://www.youtube.com/watch?v=HwbE3bPvzr4">
Video highlights</a>
```

You can also add a few simple styles to make sure the text link doesn't look out of place:

```
1.   .vid{
2.        display: block;
3.        padding: .3em;
4.        margin-bottom: 1em;
5.        background: url(../images/video.png) 5px center no-repeat #e3e0d9;
6.        padding-left: 35px;
7.        border: 1px solid rgb(175,175,175);
8.        color: #333;
9.   }
```

There's nothing too fancy going on here. We gave the link a little padding and margin to set it apart from the rest of the content, and applied a background with a video icon set to the left (**Figure 4.8**).

Now, with JavaScript, convert the link to the appropriate embed.

Figure 4.8 With some styles in place, the video link fits nicely in with the rest of the page.

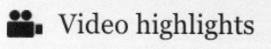

Add the following function to the `Utils` object in yass.js:

```
getEmbed : function(url){
      var output = '';
      var youtubeUrl = url.match(/watch\?v=([a-zA-Z0-9\-_]+)/);
      var vimeoUrl = url.match(/^http:\/\/(www\.)?vimeo\.com\
/(clip\:)?(\d+).*$/);
      if(youtubeUrl){
            output = '<div class="vid-wrapper"><iframe src="http://
            www.youtube.com/embed/'+youtubeUrl[1]+'?rel=0"
            frameborder="0" allowfullscreen></iframe></div>';
            return output;
      } else if(vimeoUrl){
            output =  '<div class="vid-wrapper"><iframe src="http://
            player.vimeo.com/video/'+vimeoUrl[3]+'" frameborder="0">
            </iframe></div>';
            return output;
      }
}
```

Let's walk through the function.

The function takes the URL of the video as its only parameter. It then determines if the URL is a YouTube video or a Vimeo video using regular expressions (lines 4–5). Depending on the URL type, it creates the embed markup including the containing element and returns it (lines 5–11).

Armed with the `getEmbed` function, it's easy to convert the video link to an embed. Throw the following JavaScript within the `matchMedia("(min-width: 37.5em)")` test:

```
//load in the video embed
var videoLink = document.getElementById('video');
if (videoLink) {
      var linkHref = videoLink.getAttribute('href');
      var result = Utils.getEmbed(linkHref);
      var parent = videoLink.parentNode;
      parent.innerHTML = result + videoLink.parentNode.innerHTML;
      parent.removeChild(document.getElementById('video'));
}
```

Figure 4.9 On large screens (right) the video is embedded but small screens will see a link to the video instead.

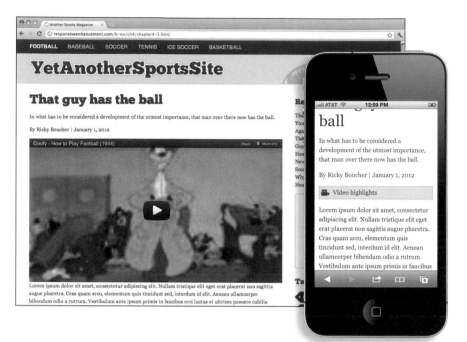

The first two lines grab the link to the video and the link's href. On line 5, the link is passed to the getEmbed function we created. Once you have the result, lines 6–8 insert it into the article and remove the text link (**Figure 4.9**).

Now the video embed is responsive, and is pulled in only when the screen size is greater than 37.5em, ensuring that the base experience won't need to make the expensive HTTP requests to embed the video.

Advertising

Another fixed asset that presents some difficulties is advertising.

Like it or not, advertising is a key part of many businesses' revenue stream online. We won't get into a debate here about advertising-based revenue versus the pay-for-content model; that's a discussion that gets ugly quickly. The reality of the matter is that for many businesses, ad revenue is essential.

From a purely technical standpoint, advertising in a responsive layout isn't that difficult to implement. You could use JavaScript to conditionally load an ad unit based on the screen size. Rob Flaherty, a developer in New York City, demonstrated a basic method:[6]

```
1.   // Ad config
2.   var ads = {
3.       leaderboard: {
4.           width: 728,
5.           height: 90,
6.           breakpoint: false,
7.           url: '728x90.png'
8.       },
9.       rectangle: {
10.          width: 300,
11.          height: 250,
12.          breakpoint: 728,
13.          url: '300x250.png'
14.      },
15.      mobile: {
16.          width: 300,
17.          height: 50,
18.          breakpoint: 500 ,
19.          url: '300x50.png'
20.      }
21.  };
```

This configuration sets up three different ads (leaderboard, rectangle, and mobile). Each ad has a width (lines 4, 10, and 16), height (lines 5, 11, and 17), URL (lines 7, 13, and 19), and breakpoint at which point the ad should load (lines 6, 12, and 18). You could use the `matchMedia` function to determine which ad should be loaded based on the breakpoint.

Even better, the ad itself could be responsive. It could consist of HTML and CSS that allow it to adjust to different screen sizes. Going this route would eliminate the JavaScript dependency and potentially allow the ad to do some cool things by playing on its interactive nature.

---

6 "Responsive Ad Demos" at www.ravelrumba.com/blog/responsive-ad-demos/

From a technical perspective, neither of these options is particularly difficult. The problem is that creating and displaying an ad has a lot of moving parts.

Most ads are served by third-party networks or the creative pieces are developed externally and then submitted according to the specifications of the site. At the moment, no major ad-serving networks accommodate varying ad sizes based on screen size.

Using an internal ad serving platform is a bit more flexible, but if the creative is developed outside your company, then you'll need to be willing to do some education. The people creating the ad materials may not be up to speed on what's going on.

More importantly, ads are currently sold much like they are in print: You pay based on the size and placement of the ad. So how exactly do you do that when the size and placement vary?

One solution is to sell ad groups instead of ads. For example, instead of selling a skyscraper ad, you sell a Premier Group ad (or whatever you want to call it). The Premier Group may consist of a skyscraper for screens above 900px wide, a boom box for screens above 600px but below 900px, and a small banner for screen sizes below that point.

Obviously, this won't be an easy transition. Creative teams, decision makers, and the salesforce all need to be educated on why this approach makes more sense than buying a defined ad space. It won't be an easy sell, but with time it should get easier.

The other consideration here is that some companies may want to target only a single form factor. Perhaps their service is something specific to mobile devices, and they decide they'd only like to serve their ads to those smaller screens. That of course throws a little wrinkle into the ad groups, as things start to get broken up.

Ultimately, I'd like to see the discussion of responsive advertising lead to fewer ad spots and a higher cost per ad. Sites whose revenues are ad-based frequently overload their pages with a plethora of ads. This makes the situation more difficult when trying to handle the small-screen experience. Do you hide all those ads, thereby limiting page views for your advertisers, or do you cram them all in there and ruin the experience for your visitors?

Instead of loading up pages with more and more ads, reduce the amount of ads on a page. Instead of ten ad slots at $1,000 per month, offer three at $4,000 each. Make the ad spaces something worth coveting. It benefits advertisers because they have fewer ads competing for attention, and it benefits users because they are greeted with a much better experience.

Unfortunately there's a chicken and the egg problem: advertising rates are currently a race to the bottom. Ads struggle to get quality click-through rates so the way to compete is to see how far you can lower the cost of entry. Someone has to be bold enough to make that first step.

Wrapping it up

Performance is an important consideration for any site. Loading images that are unnecessary or larger than needed can have a serious impact on page load time.

The CSS solution of `display:none` is not viable. It hides images from view, but they're still requested and downloaded. If you want images to show only above a certain breakpoint, the better bet is to load them conditionally, after the page load has occurred.

Responsive images are an unsolved problem. There have been many attempts at a solution but each has its own set of problems. The best thing you can do is take time before each project to consider which approach will work best for that site.

To hide background images without having to download them, include the image in a media query. Setting it in your base styles and then trying to hide it results in the image being downloaded in the majority of cases.

High-resolution displays, such as the Retina display on latest versions of the iPhone, iPad, and MacBook Pro, pose another challenge. There is a solution for CSS-based images, which can use the `min-resolution` media query.

Video and advertising are also concerns. For video, using the intrinsic ratio method can help you to scale the video appropriately across screen sizes. As always, be conscious of the performance. It may be best for users to simply link to the video on small screens and embed on larger ones.

For advertising, the technical challenges are not difficult to solve. If you're loading ads from your own system, JavaScript or some responsive HTML and CSS can help the ads change for different resolutions. The bigger problem arises in getting sales teams and third-party advertising networks to get on board.

CHAPTER 5
PLANNING

Before anything else,
preparation is the key to success.
—ALEXANDER GRAHAM BELL

Now that we've covered the basic ingredients of fluid layouts, media queries, and responsive media, we can take a step back and look at how responsive design affects the rest of the process, beginning with planning. Preparation is key, whether you're marching into battle, running a marathon, or building a responsive site. Building responsively means taking into account the diverse ecosystem of devices. Without proper preparation you'll find yourself trying to juggle the missing pieces and the quality of your site will suffer significantly. You need a plan.

That doesn't mean you'll stick to your plan from start to finish. In an environment that changes as swiftly as the Web does, you'll almost certainly encounter bumps in the road along the way. New platforms and devices emerge, deadlines shift, and priorities change. So, while it's important to have a process in place, it's equally important to be flexible and adapt. Plan to roll with the punches.

Choosing to be responsive

In 1997, in the middle of the first dot-com bubble, IBM aired a commercial featuring two businessmen seated at a conference table. One man was reading a newspaper while the other typed on a computer. The man reading the newspaper remarked, "It says here, the Internet is the future of business. We have to be on the Internet."

The other man looked up from his computer and asked, "Why?"

After a brief pause, the first man replied, "Doesn't say."

It's a humorous commercial, but it highlights a very real concern with many web projects: technology gets put ahead of strategy. Companies blindly latch onto the latest buzzword, social media craze, or hot platform, never considering whether it makes sense to do so.

The first step with any responsive project should be to determine whether embarking on the project makes any sense at all. Are you doing it because it's hip and cool? Or are you doing it because it makes sense for your specific situation?

Considerations

So, should you build a responsive site? The short and boring answer is: It depends. Before you decide, there are several factors to consider:

- Performance
- Context
- Content negotiation
- Time investment
- Support
- Advertising

If any of these considerations pose a serious roadblock, you may want to opt for a nonresponsive approach—for now. Let's look at each of them a bit more closely.

▶ **Note**
Responsive design and separate sites aren't mutually exclusive. You can (and should) still make use of the flexibility that media queries offer with a stand-alone mobile site. Read the sidebar by Tom Maslen for more.

Performance

Performance is an integral component of the user experience. What makes sense in terms of performance on one device or on one kind of network may not apply on another device.

Consider, for example, optimizing performance for mobile networks. On a wired connection, it makes sense to include styles and scripts externally. That way, the scripts and styles can be cached so the user won't have to download them again. On devices running on mobile networks, however, external styles and scripts can severely hamper your site's performance. Mobile networks suffer from dramatically increased latency, as well as reduced bandwidth, when compared to wired connections. As a result, when considering the performance of your site on a mobile connection, it often makes more sense to inline styles and scripts to reduce the number of requests.

Depending on how you swap out the images on a page, you may end up forcing the user to download multiple versions—even though he'll only ever need one. If you decide to hide content on smaller screens, that markup and CSS is still downloaded. If you're not careful about how you build your site, this can result in a site that is incredibly bloated and slow. It's possible to address these performance concerns with careful consideration, but it's not easy and, therefore, most people don't.

Context

The user experience on your site will vary depending on context. Different devices can be used for different tasks and in different environments. Mobile, in particular, can be used much differently than, say, a desktop computer.

For example, a geolocation service like Foursquare may interact in very different ways depending on the device in use. A news site, on the other hand, will work pretty consistently across different devices, because the experience doesn't rely as much on the context.

An event site might take advantage of knowing the user's location: If you can determine that the user is on his device on the day of a concert, and within a certain radius of the venue, then it would make sense to optimize the experience from his perspective, versus someone who's only considering whether or not to come to the event.

Content negotiation

You might also choose to reorganize or restructure the content of your site. Say a page has a large primary column and an aside. If you made the layout one column, the side column would be pushed below everything in the primary column. That's not always what you want. In many cases, the content in that side column may be far more important than the content toward the bottom of the primary column. If you don't reorder the content, that hierarchy will be lost (**Figure 5.1**).

Time investment

A responsive approach typically, and probably not surprisingly, requires a greater investment of time up front than a nonresponsive approach. You're considering numerous devices with varying capabilities and that takes time. You need to take stock of what devices exist, what devices to support, and how someone using a particular device might want to interact with your content. There are a lot more variables in play.

Not all of this time is lost. Much of it will be made up in the long run, when you're maintaining one site instead of many. So what you lose in the initial design of the project, you'll most likely make up in maintenance costs.

Figure 5.1 On large screens, the button to download the YAML framework is prominently displayed to the right of the screen. On smaller screens, it gets buried well out of sight.

Still, if you need to launch next month, a responsive approach is probably not feasible. If you have time to devote to creating a high-quality site, that's when you should be thinking responsively.

Support

Building a responsive site from the desktop down, as it is still most often done, presents a problem for many mobile devices. While modern Web-Kit browsers have good support for media queries, many other popular mobile browsers do not. If you start with the desktop experience, those devices will be greeted with the desktop version of the site—assuming they can handle it.

If you instead take a page from the progressive enhancement playbook and flip this approach on its head (as discussed in Chapter 3, "Media Queries") you can avoid this problem. Code for the least capable browser first. Then use media queries to progressively enhance the experience, starting with the smallest screen and building up.

If you want to capitalize on the ubiquity of the Web, building for the least capable browser first is the only responsible option. There's no guarantee that new and popular devices will be any more capable than current devices.

Advertising

The issue of advertising on responsive sites goes beyond mere technical limitations. A fundamental gap exists between how the industry is structured today, and where it needs to be tomorrow. Networks, clients, agencies—all of them need to be educated on how to create ads that will appear in different sizes on different devices.

From the technical side of things, not only does the solution have to allow for different ads to be served to different devices, but it must also allow for the opportunity for an advertiser to *not* display their ads at some resolutions. For example, an advertiser may decide that their product is best served by placing a mobile ad, and only a mobile ad. As Jason Grigsby[1] mentioned in a conversation with me about this topic "segmentation is part of advertising."

Solving the issues of selling and producing advertising for responsive designs is an important step because advertisers stand to benefit substantially from placing appropriate ads on a carefully crafted responsive site. Large banner ads are lost on small screens on a nonresponsive site. A responsive approach can ensure that an appropriate ad is served for each resolution.

Conclusion

Despite the limitations of our current tools and mindset, don't dismiss the potential of responsive design. When used carefully, and in conjunction with the right techniques, a responsive approach can be the starting point for most sites. Just remember that being responsive is not the destination. A responsive approach is a big piece of the puzzle, but in the end it's just one piece.

---

1   www.cloudfour.com

Once you've determined that a responsive approach is right for your project, you need to decide how you're going to implement it. Responsive design isn't something you can just sprinkle on at the end. You need to consider it carefully throughout the process.

Consider your analytics

With 35 billion Internet-enabled devices in use, you can't possibly optimize for each one individually. First, you need to identify the types of devices that are most important in the context of your project. Then build in a way that's aimed at these, but that will also accommodate the maximum number of remaining devices out there.

While one of the benefits of responsive design is that your layout can be almost device agnostic, this doesn't mean you should ignore the device itself—quite the opposite. Each device has different capabilities, limitations, and potential uses. Support varies from platform to platform. Devices may be used on different types of networks, which impacts performance. Depending on the form factor of a device, you may need to adjust the user interface to improve the experience (**Figure 5.2**).

Figure 5.2 Devices come in all shapes and sizes, which affects how you should design your site.

To understand which devices and form factors you should be optimizing for, you need to know what devices are being used to view your site and what they're capable of. Armed with this information, you can start making decisions about just which devices to test on, and which features to enhance for different platforms.

Carefully comb through your analytics and see what devices people are using. Find the behaviors. For example, are there devices that are used frequently, but in shorter sessions? Perhaps the experience needs to be improved for them.

Then, back up this information with market share data. For example, if you find the traffic for a particular device is very low, but the market share is quite high, that's a hint that something is lacking in that experience.

A word of caution: Be very careful that you are considering all factors when drawing conclusions from your site's analytics. Devices vary dramatically in how they communicate with your analytics program of choice as it attempts to collect data. This can lead to stats that are skewed in one direction or the other.

Skewed site analytics

For example, many analytics services, including the popular Google Analytics, use a snippet of JavaScript as the default method of tracking. That code snippet then passes along information about visitors and their devices to the analytics provider. The problem with a JavaScript-driven approach is that you may very well be missing out on a significant segment of your visitors.

Many mobile devices lack support for JavaScript. While the most common offenders are feature phones, many more capable smartphones are susceptible to this problem as well. For example, many BlackBerry devices have JavaScript support turned off by default. Since a large number of users will never enable it, they could be visiting your site without any record of them ever being there.

An even greater concern is the fact that devices have varying levels of support for JavaScript. Partial support means not only that you can't ensure that your analytics will be complete, but you also can't guarantee the analytics you do get are accurate.

One alternative is to use an image beacon approach rather than JavaScript. Google Analytics actually uses this method in its alternate "mobile" snippet. The mobile snippet is a chunk of server-side code that creates an `img` element on your page. The `src` attribute of the `img` sends the visitor and device information back to Google for tracking.

There are some potentially serious downsides to using server-side code. Unless you make adjustments to the default snippet, you'll lose ancillary information such as what version of Flash the visitor has installed, screen resolution, and level of JavaScript support. You'll lose the ability to perform event tracking and track outbound links, because the snippet cannot be adjusted to track these out of the box.

What you'll gain by using the image beacon approach is a more complete picture of the devices and browsers used to access your site. The top devices and browsers in use may shift only slightly from the JavaScript-based results, but the long tail of smaller numbers will typically extend—often significantly. You may be surprised to find how many devices are being used to access your site.

Finally, be wary of self-fulfilling prophecies. If you haven't optimized your site for different platforms and browsers, don't be surprised if that portion of your traffic is very low. When you don't water your plants, they die.

Which stats matter

After considering your existing site analytics, it's important to study the general statistical trends in the market as a whole. If a platform or browser is significantly underrepresented when compared to the broader market, it's a clue to dig a little deeper and think critically about why that might be the case. It could be that you've been dissuading those visitors by being inconsiderate of their experience with your site.

Deciding which devices to target requires taking a composite look at a variety of different metrics: There is no one stat to rule them all and bind them.

◆ **Tip**
Want the best of both worlds? Consider using server-side detection to swap between the JavaScript and image beacon methods of analytics. We'll talk more about server-side detection in Chapter 8, "RESS."

Tom Maslen

SMALL PHONE, BIG EXPECTATIONS

Tom Maslen is a senior web developer working in the BBC News web development team, leading the clientside development of m.bbc.co.uk/news. Having relaunched the mobile version of BBC News, creating a modern responsive experience for all types of mobiles and tablets, his team is now working to move the desktop BBC News experience onto the responsive code base. Maslen's a JavaScript specialist with a strong focus on browser performance and accessibility in standards-compatible web pages. Outside of work Maslen keeps guinea pigs, is Skyrim's most deadly archer, and is a long suffering supporter of Tottenham Hotspur Soccerball Club.

SMALL PHONE, BIG EXPECTATIONS

Mobile is now a part of people's everyday lives, and the rapid increase in smartphone ownership is changing how users access BBC News online. Until recently, we had a low-end mobile site for low-end devices and a desktop site for high-end browsers. But we found that more and more users were accessing our desktop site via their smartphones—clearly these users wanted a better experience than the mobile site was offering.

It was also clear that mobile users wanted—and could deal with—more information on the screen than we believed they did, even though the desktop site required lots of pinching and zooming to navigate on a touchscreen device.

One approach to fulfilling users' needs would have been to create a unique web app for every possible combination of device screen, interaction type, connection speed, and processor strength. Jakob Nielsen was right when he asserted that users on different devices have different needs.[2] But in practice, implementing this strategy would have been impossibly expensive; even Google admitted that it couldn't afford to do this.[3]

We didn't accept Nielsen's view that mobile and desktop require separate designs. Using responsive web design, we knew we could create a solution that provided a base experience to less capable browsers, with added layers of sophistication for more modern browsers depending on the abilities of the device and screen size.

Any responsive experience needed to be at least comparable in quality to what users had come to expect from the native BBC News app on their phones. This meant loading pages quickly and using touch gestures and animations in a modern manner. To test this idea, we started prototyping a responsive approach in the spring of 2011.

In addition to creating a modern experience for smartphones, we were keen not to alienate users with low-end mobile phones. Although in the West smartphones have very high market penetration, there are many markets around the world where low-end phones are still dominant.

---

2 Jakob Nielsen, "Mobile Site vs. Full Site" at www.useit.com/alertbox/mobile-vs-full-sites.html

3 Vic Gundotra, VP of engineering at Google, slide 35 from www.slideshare.net/commuterjoy/responsive-design-bbccouk-8687366

With the prototype, we proved that a responsive experience could cater to low-end devices' need for simple content delivered very efficiently, while also enhancing this base experience for smartphones. The prototype made extensive use of feature detection to test the capabilities of the client device before deciding whether to enhance the core experience or not.

ABOUT THE MOBILE-ONLY RESPONSIVE WEBSITE

In March 2012 we relaunched our mobile product. While targeting only mobile phones initially, we built the new site using responsive design principles with the idea that we would eventually use this code base to deliver the news to all users on mobile devices, tablets, and desktop computers.[4]

Having two code bases—one for desktop and another for everything else—doesn't sound very responsive, and that's because it isn't. Unfortunately much of the content on the BBC News website doesn't work on small screens. The BBC News development team is spending the next year changing the workflow that produces these different kinds of content into a format that will work with responsive web design.

For example, the work that comes out of the BBC News Specials team is very graphic-oriented. Interactive designers work with journalists to produce really great content like "Can you build a human body?"[5] However, in its current state, that page doesn't work on a small screen.

We are actively working to resolve these issues, but until we do there will continue to be a need for the legacy desktop product.

RESPONDING TO FEEDBACK

When we relaunched the mobile site, the audience feedback, as expected, was mixed. Smartphone users overall were positive about the new design, while some users on older handsets did not like the new layout.

The immediate audience analytics feedback was also interesting. Our user numbers were stable but page views were down, showing that users were viewing fewer pages per visit. We were expecting this to some extent. Our new homepage offers more information than the previous. While traffic for the homepage changed only slightly, the number of people visiting the other sections on the site dropped. We have responded by prioritizing some navigation improvements, which we released within a month of launch, and traffic to section pages, such as Technology and Business, has now risen.

Users of devices with a landscape display pointed out that the page design, which has a large image that stretches across the width of the page at the top of the screen, was too large. We are working in fortnightly iterations and after launch we added an additional breakpoint into the design. For devices with a width between 480px and 640px, a media query for landscape orientation was added. This changed the image so it was set to 50% of the width and floated left, with the title text wrapping next to it.

As more content is released onto the responsive code base, we expect usage to rival that of the desktop site. As more people access the Internet with more types of devices, the differences between the "mobile Internet" and the "Internet" will disappear, and responsive web design will become the industry standard.

---

4 BBC News Mobile site at http://m.bbc.co.uk/news

5 "Can you build a human body" at www.bbc.co.uk/news/health-17235058

Jason Grigsby's blog post "A 'Comprehensive' Guide to Mobile Statistics"[6] is an excellent resource for anyone trying to figure out which statistics to pay attention to. While the post is targeted at mobile statistics, the advice can easily extend to planning a responsive project as well. For web developers, Grigsby recommends paying attention to three metrics in particular:

- **Mobile Web Metrics**

  Mobile web metrics tell you which devices and browsers are being used to access the Web. This is an incredibly important metric. If 5 million people own the same type of device, but no one uses it to browse the Web, then you have to question whether it makes sense to optimize for that device—even with its high popularity.

- **Demographic surveys**

  Demographic surveys help you to identify how people use different devices. People of different ages, backgrounds, and income levels may use devices in very different ways. Understanding their behavior ensures that your site will not only work on their device, but also fit your target audience's needs.

- **Installed base market share**

  Stats about installed base market share look at how many devices are being used—not just sold. It's important to pair this information with the information provided by mobile web metrics and demographic surveys. Try to find that sweet spot where the installed base is high within your specific target market.

Since a responsive approach is not just about trying to meet the needs of mobile users, you need to give equal attention to these same metrics across the many other kinds of devices that sport a web browser. You can find this data through any number of third-party sources.

---

6 A "Comprehensive" Guide to Mobile Statistics at www.cloudfour.com/ a-comprehensive-guide-to-mobile-statistics/

Skewed market share statistics

Market share stats can be skewed for a number of reasons. The accuracy of the collection method is the primary issue, but the way a specific platform behaves can also cause problems. Consider the BlackBerry. Web traffic from BlackBerry devices is routed through RIM's proxy servers, which happen to be in Canada. As a result, when you look at the IP address, it will appear as though the visitor is coming from Canada. This results in the US market share of BlackBerry web traffic often being underreported.

Consider your content

We've all been there. You're told to design a site, or worse yet, to start creating the markup and CSS without knowing what the actual content will be. For the majority of sites on the Web, content is the backbone. It's what brings people to a site in the first place. Isn't it amazing then that, for so long, it's been treated as an afterthought for most projects?

From a designer's point of view, how can you design without being familiar with the content? Design isn't about choosing pretty colors and rounded corners. Design adds meaning. It helps to tell the story the content is trying to relate. It's awfully hard to tell a story you *don't know*.

Of course, you can't wait until all the content is final before beginning layout and related tasks. Try to do that and you're doomed to failure. Content is an ongoing job, one that must be considered carefully throughout the lifespan of the project. Instead of having *all* the content in place before starting, focus on understanding the types of content you need to support and where that content needs to go.

Designers and developers should be kept informed all along, otherwise you end up needing to restructure the markup or rearrange the design to accommodate some chunk of content you didn't know was coming. And if you thought that was inconvenient in the world of the desktop, read on.

Understanding the structure and hierarchy of your content is incredibly important in a responsive site. As you adjust the design for different resolutions, simply reducing the number of columns for viewing on smaller screens is not enough. Often you'll have to decide whether or not to change the way the content is supposed to display.

For example, for a news site on a large screen, it may make sense to show the title, description, and image of the 10 most recent articles. As the screen gets smaller, it might make sense to display only the last five posts. At its smallest size, it might serve the design best if those five were instead displayed as an unordered list.

A firm understanding of the types and structure of the content that will be displayed on a page makes these kinds of decisions easier. As you adjust the design, this knowledge will help you determine what content should be displayed, what content can be tucked away, and what content should take priority.

At this stage in the process, you should be answering questions like:

- Who is the intended audience?
- What content is already available?
- How can existing content be simplified and condensed?
- What is the key message?
- Is there any content that does *not* support the key message?
- What is the hierarchy of the content?

Two deliverables in particular can help you answer these questions: the content audit and page tables.

Content audit

At the very least, you should know what content you have now. A content audit accomplishes that. The content audit is an assessment, or inventory, of all the existing content on a website. Conducting a content audit serves many purposes. The audit reveals information about the structure, location, and maintenance of each page of content. It can also reveal the gaps in your content: what's missing that should be added going forward. Finally, a content audit serves as an excellent aid in content migration. It provides a roadmap from the old site to the new one, eliminating a lot of the guesswork that is often involved in the process of migrating a site to a newer design or a different CMS.

To conduct an audit, you go page by page through your site, recording information about each piece of content in a spreadsheet. This spreadsheet becomes a resource you can turn to when you need to remember who maintains a specific page, or where certain content resides.

Henny Swan

RESPONSIVE DESIGN AND ACCESSIBILITY

Swan is a UK-based web accessibility specialist who focuses on video on demand and mobile. She currently works for the BBC on iPlayer and is writing mobile accessibility standards and guidelines. She can be found on Twitter as @iheni and at her blog, www.iheni.com.

Building a responsive site is probably the most efficient way to make content accessible to diverse users. A single code base with good structure, alternatives, labels, and editorial—built with respect for the principles of progressive enhancement—can go a long way toward ensuring cross-device accessibility. But it's not a silver bullet. What works well on a desktop may introduce issues when viewed on a tablet or mobile, so it's important to understand where the breakpoints are, that is, where accessibility breaks depending on the device.

An essential ingredient of accessible sites is structure. Correct use of headings, WAI-ARIA (Web Accessibility Initiative-Accessible Rich Internet Applications) landmarks, paragraphs of text, and lists group related information in a way that can be understood by assistive technologies such as screen readers and voice input software, and provides navigation within a page. Content that's made up of five H2s with text paragraphs under them on a desktop might be reduced to a list of five links on a mobile device. Main navigation that comprises six links on desktop might

pack away into a single drop-down menu on mobile. This reduction for mobile makes coding the five headings as H2s redundant, as they're now a list. Mobile has also engineered itself out of needing a navigation landmark. In fact, keeping the H2s and landmarks in this instance could introduce a degree of verbosity and clutter for screen reader users.

While we often concern ourselves with how well WAI-ARIA or HTML5 is supported across devices, there are breakpoints for HTML 4. Coding techniques we rely on for desktop may not be supported on mobile. Using tabindex="-1" around repeated links works fine on desktop, but is not supported on mobile. Hover states, title, abbr, and span also suffer.

Despite the breakpoints, responsive design remains the most efficient way to include diverse users. Smart use of media queries should help reflow content in a way that's understandable regardless of the user's ability, how content is accessed, or what the content is viewed on.

	A	B	C	D	E	F	G	
1	Page ID	Page Name	Link	Document Type	Topics, Keywords	Owner/Maintainer	ROT?	Notes
2	2.0.0	About Yet Another Sports Site	/about	default_page.php	All pages in this section use Standard Meta Tags	Jeff Lenz		
3	2.1.0	Editorial Staff	/about/editorial	default_page.php		Jeff Lenz		
4	2.1.1.0	Erik Pennycuff	/about/editorial/erik-pennycuff	bio.php		Jeff Lenz		
5	2.1.2.0	Derek Lehman	/about/editorial/derek-lehman	bio.php		Jeff Lenz		
6	2.1.3.0	Michael Weideman	/about/editorial/michael-wiedeman	bio.php		Jeff Lenz	O	Broken image
7								
8								
9								
10	Major Sub-Section							
11	Top-level, section top page							
12	Cross-link							

Figure 5.3 A content audit details the structure, location and maintenance considerations of content across your site. You may find that you need additional columns, or fewer, depending on your project.

There are many templates out there to get you started, but my favorite was first mentioned in an article by Jeffrey Veen way back in 2002.[7] The template (pictured in **Figure 5.3**) is very simple, you won't get caught up in bells and whistles. The template includes columns for:

- **Page ID:** A unique identifer for the page.

- **Page Name:** The title of the page.

- **Link:** The url where the page resides.

- **Document type:** The template the page uses.

- **Topics, keywords:** The topics the page is about and the keywords to be used.

- **Owner/Maintainer:** Who is responsible for the content on the page.

- **ROT:** Redundant, out of date, or trivial. Indicates if the page should be removed for the new site.

- **Notes:** Any general commentary about the page. This could be broken images, HTML problems, or just reminders for later.

By going through your content with a fine-tooth comb, you also become aware of the quality of different content on the site. This can help you make decisions about prioritization, and in some cases, even help you determine whether a page could be condensed or removed completely. If your content isn't contributing to your primary message or providing value for your visitors, then what is it doing on your site in the first place?

For responsive projects, a content audit can help to highlight the similarities between different pages. This helps you to determine your content types as well as determine the rules for how each content type needs to be adjusted as the site adapts to different resolutions.

---

7 "Doing a Content Inventory (Or, A Mind-Numbingly Detailed Odyssey Through Your Web Site)" at www.adaptivepath.com/ideas/doing-content-inventory

Page tables

Once you know what content you have, it's time to take a page-by-page look at how to structure it.

Wireframes can help with this to some extent, but typically they only show a small selection of pages within a site. Also, they offer no guidance as to how content will be maintained or what the key message is for each page. To overcome this gap, we need to introduce another kind of deliverable: the page table.

Page tables, sometimes referred to as content templates, offer a detailed exploration of content on a page-by-page basis. A page table contains information about what content is included on a page, what the key message is, and how the content will be maintained. You can see an example of what a page table might look like in **Figure 5.4**.

About Yet Another Sports Site

Page objective: Provide information about who, and what, Yet Another Sports Site is.
Source content:
Scope: In scope

Page title	About Yet Another Sports Site
Main content	**Message:** We are your one stop destination for sports related news Provide some general information about what information is available on Yet Another Sports Site, as well as what sports are covered. List of sports covered includes: • football • baseball • soccer • tennis • ice soccer • basketball Provide some general information about what information is available on Yet Another Sports Site, as well as what sports are covered.
Secondary	Links to editorial staff member bios. Information about advertising with Yet Another Sports Site.
Third	Footer and standard links.

Content creation: The content is not web ready. It will need to be edited and fine-tuned from its current print-based version.

Maintenance: Should be reviewed every 6 months to make sure that the information is up to date.

Technology / Publishing / Policy implications: None.
Reliance on third parties: None.

Outstanding questions: None.

Figure 5.4 Page tables detail the structure and key goals for each page, helping to guide decisions about how to lay that content out at different resolutions.

Notice that the page table is very low fidelity. Keeping the page table low fidelity ensures that no one will be confused about its permanence. It also means that these page tables can be created and modified very quickly.

Page tables have the added benefit of making it easier to get needed content from stakeholders and clients as they know exactly what kind of content needs to be there and what it needs to communicate. Having the content mapped out in this way helps to keep everyone on the same page, as well as hold people accountable for their role in the process.

Arming yourself with information about the hierarchy of content on a page is essential—particularly for a responsive approach. As you adjust the layout of your site from one device to the next, keep that hierarchy in mind.

There are more steps you can take to ensure that your content is solid. We'll come back to this topic in Chapter 7, "Responsive Content," but for detailed information about content, check out *Content Strategy for the Web* by Kristina Halvorson and *The Elements of Content Strategy* by Erin Kissane.

Consider where you're going

Armed with knowledge about your audience and your content, you can start to consider *where* to present your content. While it makes sense to make your website accessible on as many devices as possible, you do need to decide which specific platforms, devices, and capabilities you will optimize for. Site analytics are invaluable for this.

It's not about aiming for the lowest common denominator or serving only the most capable devices. It's about creating a site that can be experienced on a large spectrum of devices in a way that best suits those devices' capabilities and form factors.

Optimized for some, accessible to many

As important as it is to identify the most common devices and platforms being used to access your site, it's just as important to remember that you can't anticipate them all. You may not be able to optimize for all devices, but you should attempt to support them by making your content accessible.

Brad Frost, a developer with R/GA in New York, discussed the difference in his blog post, "Support vs. Optimization":[8]

> It's just about being more considerate and giving these people who want to interact with your site a functional experience. That requires removing comfortable assumptions about support and accounting for different use cases. There are ways to support lesser platforms while still optimizing for the best of the best.

The way to do this is to very carefully apply the web stack with progressive enhancement always in mind. The goal isn't for every browser and device to receive the exact same layout and experience—that's simply not realistic. If an older device has a few wrinkles in the experience, that's all right. Just make sure the experience is functional. This is the difference between optimizing for a device and supporting a device.

Consider the cross-device experience

How many devices do you use in any given day? If you're like many people, the answer is several—often for the same task. According to a study released by Yahoo!, 59 percent of people sometimes visit a site on their mobile device and then follow up on their desktop. 34 percent of people do the opposite: they start on the PC and then follow up on their mobile device.[9] As you start introducing all the other web-enabled devices a person owns, shifting becomes an increasingly difficult reality to ignore.

When asked about experiences he liked, Madhava Enros of Mozilla said that mobile usage is about a constellation of devices (**Figure 5.5**):[10]

> Another that I really like is the Kindle. I love the hardware itself, but Amazon really seems to have understood that mobile usage is about a constellation of devices. It's not just about the one phone you have. It's being able to read at home on your e-reader, but then read on your Android phone when you're on the train, or pick up your iPad when you're elsewhere. That kind of consistency of getting at your stuff across a bunch of devices is a really great insight.

---

8 "Support vs. Optimization" at http://bradfrostweb.com/blog/mobile/support-vs-optimization/

9 "Mobile Shopping Framework: The role of mobile devices in the shopping process" at http://advertising.yahoo.com/article/the-role-of-mobile-devices-in-shopping-process.html

10 "On a small screen, user experience is everything" at http://radar.oreilly.com/2011/03/mobile-design-user-experience.html

Figure 5.5
The Kindle syncs your notes, highlights, and reading progress so that you can pick up where you left off across a number of different devices and experiences.

We can frame that in another way: web use is about a constellation of experiences. Each individual experience a user has with your site should be able to stand alone. However, those experiences also need to come together to create a greater, unified experience.

This has many implications, but the most elementary is that of coherence: the experience on one device should be familiar to someone who has first interacted with your site on another. Navigation paths should be familiar and the user should never feel as though some important piece of content isn't there.

Keep the cross-device experience in mind from the beginning. Consider how the experience must change based on dimensions and capabilities, and what you can do to make sure it remains familiar from device to device.

It comes down to understanding that we can't continue to view the Web as a mobile web, desktop web, and so on. We need to understand, and embrace, that the Web is just the Web. The devices we use to access it may vary, as may the context. As a result, the design and even some of the content may vary as well. In the end, however, it's still one Web—and users will expect that they can interact with it that way, regardless of what device they may be using at the time.

Prepare your test bed

Of course, you'll need to test all your hard work, starting early on with collaborative design briefs (discussed in the following chapter). This is the part where everyone starts sweating buckets. How on Earth do you test across so many browsers and devices without taking out a second mortgage?

First, remember the difference between optimization and support. You can't test your site on every device and browser—it's just not possible. Identify your key ones and focus on those.

For those devices and browsers you will be testing on, you have a few options:

- Actual devices
- Emulators
- Third-party services

Actual devices

The best way to test your site, hands down, is to test on real browsers running on real devices. Testing on devices gives you the clearest picture of how your site will be affected by considerations such as performance, network, form factor, and capabilities. You just can't get this kind of information by simply resizing your browser window or testing on emulators. If you really want to see how it feels to use your site, then you have to use it in real-world scenarios, just as your users would.

Get out of your office and away from your super high-speed Internet. Use a slower Wi-Fi connection. Connect to a mobile network. Use your site while waiting at a noisy bus stop. Visitors won't always be browsing from the comfort of a chair and with access to a high-speed network. You shouldn't be testing as if they will.

Getting real with your testing is easily the best method. Unfortunately, there are a lot of devices out there and they're not exactly cheap. Getting your hands on them is important, but doing so without breaking the bank is too. How do you decide which devices to purchase?

The answer depends on your specific situation. In her post, "Strategies for choosing testing devices",[11] Stephanie Rieger lists five criteria for determining which devices to purchase for testing:

- Existing traffic
- Regional traffic and market
- Device-specific factors
- Project-specific factors
- Budget

It's worth taking a closer look at these to see how they guide your decision.

EXISTING TRAFFIC

Once again, site analytics prove their worth. The best starting point to determine what devices you may want to purchase is knowing what kind of devices are accessing your site. Pay attention to the devices themselves, but also platforms and versions. From this analysis, you should be able to come up with a lengthy list of possibilities.

---

11 "Strategies for choosing testing devices" at http://stephanierieger.com/strategies-for-choosing-test-devices/

Figure 5.6 While touch-enabled screens are increasingly popular, many devices, including many popular Black-Berry phones, feature trackballs or qwerty keyboards for input.

REGIONAL TRAFFIC AND MARKET

As with decisions about grouping and breakpoints, you can't rely solely on your own analytics, however. Make sure that self-fulfilling prophecies aren't obscuring your statistics. Find out what devices and platforms are dominant in your area. Compare them to the devices you found in your own analytics to see what's missing and what overlaps.

DEVICE-SPECIFIC FACTORS

While it's important to have a variety of platforms represented in your test bed, that's not enough. Make sure you use a variety of different form factors, sizes, and capabilities. The same platform can run very differently on a high-end device than it does on a mid-tier or lower-end device. The methods of input can also have a large impact on how you should design your site (**Figure 5.6**). Make sure these different features are represented.

PROJECT-SPECIFIC FEATURES

Consider the specific features your project requires or would benefit from. In her post, Rieger uses geolocation as an example. If your site makes heavy use of location services, then you'll want to use devices capable of supporting geolocation. You'll also want a few that aren't capable so you can test your fallback options accordingly.

BUDGET

Unless you're sitting on piles of money (and if you are, may I suggest buying another 10 or so copies of this book), you'll have a limited budget for building your testing suite. Keep an eye out for used devices for sale cheap. Remember, it's OK to get an older model. Most visitors probably won't be running the latest and greatest device. Often, having a slightly older device is a much more realistic representation of your audience.

Be sure to shop around. Phones and tablets aren't cheap, but if you pay attention to sites like Craigslist and eBay, you'll find some fantastic deals on excellent testing devices. Just be sure not to be *too* thrifty. It's good to have those cheaper, older, low-end models around, but they shouldn't be the only ones you test on.

Don't be afraid to make use of your local carrier stores. Walk into them, explain what you're doing, and you'll be surprised at just how willing they can be to let you test your site for a few minutes on their devices.

Finally, ask around your office. If you've got a group of people you're comfortable with, find out what kind of devices they own. We took a poll at our office of just under 30 people and the diversity was pretty impressive. You may be surprised to find the mobile test bed you have sitting right there in your office.

LOAD UP ON BROWSERS

Armed with your array of testing devices, your next step will be to grab any and every browser you can and load those devices up. Many of the devices will have several browser options available. Get them all.

This applies to your desktop as well. Grab Safari, Chrome, Firefox, Internet Explorer, and Opera and install them. Where you can, load up multiple versions so you're not just testing on the latest and greatest browser versions.

▶ **Note**
For an in-depth look at some different emulators, visit http://www.mobilexweb.com/emulators and check out Maximiliano Firtman's "Mobile Emulators & Simulators: The Ultimate Guide."

Emulators

Emulators are far from perfect. They usually require a hefty SDK, so you need lots of space to store them. They give you no sense of how it feels to interact with your site on a real device. They're essentially ports of the browser or operating system, which means they're prone to errors and differences. Some bugs that appear on an actual device look just fine on the emulator.

That being said, testing on an emulator is better than testing nothing at all. If you can't have a real device in hand, this may be your next best option.

Adobe Shadow

Having a large selection of testing devices is fantastic, but you still have to go through and manually load your site on each of the devices to see how it performs and displays. This is decidedly less fantastic. Enter Adobe Shadow.

Adobe Shadow is an inspection and preview tool that aids testing on actual devices. To use it, download the helper application onto your computer and install the Chrome extension. Then, install the appropriate Adobe Shadow on each device (at the time of writing, only Android and iOS devices are supported).

With everything installed, you can then use the Adobe Shadow application on the devices to connect to your computer (no wires necessary). Once connected, the page open in Chrome will be displayed on all connected test devices as well.

Here's where the magic kicks in. Let's say that you have ten different devices all connected to your desktop through Adobe Shadow. If you move to a different page in Google Chrome, *each connected device* will also move to that url. This means you can walk through an entire site on your desktop and all the devices that are connected will follow along, saving a tremendous amount of testing time.

Among its many other impressive features are the ability to:

- take screenshots of any connected device
- take a screenshot of all connected devices at the same time through the Chrome extension
- remotely inspect the HTML, CSS, and DOM structure of connected devices
- control the cache on any connected device

Seemingly overnight, Shadow went from being released to being an essential tool in the web developer's toolbox.

Third-party services

Third-party services such as PerfectoMobile (www.perfectomobile.com) and DeviceAnywhere (www.keynotedeviceanywhere.com) have many mobile devices available and you can see how your site renders on them. The cost of these services can really add up though, so be careful how often, and for how long, you use them.

While third-party services are more accurate than emulators, the cost means that they'll typically be your last resort. If your budget allows for it, start with real devices where possible, fill in the blanks with emulators, and fall back on the third-party services only when needed.

Wrapping it up

Responsive design is a powerful technique, there's no doubt about that. It's not a silver bullet though. Getting the maximum value from your site takes a lot of time and very careful consideration. You must integrate responsive design into your planning for the project.

Study your analytics, but keep in mind that they have a way of lying. Consider your content carefully. It needn't be finalized before design and development begins, but you should know the structure of it.

Consider the cross-device experience. People will be using different devices to access your content. They will expect the experience to be familiar, yet optimized for their device.

Finally, test your site on actual devices whenever possible. It can be a little intimidating, but building your own test suite doesn't have to break the bank. By taking the time to determine which devices will benefit your project the most, and keeping your eyes peeled for deals, you can slowly build a powerful suite of devices.

In the next chapter, we'll look at how a responsive project affects the entire workflow, from the way teams work together to the way sites are designed and built.

CHAPTER 6
DESIGN WORKFLOW

Our "Age of Anxiety" is, in great part,
the result of trying to do today's job with
yesterday's tools—with yesterday's concepts.
—MARSHALL MCLUHAN

When you toss a stone into water, it makes a splash that causes a series of expanding ripples. While the point of impact is small, the effect is far-reaching.

If our modern work process is the water, then responsive design is the stone. This one change sets in motion a series of ripples that affects everything about the way we work with the Web.

Technology changes. It evolves, it matures. It becomes capable of performing new tasks. When this happens, we must learn to change as well. Our tools and techniques, our thought processes—they must evolve as well in order to keep up.

The impact of new technology on the design workflow is tremendous. It can also be unsettling as we come to terms with the fact that so many of our current practices may be flawed. Our workflow must become more flexible. We must shed our old ways of working, and try to find a better way to manipulate this incredible medium.

In this chapter, we'll explore:

- The interactive nature of the Web and its impact on workflow
- The importance of thinking mobile first
- The benefits of designing in the browser
- Tools and techniques such as wireframes, sketches, and style guides

Your mileage may vary

Dan Brown has a great line in his book *Communicating Design:* "Anyone who tells you the design process is absolute doesn't make a living doing it."[1] The design process is an art, not a science. There are very few rules involved. Ultimately, each client, each project, each team works differently. You need to find the process that works best for you and your project.

A number of different criteria factor into what that process entails: the size of the team, the budget, the capabilities of the designers and developers, the timeline—these all dictate what deliverables and steps are necessary for a specific project.

---

1   Dan Brown, *Communicating Design*, Second Edition (New Riders, 2010)

Remember that the individual steps in the process are less important than adhering to a few key concepts:

- The Web is interactive. Your tools and deliverables should reflect that.
- The process needs to be collaborative.
- It's not about pages anymore. It's about systems.

An interactive medium

We need to move away from working with the Web as if it were a static medium. It's not. It's flexible. It's unpredictable. Settling into a rigid workflow with rigid, static deliverables doesn't help us maximize on this potential. It limits us by applying arbitrary constraints where there are none.

To date, our approach to designing for the Web has closely resembled designing for print. We use many of the same tools for designing a website as we would for designing a poster. But print isn't an interactive medium; the Web is. People don't just look at a website, they interact with it. They click. They hover. They tap. The Web is a living, breathing canvas that they can manipulate and bend to their will. The Web is much closer to being software than it is to being print.

Our tools, techniques, and deliverables should better reflect the Web's dynamic nature.

Collaboration

For most of the Web's existence, the workflow has been mostly linear. The designer creates the design, and once approved, passes it off in the form of a static mock-up or two to the developer to build. Unfortunately, a lot of information can get lost in the exchange. Things like error messages, hover states, open and closed navigation—these are the components that sometimes can be overlooked in the handoff.

With a responsive project, because you're focusing on serving such a wide variety of different devices, the workflow necessarily becomes much more indirect. Not only must you be aware of the kind of interactions people can have with the site, but you must also consider how the site will respond to different sizes, capabilities, and methods of input. You can't expect the designer to anticipate everything that will come up, and you can't expect the developer to accommodate each interaction in way that is 100 percent in sync with the designer's original vision. A higher degree of collaboration is necessary.

Ethan Marcotte discusses this in his book *Responsive Web Design:*[2]

> The responsive projects I've worked on have had a lot of success combining design and development into one hybrid phase, bringing the two teams into one highly collaborative group.

This hybrid approach makes much more sense. It provides developers and designers alike with opportunities to discuss how pages should behave at different sizes and when interacted with. Together, they can discover the interactions and components that may be less obvious, and make decisions about how to handle those different devices and input methods.

Collaboration ensures that fewer things slip through the cracks. Especially when designing in static programs, it's easy for a designer to envision one ideal scenario, with a flow that assumes the best possible support and functionality. If the designer and developer work closely together throughout the design process, the developer can point out other possible scenarios: What happens when touch is supported? What happens if there's no geolocation? Working together, these scenarios can be designed for as well.

This same benefit becomes apparent during development. The developer may not be fully aware of the designer's vision. She may not understand why certain decisions were made about flow and visual aesthetics. With a designer working alongside her, that original vision can be maintained. When a scenario crops up that wasn't originally planned for in the earliest designs, the designer can work with the developer to create a solution that maintains the integrity of the design.

The collaborative workflow can also lead to innovative solutions. Like rubbing two stones together, the friction provided by two different perspectives can spark an idea. We solve problems based on our prior experiences, which means that our solutions are limited by what we know. When you bring people together, their collective range of experiences expands and so does the likelihood of finding a high-quality solution to any problems that arise.

Successfully adopting a collaborative workflow requires communication, iteration, and respect.

---

2 Ethan Marcotte, *Responsive Web Design* (A Book Apart, 2011)

COMMUNICATION

From the very first kick-off meetings, designers and developers should both be involved. By involving designers and developers early on, you create the opportunity for much stronger results from both sides. Designers can make sure their original vision is coherent from page to page and interaction to interaction. Developers can identify potential concerns before they grow into serious issues.

Instead of a simple hand-off, a more collaborative workflow thrives on design briefs: meetings involving both designers and developers.

During these design briefs, the site should be viewed on as many different target devices as possible. This will alert you to any faults in the design and clue you into additional adjustments you can make to optimize the experience for a given device.

During these briefs, people on both sides of the table can answer questions such as:

- Are the touchpoints on a touch screen device large enough?
- At what sizes does the design start to show stretch marks?
- How cumbersome is it to interact with the dynamic elements?
- Would another breakpoint improve the design?
- Can the experience be enhanced for a given device?
- What minor adjustments could help support a broader range of devices?

ITERATION

As these questions are answered, you iterate. You tweak the design to accommodate changes, then rinse and repeat. Ideally, you're taking small steps—not making big changes with each iteration. This makes it much easier to fine-tune the experience and avoid getting too caught up in one large, overarching view of the experience.

This might sound time-consuming. It is. It's also an incredibly important step toward ensuring that the end product will be an enjoyable experience for the people who use it.

It's about immersing yourself in the medium you're creating for. We have a limited knowledge of the specific and unique quirks of the cornucopia of devices. Trying to anticipate layout issues as the site scales and is interacted with is a losing proposition.

RESPECT

Of course, this whole process falls apart if there's a lack of mutual respect between the designers and developers working on a project.

Solid communication helps to some extent. By working so closely with one another, designers and developers alike will gain a deeper respect and better understanding of the challenges they each face.

A little knowledge goes a long way. Respect, as it turns out, is very difficult to give to something you don't understand. If you're a designer, taking the time to dabble in some programming gives you a deeper understanding of the developer's work. Likewise, as a developer, exploring design concepts helps you realize that design is much more than just pretty colors and fonts.

COLLABORATION WITH THE CLIENT

Collaboration shouldn't stop internally; it should extend to your interactions with the client as well. Get her involved early on, and make her a part of the process throughout. The typical waterfall approach—where designers and developers come up with a solution, then hand it off to the client for approval—can result in an "us versus them" mentality. It can turn into a game of one-upmanship. The client feels the need to request changes to get herself involved. The designers and developers feel the need to defend their decisions and combat the changes the client tries to interject.

If you keep the client involved throughout the process, however, then it becomes a team effort. The wall between the client and the design team gets torn down. Both sides have their voices heard, and every solution is arrived at with input from each.

Better collaboration with the client is also an incredible educational experience for both parties. The design team learns about the unique requirements and constraints that the client has to deal with, things like legacy systems and company politics. The client gets to see how decisions about design and support are arrived at. If the client is involved in those design briefings, she gets to see how the design of a site necessarily varies from device to device and browser to browser.

Brad Frost

SELLING RESPONSIVE DESIGN

Brad Frost is a mobile web strategist and front-end designer at R/GA in New York City. He is the creator of Mobile Web Best Practices, a resource site aimed at helping people create great mobile and responsive web experiences. He is also the curator of WTF Mobile Web, which teaches by example what not to do when working with the mobile web. He is passionate about mobile and likes to tweet, blog, and speak about it.

It's essential to get the client on board with responsive design up front because going down the responsive path affects the process, timing, budget, and, ultimately, the final product. It's important to be honest with clients and show them the challenges as well as the opportunities of responsive design. Educated clients are more willing to invest in the project and ensure that it's done right. The rest of the process runs relatively smoothly when you convince the real decision makers.

I've found that showing, rather than telling, does absolute wonders for client education. In a few pictures I can demonstrate that the web landscape is increasingly complex and that the client needs to address that fact. Examples can describe responsive design in ways that words really can't. One of my favorite things to do is to make a page or two of the client's existing site responsive. While it's certainly not how you'd want to build the new site, it helps the client understand the concept of adaptive layouts. Clients often have a hard time thinking outside the box ("but we're not a newspaper!"), so that exercise keeps the focus on the responsive opportunities.

A few factors play a part in what pages to choose. One is ease of implementation.

Obviously you wouldn't want to pick the most challenging page on the site for a basic responsive proof of concept. Pages with a higher percentage of mobile views are good candidates. I also like to show that responsive is more than just layout adjustments, so I use pages that have good opportunities for a simple swipe carousel to get a little sexy on them. A lot of it comes down to the art of presentation, which means showing it on real devices, but as I learned, you should lead with the squishy window resize so the client gets the concept before viewing it on real devices.

Sometimes, a responsive approach isn't the right one. Certain projects need camera API access. Certain microsites have a shelf life of only a couple weeks. Certain clients have products that cater to millionaires so they can afford to build a customized iPhone app.

However, even if a project isn't responsive, I *always* ask the important questions about mobile compatibility: How are those videos going to be handled for mobile devices? What's the page size? What if a device doesn't support this font?

At the very least you want to have mobile consideration, and, at most, a full-blown optimized and adaptive experience.

Thinking in systems

Think back for a second to Chapter 5, "Planning," and our discussion about the cross-device experience. Coherence is one of the primary principles that emerge from that discussion. A site needs consistency—not just page to page, but device to device.

Achieving coherence requires us to stop thinking about the site on a page-by-page basis and start thinking in terms of systems and their components: headers, footers, navigation systems, and so on. Thinking about the individual components decouples us from the page, forcing us to consider how these components work in relation to the entire site experience.

This has always been important, but never more so than today. Sites have to work on more devices and browsers than ever before. Considering how the individual components of a site work in different environments, and then how those components come together in a unified way to create a broader experience, is essential to the success of any responsive project.

In addition, this way of approaching design helps to improve consistency and productivity. There's no need to reinvent solutions over and over: as you design, you are creating a library of them that you can reuse whenever it makes sense.

Thinking mobile first

As we've discussed earlier, increasing fragmentation has turned our typical processes on their heads. The rallying cry of the day is to start by designing the mobile experience first.

The concept of mobile first was spearheaded by Luke Wroblewski. In his original post on the topic, he cited three reasons why the mobile experience should be the first one created:[3]

- **Mobile is exploding**

    "Building mobile first ensures companies have an experience available to this extremely fast-growing user base widely considered to be the next big computing platform."

---

3 "Mobile First" at www.lukew.com/ff/entry.asp?933

- **Mobile forces you to focus**

  "Mobile devices require software development teams to focus on only the most important data and actions in an application. There simply isn't room in a 320 by 480 pixel screen for extraneous, unnecessary elements. You have to prioritize."

- **Mobile extends your capabilities**

  "Building mobile first allows teams to utilize this full palette of capabilities to create rich context-aware applications instead of limiting themselves to an increasingly dated set of capabilities."

Let's explore each of these reasons a little more closely.

Mobile is exploding

Mobile devices are increasing rapidly both in quantity and quality. One report estimates that by the year 2020, there will be 12 billion mobile subscriptions.[4]

With the proliferation of devices come more and more people who access the Internet only via their mobile device. No laptop, no desktop: their only interaction with the Internet is through that little device they carry in their pocket. In the United States, 25 percent of mobile users access the internet only through their mobile device. In the United Kingdom, that number is 22 percent.[5]

If those numbers seem high, they shouldn't. Compared to the rest of the world, 25 percent is actually pretty low. Egypt, for example, leads the way with 70 percent of mobile users being mobile-only (**Figure 6.1**).

Africa is another very interesting example. There, more people will soon have access to a mobile device than to electricity.[6] This means that to charge these devices they're using things like car batteries.

---

4 "GSMA Announces That the Proliferation of Connected Devices Will Create a US$1.2 Trillion Revenue Opportunity for Mobile Operators by 2020" at www.prnewswire.com/news-releases/gsma-announces-that-the-proliferation-of-connected-devices-will-create-a-us12-trillion-revenue-opportunity-for-mobile-operators-by-2020-131484733.html

5 "Global mobile statistics 2012: all quality mobile marketing research, mobile Web stats, subscribers, ad revenue, usage, trends…" at http://mobithinking.com/mobile-marketing-tools/latest-mobile-stats

6 "The Significance of Mobile Web in Africa and its Future" at www.wfs.org/content/significance-mobile-web-africa-and-its-future

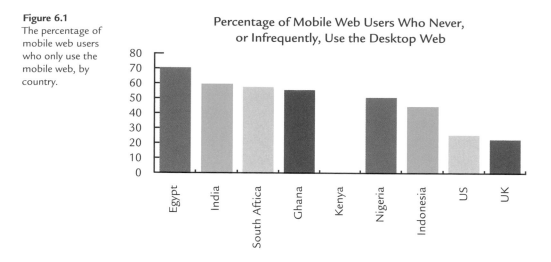

Figure 6.1
The percentage of mobile web users who only use the mobile web, by country.

What's really interesting about these numbers is the way this impacts how the Web is perceived in these countries. It's hard to fathom, but try to imagine what it means to be living in a place where your neighbor is more likely to have a mobile than to have electricity. Think about how your perception of web use would be different if you and 7 of your 10 friends always viewed the Internet through the small screen on your phone.

The number of devices, and the number of people using them to access the Web, will continue to grow—rapidly. It makes sense to consider the mobile platform, already the predominant one in some countries, first.

Mobile forces you to focus

Designing for mobile first also helps to focus the discussion on the content that matters most for your site. We've all worked at companies, or for clients, where everyone in the company had a different idea of what should go on the home page. Of course, every department wants its own material to be up front and center. This leads to crowded designs. We cram our sites full of tabs and collapsible elements and leave very little room to breathe (**Figure 6.2**).

Figure 6.2
The article (the highlighted portion) is the content that matters to the visitor, but it's buried amidst a pile of distractions.

On a mobile device, it's much more difficult to get away with this. These devices typically have smaller screens. This means there's less room to cram a bunch of content into. As a result, you're forced to home in on the content that's most important to your visitors. What features and functionality are vital to your site? Which are simply nice to have? Better yet, which don't belong on your page at all?

The discussion about what content matters and what doesn't often spills over into your larger screen layout as well. If you've determined that a chunk of content isn't important enough to be on the home screen for a mobile display, is it really important enough to be there on a larger screen?

◆ **Tip**
Simple and Usable, by Giles Colborne, is an excellent book for anyone trying to figure out how to simplify a site to its core and reduce clutter in the process.

Mobile extends your capabilities

Today, many businesses approach their mobile sites as limited, stripped-down versions of their desktop sites. Perhaps it's because of the limiting characteristics we historically assign to the label "mobile." Or perhaps it's because we've resisted the idea that great things come in small packages. Whatever the reason, many seem intent on simplifying the mobile experience to an extent that makes it feel crippled next to the desktop site, or as some call it, the "full site."

This is an inherently flawed way of thinking, and in practice, makes very little sense. As Josh Clark, a mobile consultant, says: "Saying mobile design should have less is like saying paperbacks have smaller pages, so we should remove chapters."[7]

The truth is that mobile devices aren't limited alternatives to their larger brethren; they're often far more capable. They can make heavy use of geolocation to optimize the experience. They can switch layouts depending on the way they're held. Many of them support a rich, multi-touch interface. These devices are very often capable of providing a much richer user experience than their desktop counterparts.

Devices are also loaded with an ever-increasing number of sensors. While many are not yet accessible from the browser, keep an eye on the future and consider how these sensors can be used to create an enhanced experience. Mobile devices shouldn't be given a dumbed-down version of your site; they're a gateway to a far more personal experience than has ever been possible before.

What all this adds up to is this: It makes sense to consider the mobile experience first in your design process. There's a transition period of getting used to mobile-first, but once you do, you'll find it helps you to focus on the key components of your site and saves you time.

---

7 "Josh Clark debunks the 7 Myths of Mobile Web Design" at The Next Web (TNW)
   http://thenextweb.com/dd/2011/11/07/josh-clark-debunks-the-7-myths-of-mobile-web-design/

The tools

The tools presented here are ones that I've found to be valuable in my own process. Not every project includes them all. Some projects include more. These are the core deliverables, the ones I keep coming back to most often. As noted earlier, your mileage may vary from project to project. The process is not rigid. You should use the right tool for the right job.

Wireframes

When you create a design, you don't want to get caught up in the little details too early on. If the first thing you create is a high-fidelity mock-up or prototype, it will be very difficult to see past the colors and typography through to the actual structure of the design.

Instead, it's helpful to start by creating low-fidelity wireframes. A wireframe is a diagram that demonstrates what content will appear on a page. Wireframes typically do not include color, font choice, or images. The purpose of a wireframe is not to demonstrate the site layout, but to help determine the page structure, including what kinds of content will be displayed and the priority of that content.

Keep your wireframes as simple as possible. The higher the fidelity of your wireframe, the more resistance you'll run into. Too many details and people start to get distracted. At this stage, you don't want to focus on fonts or colors—you want to zero in on the elements of a page and their structure. The lower the fidelity of the wireframe, the easier it is to focus on the page structure, hierarchy, and behavior.

Stephen Hay likes to use what he calls "content reference wireframes." A content reference wireframe is a low-fidelity document intended to show roughly where the different types of content will reside on a page. Using the content audit and page tables (discussed in Chapter 5, "Planning"), you know the content to be included on a page and its general hierarchy. Using this, you can create a content reference wireframe showing where that content will reside (**Figure 6.3**).

Figure 6.3 Content reference wireframes demonstrate where each chunk of content will reside on a given page.

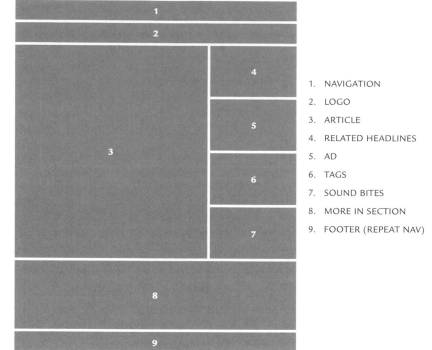

1. NAVIGATION
2. LOGO
3. ARTICLE
4. RELATED HEADLINES
5. AD
6. TAGS
7. SOUND BITES
8. MORE IN SECTION
9. FOOTER (REPEAT NAV)

Because content reference wireframes are so low fidelity, you can create them very quickly. In just a few minutes you can produce wireframes for several different basic screen sizes to show to the client or stakeholders. And because content reference wireframes are easy to create, you won't be pulling your hair out every time the client requests a change: with only a couple of minutes of work, you're all set.

START WITH SKETCHING

Whatever format you prefer for your final wireframes, you should start with sketching. The power of sketching lies in quantity, not quality. Sketches can be created very quickly, allowing you to rapidly work through a number of different possibilities and different sizes (**Figure 6.4**). This is particularly important for a responsive project, where you will want to sketch out the layout for a number of different resolutions.

Figure 6.4 Sketching allows you to quickly work through many ideas and scenarios.

Sketches are also as low-fidelity as they come. If people see a sketch on a piece of paper, they recognize that it is a rough idea. A sketch is very informal: its rough lines imply that it shows creative thought in process, not a refined and polished idea. This encourages more participation and conversation when people see it, since they recognize that it's still being worked on. The lack of details helps you avoid tunnel vision and see the bigger picture.

After sketches have been created and reviewed, some designers will move to a slightly higher-fidelity wireframe. One common next step is what Jason Santa Maria termed the "Grey Box Method."[8]

Using the Grey Box Method, your next step is to create a wireframe consisting of, you guessed it, grey boxes to represent the different sections of content. This is typically done using Adobe Illustrator, Photoshop, or any number of tools specifically created with wireframing in mind.

Grey box wireframes have become so common that many stakeholders have come to expect them. However, it's at this point that we should consider

---

8 "Grey Box Methodology" at http://v3.jasonsantamaria.com/archive/2004/05/24/grey_box_method.php

breaking away from our typical approach. Wireframes are very good for relating a quick idea about the structure of a page, but they're not good at doing much else. Some people will go to great lengths to create high-fidelity wireframes, but there's only so much information they can convey. It's about using the right tool for the right job.

Instead of introducing grey boxes, consider moving from paper sketches to something a bit more interactive.

Mock-ups

Part of maturing is letting go. You probably had a favorite toy or stuffed animal when you were a kid, but at some point, you outgrew it.

It's time to outgrow the desire for pixel-perfect control.

Sometimes, in order to support a maximum number of people, you need to be willing to sacrifice perfection. We can attempt to create pixel-perfect designs that reach only a subset of the potential audience, or we can accept the ebb and flow. We can create beautiful sites, allowing for some imperfections, and provide a much larger audience with an enjoyable experience.

Imperfection is a good thing. Imperfections breed character and allow for malleability. In fact, imperfect but flexible trumps perfect and inflexible just about every time. Like Play-Doh, people want something they can customize and make into their own.

The question "does a website have to look the same in every browser" has been taunting our industry for years. Many have argued that it doesn't have to. Yet we've tried—hard.

Consider the elaborate lengths we've gone to in order to make our sites look as identical as possible, regardless of the browser. Most of us have implemented a rounded corners solution, back before vendor-prefixes let us serve them up to most modern browsers. These convoluted solutions typically required several extra divs and multiple images.

For a long time, bringing opacity in PNGs to Internet Explorer was another point of agony. Since IE didn't support 24-bit transparent PNGs, we created endless numbers of third-party scripts to trick IE into displaying them correctly.

These solutions were hacks, costly ones. They added time to the development process and weight to the pages. They added unneeded complexity to our projects.

The idea of creating pixel-perfect experiences is very tempting. That's why so many people get excited about what they can do with native iOS applications. They have absolute control over the way their app is designed and laid out.

That same precision doesn't exist on the Web. There are too many variables. The user can zoom in or out of the page, altering the way the page appears. The user may decide not to keep the browser fully maximized. Any number of different browsers and devices, each with its own capabilities and levels of support, may be used to access our sites.

The idea of a design that looks identical across browsers is a fallacy—and potentially a harmful one.

Clients and stakeholders are often the ones speaking up the loudest when a design doesn't look the same in IE 6 as it does in the latest version of Google Chrome. We can't point fingers, however, because if we dig deep enough, we find that the root of the problem may very well be one of our own practices: static mock-ups.

THE TROUBLE WITH STATIC MOCK-UPS

The traditional approach for creating initial design mock-ups for a site has been to use a graphics program like Adobe Photoshop or Fireworks. You churn out a static mock-up, perhaps print it, and then show it to the client. Together, you review the design and note any adjustments that should be made. Then it's back to Photoshop.

Once you have the mock-up finalized and approved, you hand it off to your front-end developers to start implementing the mock-up into HTML and CSS.

This feels comfortable. It's tradition. It's the norm. It's also fundamentally flawed.

There's no doubt that these graphics programs are powerful. They give you a tremendous amount of tools and control. You can fine-tune the typography, colors, borders, layout, and more. This makes them fantastic tools for image editing, icon design or designing for print; it makes them a poor choice for a nonstatic medium like the Web.

When you open Photoshop and create a new document, the first thing you have to do is specify the file dimensions; at that point you're already disconnected from the very medium you're creating for. It's no wonder we build so many fixed-width sites.

There are lots of problems with static mock-ups. They provide a very limited perspective of what the end result will look like. They can't demonstrate how a design will appear at different screen sizes. They don't show what the page looks like when it's interacted with—the hover and focus states for example. There's no hint at the many inconsistencies of rendering across a bevy of different browsers.

This is a big problem when it comes to communicating the design to a prospective client or a manager. We give them these static mock-ups with their perfectly laid out colors and fonts and then complain when they get upset that the site doesn't look the same across browsers.

The control these static mock-ups provide creates false expectations about how the design will actually behave on the Web—on different browsers and different devices.

This also causes a disconnect between designers and developers. The designer hands the developer the approved static mock-up, but this often means that there's nothing to demonstrate to the developer how to handle the visual styles when an object is interacted with.

In turn, graphics programs give the designer the illusion of having much more control over the precise layout of a site. Any front-end developer I've ever talked to has complained at one point or another of being handed a mock-up of a site that just wasn't realistic, or if it was, was terribly inefficient.

Particularly with a responsive approach, serving up multiple static mock-ups is a fool's errand. How many mock-ups will you be creating? What happens when the CEO gets a new device with a different screen size and wants to see another mock-up? As with separate sites, this method doesn't scale particularly well.

DESIGNING IN THE BROWSER

An alternative approach is to design in the very environment where the site will actually live: the browser. This eliminates many of these issues.

A live, HTML-driven mock-up will better demonstrate what happens when users interact with elements on the page. You can show how the mock-up needs to change depending on the capabilities of the device or the browser in question and see how the design looks on variously sized screens.

Designing in the browser has the added benefit of putting the focus on the content and its structure. Considering the form of the markup this early in the process can only be a good thing. After all, for most sites, it's the content that brings the visitors.

This isn't for everyone though. Designing is a creative endeavor; you can't do it well using tools you're not entirely comfortable with. There's a certain level of familiarity and comfort for most designers when working in a graphics editor. That same level of familiarity might not be present when designing in the browser.

This isn't a fault of the approach itself, but rather of our tools and our own habits.

OUR HABITS

Just like a Whac-a-Mole game, the debate about whether or not a designer should know how to code keeps popping up. It's hardly a new topic. In 1990, Mitchell Kapor was arguing that designers should know how to program:[9]

> Designers must have a solid working knowledge of at least one modern programming language (C or Pascal) in addition to exposure to a wide variety of languages and tools, including Forth and Lisp.

I'm not willing to take quite that hard of a stance. I don't think a designer needs to know how to program (though that's certainly a bonus), but I do think a designer should know how to write HTML and CSS.

The Web is an interactive medium. In many ways, it's much closer to software than it is to print. Yet, historically, we haven't treated it that way. Perhaps because the Web evolved largely from a print background, the document-centric approach has driven the work process.

This is a flaw and a limitation, but a predictable one. It's Marshall McLuhan's rear-view mirror theory in full effect (**Figure 6.5**).

A common retort from people who believe designers shouldn't code is that you wouldn't want your architect to build your house, and that's true. But I also wouldn't hire one who didn't know how to. I'd expect the architect to be very knowledgeable about building a house. I'd want her to know all about the construction materials that could be used, and the pros and cons of each. I'd want her to have a solid understanding of how to build a stable foundation and how to compensate for the natural stress that a building has to endure.

The same is true of a web designer. The designer doesn't necessarily have to build the site by herself, but she should have a deep understanding of the medium. She should know the language of the Web and that means HTML and CSS, at the minimum. She should understand the constraints as well as the unique characteristics and the possibilities.

---

9 Terry Winograd, *Bringing Design to Software* (Addison-Wesley, 1996)

Figure 6.5
"We look at the present through a rear-view mirror. We march backwards into the future."
—Marshall McLuhan

Maturing is hard—just ask any acne-ridden teenager. It is necessary though. If we're ever going to embrace the full potential of the Web, we need to move beyond our comfort zones now and again.

The Web is an interactive medium: one that's based on movement and interactions, one that can be manipulated at the user's whim. It makes little sense not to embrace this in the earliest stages of a project.

OUR TOOLS

Graphic editors are too restrictive and don't reflect the nature of the Web. Unfortunately, for many designers, working in code removes the ability to be creative and experiment. We need to build the skills necessary to work better in this interactive medium, but we could use a little help from our tools.

In a presentation entitled "Inventing on Principle," Bret Victor discussed the need for immediate feedback from our tools to foster creativity:[10]

> Creators need an immediate connection to what they create. And what I mean by that is when you're making something, if you make a change or you make a decision, you need to see the effect of that immediately. There can't be any delay, and there can't be anything hidden. Creators have to be able to see what they're doing.

10 "Inventing on Principle" at https://vimeo.com/36579366

Static mock-ups still have their place

It's not likely that we'll ever eliminate graphic editors from our workflow entirely; that's all right. That shouldn't be the goal. Graphic editors are great for look and feel and intense graphics. We just need to be aware that as a tool, they have serious limitations.

While it's highly unadvisable to consistently use static mock-ups to present your designs to clients, they can still be useful at times. For those tricky look-and-feel graphics, it can be beneficial to quickly mock something up and present it for discussion.

Just make sure that you hop back into the browser as soon as possible after getting feedback from the stakeholders.

This lack of an immediate connection to what we create is what causes many designers to feel restricted by designing in the browser. Our tools today don't do a very good job of bridging that gap.

Until the wonder-tool comes along, it's important to work toward loosening the grip of your favorite graphic editing program. Don't remove it entirely, but start moving toward a more agile approach. Create the visuals as you code. Tackle the two hand-in-hand and you'll be much better equipped to work on the Web.

Style guides

To aid in this process, you should create a visual style guide and pattern library. Style guides have been quite popular among large brands for quite some time. A purely visual style guide lets people know how the visual identity of a brand—the fonts, the images, and the logos—should be used. It ensures that even though the designer won't be directly involved in the creation of the materials, the brand's voice will still be heard in the final piece.

Applying this same concept to development brings us to the front-end style guide. The guide demonstrates how different components should be displayed throughout the site. This can include things such as tables, buttons, error messages, typography, images, and so on.

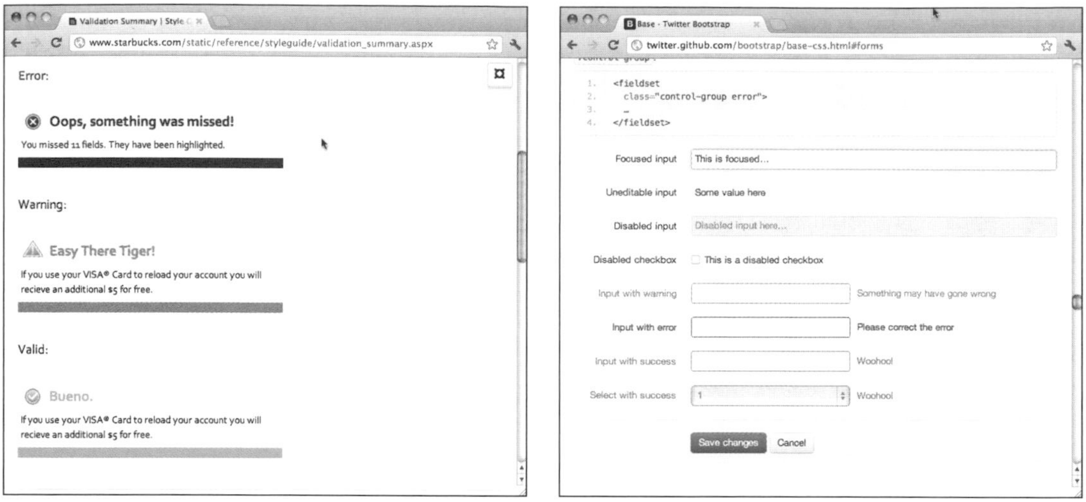

Figure 6.6

The Starbucks (left) and Twitter Bootstrap (right) style guides are excellent examples of how useful a comprehensive style guide can be.

The guide also serves as an example for any markup patterns you should be using. For example, when demonstrating how a table should appear, you should show how the markup for that table should be written, including the structure and attributes. Doing this ensures that not only will your site maintain a consistent visual appearance, but the code will also maintain a consistent form, greatly simplifying maintenance.

Since these style guides are created in HTML and CSS, they're an excellent way to test how styles will behave across different browsers and different widths. With all your components on one page, you need only load that page in a different browser or on a different device to see at once how all the elements behave in that environment. You can resize your window or adjust the text size and see instantly how those changes affect the individual components.

If you decide to change a few styles, just adjust the guide and retest that page across your target devices to quickly see how things will behave. When a browser lacks support for a specific feature, are the elements still consistent with the overall look and feel? When you view the guide on a small-screen device, does the typography still work? Do you need to adjust the font size on a large screen?

Style guides are becoming increasingly common. One of the best-known guides is Twitter's Bootstrap (**Figure 6.6**). Bootstrap demonstrates how everything from media blocks to typography to modal boxes should be written and stylized. A new developer inheriting a project with this kind of resource available will have no trouble getting up to speed.

CREATING YOUR STYLE GUIDE

There's no right way to create a style guide. As long as the process you choose leads you to a guide that's simple to maintain and easy to test and review, then it's the right process.

One tool to consider is Paul Robert Lloyd's Barebones. Barebones is a freely available, multi-purpose framework that serves as an initial directory setup, style guide and pattern library.

▶ **Note**
You can download Barebones from GitHub at http://github.com/paul-robertlloyd/bare-bones.

Setup is straightforward: download the code to the location of your choice and you should be ready to go. The code creates the following directory structure:

- _assets: An empty folder intended for images and fonts for your site
- _css: A folder for storings your CSS
- _inc: An empty folder intended for PHP includes
- _js: An empty folder intended for JavaScript files
- _patterns: A folder for storing patterns for the pattern library
- _patterns.php: The page that will display the pattern library
- _styleguide.php: The page that will display the style guide

The two files of primary interest for this book are _patterns.php and _styleguide.php.

The style guide (**Figure 6.7**) shows how the base markup (things like lists, header elements, and horizontal rules) will display with the site's styles. It's a static page: if you want to add an element to the guide, you edit _styleguide.php directly and then add the styles to the _patterns.css file located in the _css directory.

In addition to being a nice visual reference of how elements should appear on the site, the style guide also includes information about when and how certain elements should be used.

The pattern library (**Figure 6.8**) shows how different snippets (like a tooltip or an error message) are styled and displayed. In addition, the markup is displayed demonstrating how the snippet should be marked up in HTML.

All of the snippets included on the pattern page are stored as individual html files in the _patterns directory. The pattern page searches through the folder, displaying each snippet and its markup. Adding a new pattern is as simple as creating a new file in the folder with the appropriate snippet and including the styles in the _patterns.css file.

Figure 6.7
The default style guide included in Barebones shows how base markup is styled.

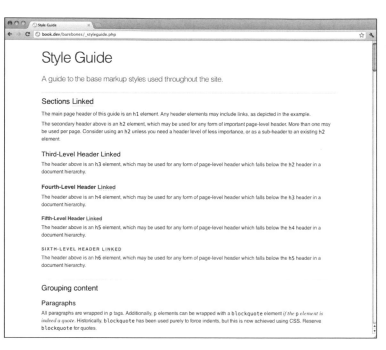

Figure 6.8
The Barebones pattern library displays how common snippets will display, as well as the markup used to create them.

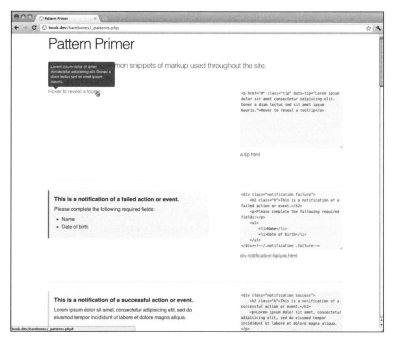

Let's take a look at the PHP to see what's going on here. Don't worry, it's pretty simple code:

```
1.    $files = array();
2.    $patterns_dir = "_patterns";
3.    $handle = opendir($patterns_dir);
4.    while (false !== ($file = readdir($handle))):
5.        if(stristr($file,'.html')):
6.            $files[] = $file;
7.        endif;
8.    endwhile;
9.    sort($files);
```

This section of the code is opening our patterns directory (line 3), reading out the contents of each one (lines 4–8) and putting them into an array. It then sorts them alphabetically by filename (line 9).

Now that it has a sorted array of all the snippets in the pattern directory, it loops through that array, spitting out the content of the files into the style guide.

```
1.    foreach ($files as $file):
2.        echo '<div class="pattern">';
3.        echo '<div class="display">';
4.        include($patterns_dir.'/'.$file);
5.        echo '</div>';
6.        echo '<div class="source">';
7.        echo '<textarea rows="10" cols="30">';
8.        echo htmlspecialchars(file_get_contents($patterns_dir.'/'.$file));
9.        echo '</textarea>';
10.       echo '<p><a href="'.$patterns_dir.'/'.$file.'">'.$file.'</a></p>';
11.       echo '</div>';
12.       echo '</div>';
13.   endforeach;
```

As it loops through the snippets, it inserts the snippet into a div (lines 3–5) and the raw HTML into a text area (lines 6–11) so you can see the markup that creates the snippet.

This deceptively simple tool makes it remarkably easy to add to the style guide. Any time you have a new element you need to style, just include the snippet in the patterns library and it will automatically show up on your guide. Maintenance is a piece of cake and you get all the value of having your styles and snippets all displayed together on a single page.

Wrapping it up

Responsive design is more than a simple strategy: it's the trigger for a completely new way of approaching projects for the Web, a new workflow that better utilizes the unique strengths of this remarkable platform.

This new workflow must be agile and flexible. Because of the collaborative nature of the new approach, communication, iteration, and especially respect are absolute musts. Designers and developers should work closely throughout every project.

Thinking mobile first helps you focus and recognize interesting new methods of enhancing the experience for visitors. Mobile devices are becoming more and more prevalent, and more and more capable, opening doors to new methods of interaction and discovery.

Deliverables have to mature as well. Wireframes help you avoid getting too caught up in the details early on in a project. Keep them as low fidelity as possible—there's power in the implied malleability of a sketch.

Embrace the interactive nature of the Web and start creating mock-ups in the browser. There's only so much a flattened image file can portray about a site: without the ability to show how the design behaves when users interact with it, handoffs can become complicated.

Designing in the browser means it's time for designers to brush up on their HTML and CSS skills. It may be painful, but embracing the interactive nature of the medium is a must. This doesn't mean graphics editor programs are completely removed from the picture, just that they should no longer be the place we start by default.

Thinking in systems can help us navigate the tangled diversity of browsers and devices. Thinking page-to-page is not good enough. Style guides help by forcing us to consider the individual components in a site and how they relate to one another.

In the next chapter, we'll look at how to create content that can be reused across platforms as well as how we can adjust it and when.

CHAPTER 7
RESPONSIVE CONTENT

Technology will change. Standards will evolve.
But the need for understanding our content—
its purpose, meaning, structure, relationships,
and value—will remain. When we can embrace
this thinking, we will unshackle our content—
confident it will live on, heart intact, as it
travels into the great future unknown.
—SARA WACHTER-BOETTCHER

Imagine you're looking to buy a house. You find one online and the photos look fantastic! There's lovely hardwood flooring and plenty of space. The kitchen has clearly been redone recently: the cupboards are all new and the counter-tops sparkle. There's a sunroom, a large family room, and a wraparound deck. There's even a heated pool. It couldn't possibly get any better!

You go to look at the house and as you pull up, you notice to your bewilder-ment that this lovely-looking home is crooked. The foundation is uneven and cracked. It's amazing the thing hasn't collapsed.

A house is only as good as its foundation. You can spend all the time and money you want on hardwood floors, granite countertops, and fancy light fixtures, but if the foundation isn't solid, the house won't last very long.

Building a site without considering the content and, more importantly, the message that content is trying to convey, is the equivalent of laying a beautiful hardwood floor over compacted dirt. Understanding content and its purpose is vital to the success of any project.

In this chapter, you'll learn

- Why it's important to consider content from the very beginning
- How to determine content structure and why it matters
- What content to display, and when—and why you can't simply rely on View Desktop
- How to enhance content for different devices
- When content order should change
- How to plan and structure content in a future-friendly way

Starting with the content

As we discussed in Chapter 5, "Planning," it's important to consider content from the very beginning of your project. Content is the backbone of most sites. To not give it attention early on in the process is to undervalue the primary reason people come to your site.

For many the rallying cry has been "Content First!" As a general concept, this works just fine. However, as tends to happen with these sorts of things, some have taken it literally and believe that it means that design should not happen until all content is finalized.

This is neither realistic, nor ideal. Content is an ongoing discussion that needs to take place throughout the design process, and long after. As designer Cennydd Bowles pointed out, design and content go hand in hand:[1]

> Style and substance are irretrievably linked. Like space and time, they are neither separable nor the same thing—there exists no hierarchy between them, no primacy. One informs the other. The other informs the one.

A more realistic strategy would be "content structure first": while you can't expect finalized content before you begin a project, you should have a solid understanding of the different types of content, how each will be created, their purpose, and their structure.

Along with this understanding of content structure, it's helpful to have some sample content to work with. Again, you don't need everything at this point, but having a sample news article, recipe, staff biography—whatever your types of content may be—will guide the design while reaffirming that your planned course of action for dealing with content is accurate.

But the truth of the matter is that you must start with *communication*: the message you're trying to get across. Only by knowing what you're trying to communicate can you determine the structure of your content, not to mention the design of your site.

Content types

It's important to know what types of content you'll be displaying on a site. For example, a news-based site will most likely have, at the very least, articles, blog posts, and comments. Most news-based sites will be a little more granular. Instead of "article," some example content types might be an interview, a review, and an editorial.

Similarly, in addition to blog posts and articles, a cooking site might include content types such as recipes and chef bios. Determining content types is an important step for *any* site: all sites have content that can, and should, be broken out into types.

---

1 "What bugs me about 'content-out'" at www.cennydd.co.uk/2011/what-bugs-me-about-content-out/

Knowing content types also helps frame discussion about structure, creation, and purpose. Each of these considerations will in turn guide decisions about how to reorganize the hierarchy of content as the site adapts to different resolutions and capabilities.

Purpose

For each type of content, you must know its intended role. If you're not sure of the purpose of your content, how can you possibly make decisions about what content should take priority in which scenarios?

Responsive design inevitably results in you having to shuffle the location of content around on a page. Having an intimate knowledge of the purpose of your content helps you determine how to reorganize your content while maintaining the hierarchy.

Creation

Figure out how each kind of content is created. Who's responsible for content creation? Who edits and maintains the content? What's the process for getting, say, a new article on the site? For example, is there an editorial process that the content must go through? Who has to approve the content before it's published? Who gives final sign-off?

These kinds of questions play an important role in helping you determine how to build your site or application.

Structure

Designing a site for different devices and platforms means that your content has to evolve, to shift between contexts. Each change in context creates a potential shift in the priority of your content.

When I talk about structured content in this sense, I'm not talking about semantic HTML markup, though that's obviously very important (and related). Instead, I'm talking about structured content at the database or model level. Each content type contains any number of specific chunks of content. An article, for example, must have a title, a body, an author, and a creation date. You determine these different chunks through a process called content modeling.

CONTENT MODELING

Content modeling is the process of determining and documenting the structure of your content. Each chunk of content should have a very specific meaning and purpose: This will help guide decisions about how to utilize it on different platforms and devices.

These chunks of content should also be stored as discrete entities (e.g. database fields) so they can be found easily and utilized where appropriate. If everything is clumped together in one big blob, with no *metadata* to break it up, you won't be able to reprioritize the content when necessary.

A great example of this is any product information page. Such a page typically contains a photo, the name of the product, a description, some reviews, pricing, and additional suggested purchases. Each of these are individual entities or fields that should be stored separately. If the description and pricing are lumped together in one field, you have virtually no control over how those components will be adjusted to work at different resolutions. They're too tightly coupled to manipulate the method, and order, of their display. Likewise, if there's no appropriate metadata attributed to the product itself or to the potential suggestions, you won't be able to make intelligent decisions about which additional items to display.

If, instead, each component is stored separately, with appropriate metadata, you can arrange them however you like to ensure that hierarchy is maintained.

Content modeling requires that you do a deep-dive analysis of your content. How modular does it need to be? What types of content will need to be reused in different locations? Does some content need to be displayed in a completely different way depending on the page? Will you need to sort or filter the content? What are the time constraints of your content creators? Answers to these questions, and more, are necessary for creating an accurate and successful content model.

Don't try to do any content modeling until after you understand the higher purpose of the content: who will be consuming it and what it needs to communicate. Remember, without an understanding of the purpose of your content, you can't possibly determine how to structure it to ensure reusability and adaptability.

● *Metadata*
Data that provides context for a chunk of content. For example, tagging something as "travel" is a way of indicating that a chunk of content contains information about traveling.

Because of the deep level of analysis it requires, content modeling not only helps you determine the different chunks of content you need but also guides fundamental decisions about how content will behave in a responsive site. Specifically, content modeling can help you determine:

- What content to display, and when
- Whether the order or priority of content should change for different circumstances

What content to display, and when

Armed with information about your content structure and hierarchy, you can make informed decisions about how your content should be displayed as your design adjusts to accommodate different sizes and contexts. If you've taken the time to understand the content's purpose and structure it properly, you now have adaptive content.

In her book *Managing Enterprise Content: A Unified Content Strategy*, Ann Rockley defines adaptive content as "content that can be displayed in any desired order, made to respond to specific customer interactions, changed based on location, and integrated with content from other sources."[2]

There are two basic strategies here:

- Removing content
- Enhancing content

Removing content

If you're thinking about removing content entirely for a certain context, be very careful. Specifically, I'm referring to the alarming trend of hiding content on mobile devices and offering a View Desktop or View Full Site link for anyone who might want the "full experience" (**Figure 7.1**).

Figure 7.1 An all too common practice on mobile sites is to provide a limited subset of content and a link to view the "Full" or "Desktop" version of a site.

---

2 Ann Rockley and Charles Cooper, *Managing Enterprise Content: A Unified Content Strategy* (New Riders, 2012)

VIEW DESKTOP IS NOT A SOLUTION

Let me paint a scene for you.

You're a regular reader of your local newspaper. You're also opposed to the unnecessary waste of paper, so you subscribe to the online version. Everything is great. The content is of high quality and you become very familiar with how to navigate the site to find your favorite types of content.

Then you open the site on your phone. The only pieces of your favorite paper that are left intact are the top five stories from this week and a few of the most popular categories. The rest of the content has been removed.

Reluctantly, you click the View Desktop link to see the version of the site designed for larger screens. At least you know you can find the content you wanted to read there —even if the formatting is less than ideal on your small screen.

This scenario happens all too often on today's Web. The powers that be— whether that's the developers, the designers, or the people who sign their checks —decide that mobile users don't want the full site. They want this simplified version of the site with only the most popular content. If visitors want to browse the site in detail, well, that's what the View Desktop link is for.

The problem is that these assumptions about what mobile users want are driven by outdated views of how users interact with the Web on their mobile devices.

The traditional view of the mobile user goes something like this. He's in a hurry and on the go. When he goes online on his phone, he's doing so because he wants to get at a specific piece of information and doesn't have time to waste in doing so. This is not casual browsing—mobile users are very task oriented.

That's often not the case anymore. The capabilities of smartphones have improved so much that the browsing experience on a mobile device is no longer unbearable. In fact, on the right device, the mobile browsing experience is quite enjoyable. Further complicating the matter is the changing definition of a "mobile device"; tablets have further muddled the situation.

There are still times when a mobile user has a specific piece of information he's after, but just as often he simply wants to browse for a bit. He's using the device at home, in the waiting room at the dentist, and in the car while waiting for his kids to get out of school. These aren't your traditional scenarios of mobile use— this is recreational, casual browsing.

In these situations, what the user wants is not a crippled experience, but the full one. He wants a design optimized for his device, but the content needs to be the same and the experience needs to be familiar. If he feels that a site is holding back information that would be accessible on the desktop, he'll start hunting for that link to the desktop version.

We can't use the View Desktop link as a cop-out. If the user has to click that link, then we've already failed him. He may have access to the content he wants, but the experience is no longer very enjoyable.

When a site is viewed on a mobile device it should be simple and easy to use, but not dumbed down.

TRUST

It all boils down to trust. Right now, people don't trust the mobile version of sites—particularly when they see that View Desktop or, even worse, the View Full Site link.

They've been burned by these mobile versions too many times. Content has gone missing, navigation paths have become unfamiliar. They've struggled with these issues so many times that they no longer trust the design you've put on their phone, no matter how pretty it might look.

We can't make fundamental decisions about which content to display and which to hide based on assumptions driven by the kind of device in use.

Enhancing content

Rather than removing content entirely, a better practice is to design each experience and then *enhance* the content so it responds as you've planned.

It's entirely possible that all of the content displayed for one variation of your design doesn't need to be displayed for another. For example, if you're designing a page that sells clothes, it might make sense to display 10 related items on a large screen, but only two or three on a small-screen device. Perhaps it even makes sense for your core experience to not list related items at all, but to simply display a Related Items link.

It may also make sense for excerpts to be shortened on smaller screens. For example, on large screens it might make sense to show a teaser paragraph followed by a Read More link, but to conserve screen space, it might be better to reduce the paragraph to a single sentence for mobile devices.

Figure 7.2 Currently, the latest headlines are all listed out on the small screen layout, consuming much of the screen real estate.

Let's take a look at a simple example of conditionally loading content using JavaScript.

Looking back at the article page for *Yet Another Sports Site,* we can see the related headlines content in the sidebar (**Figure 7.2**). We decide that to save space on small screens we don't want to list the latest headlines by default. Instead, we'll display a link to view the latest headlines. When that link is clicked, the articles will appear.

To enhance the experience when necessary, we'll use what Scott Jehl dubbed the *anchor-include pattern.* The anchor-include pattern is a pattern for making an already functional link work as a client-side include through progressive enhancement. Jehl's snippet requires jQuery, and while there's nothing wrong with that, for demonstration purposes we'll build ours using vanilla JavaScript.

We'll cheat a little bit, though. Using XMLHttpRequest appropriately cross-browser requires a bit of tweaking that's beyond the scope of this book. So, when it comes to the Ajax portion of the function, we'll use Reqwest.js—a small, compact module for including Ajax functionality. If Reqwest isn't your cup of tea, you can use the Ajax helper of your choice—it should be interchangeable.

▶ **Note**
Visit http://filament group.com/lab/ ajax_includes_ modular_content/ to see Jehl's jQuery snippet and read a post on the technique.

▶ **Note**
Reqwest is included in the example files. Or you can go to https://github. com/ded/reqwest to download it from GitHub.

Let's start by considering the base experience. If JavaScript isn't enabled, or if the screen is below a certain size, we want just a basic link to appear:

```
1.    <section class="related">
2.        <a href="headlines.html" id="lazy">View the latest headlines</a>
3.    </section>
```

We're using the id attribute to provide a hook for the JavaScript—a way to identify the link in the script. We'll also need to know what element the resulting content should be placed into. For that, we'll use the new data-* attribute in HTML5. The data-* attribute lets you create your own attributes to place data into instead of overloading existing attributes. You can name your data-* attribute anything you want provided it begins with the data- prefix. In this example, since the attribute is telling the script which element to target, naming the attribute data-target seems to make the most sense:

```
1.    <section id="related" class="related">
2.        <a href="headlines.html" data-target="related" id="lazy">
          View the latest headlines</a>
3.    </section>
```

We've simply used a data-target attribute to identify which element we'll put the result into once we've grabbed the content.

▶ **Note**

In production, it might be better to extract this snippet from within an entire page. That way, if JavaScript isn't enabled, the visitor will still get a full page when they click the link. For demonstration purposes, a snippet will work fine.

Before writing the JavaScript, let's take a look at the headlines.html page:

```
1.    <h2>Related Headlines</h2>
2.    <ul>
3.        <li><a href="#">That Guy Knocked Out the Other Guy</a></li>
4.        <li><a href="#">Your Favorite Sports Team Lost. Again.</a></li>
5.        <li><a href="#">The Yankees Buy the Entire League</a></li>
6.        <li><a href="#">Guy Says Something Stupid in the Heat of the
          Moment</a></li>
7.        <li><a href="#">New Record Set as Neither Team Scores</a></li>
8.        <li><a href="#">Why Haven't You Clicked One of Our Headlines
          Yet?</a></li>
9.    </ul>
```

As you can see, there's not much going on here. It's just the snippet that used to be in the article page by default.

Now, add the anchorInclude function to the Utils object (first introduced in Chapter 3, "Media Queries").

```
1.    // anchorInclude turns a functioning link into an client-side include
2.    anchorInclude : function ( elem ) {
3.        //grab the link's url
4.        var url = elem.getAttribute('href');
5.        //grab the target element where our result will appear
6.        //set on the link using the data-target attribute
7.        var target = document.getElementById(elem.getAttribute
          ('data-target'));
8.        //make our ajax request
9.        //using reqwest.js for demonstration purposes
10.       reqwest(url, function (resp) {
11.           //place the result into our target element
12.           target.innerHTML = resp;
13.       });
14.   }
```

The anchorInclude function takes a functioning link (elem) as a parameter (line 2). Once the script has the link, it grabs the link's URL using the getAttribute method (line 4). The same method is used to get ahold of the target element (line 7).

Next, the script makes an Ajax request (lines 10–13). Again, I'm cheating here and using Reqwest, but you can use the Ajax helper of your choice. The request is made to the URL that was already grabbed from the link. The response is then inserted into the target element using the innerHTML property (line 12).

You now have a working anchorInclude function. If you grab the lazy loading link and pass it to the function, you should see the headlines appear in place of the link:

```
var lazyLink = document.getElementById('lazy');
anchorInclude(lazyLink);
```

All that's left is to tell the function when to fire. Since you're already using matchMedia to check the breakpoint for lazy-loading the images, you can just drop the anchorInclude function call in there as well:

```
if (window.matchMedia("(min-width: 37.5em)").matches) {
    Utils.anchorInclude(lazyLink);
    ...
}
```

If the device matches the media query, the conditionally loaded content will appear. If not, the basic link will display.

You can actually enhance this further. Currently, on a small screen device, when you click on the link you'll continue to the linked page. This may be fine, but you could improve the experience for those with JavaScript enabled if you instead loaded that conditional content on click. To do so requires only that you add an else to the if statement:

```
1.   //only run this function when the screen's width is at least 600px
2.   if (window.matchMedia("(min-width: 37.5em)").matches) {
3.       Utils.anchorInclude(lazyLink);
4.       ...
5.   } else {
6.       //if the screen is less than 600px wide
7.       //load the headlines only if the link is clicked
8.       lazyLink.onclick = function() {
9.           Utils.anchorInclude(this);
10.          return false;
11.      }
12.  }
```

Enhancement through truncation

Another way to optimize the experience for the small screen may be to truncate some of the text. For example, let's say you have a teaser paragraph for an article with a link to the full piece at the end. You could reduce that to simply be a link to the full piece, or you could decide to leave a little bit of a summary there to entice people to read more.

If you have a "teaser" field stored in your database, you can do this by ensuring that the hook of the story is contained within, say, the first two sentences of the blurb. That way, no matter whether the truncated or complete teaser is displayed, the main gist of the article is still shown to the visitor.

Just be sure you don't truncate key content. A teaser is a good example of something you could truncate. You wouldn't want to truncate the article itself, or anything that could then lose its meaning. It's easy to get carried away and start removing content that's important for the user to have access to in order to provide consistency. Truncation is a strategy that must be applied with care.

Figure 7.3 With the JavaScript in place, large-screen displays will see a list of headlines (left) while small screens (right) will see a link to the headlines, conserving screen real estate.

The result is that the content will always be conditionally loaded (provided JavaScript is enabled)—it's just a matter of when (**Figure 7.3**). This is progressive enhancement at its finest. If JavaScript is not supported, or it's turned off, the visitor gets a completely usable site and all the content is still intact. If JavaScript support is available, the experience is enhanced, regardless of the dimensions of the screen.

When should content order change?

As I mentioned before, adjusting the layout of your site for multiple devices and resolutions means you'll have to make decisions about the order of content at those different screen sizes. The inability to negotiate content order is currently one of the biggest limitations in a purely front-end driven responsive approach.

Take, for example, the *Yet Another Sports Site* article page. Imagine, for a second, that the sidebar contains content relevant to the article, like a photo gallery or videos associated with the article.

▶ **Note**
Chapter 8, "RESS," discusses feature and server-side device detection. Combining responsive design with detection can help you negotiate the order of content.

Figure 7.4 All of the sidebar content is pushed below everything in the main column, but sometimes that doesn't make sense.

● **WYSIWYG**
What You See Is What You Get. A WYSIWYG editor (sometimes referred to as a rich text editor) gives the content creator the ability to style content during the editorial process through a series of buttons.

On a large screen, this layout would make sense. The sidebar content would be shown inline with the article so users would have quick access to it.

But what happens when the layout is suddenly converted to a single column on a small screen? Suddenly, because of the way the HTML is created, the sidebar content is pushed below the main column (**Figure 7.4**). Is that really what should happen, however? Is the sidebar content suddenly that much less important than the ancillary content in the main column?

You may also want to emphasize certain bits of content depending on the type of device in use. If a smartphone is being used to access a restaurant site, for example, then the restaurant's contact or location information should definitely be front and center.

Structure, again

These kinds of scenarios are exactly why content structure is so important. If that content is all one *WYSIWYG* (What You See Is What You Get)-generated blob, there's not much you can do. In fact, your decision becomes binary: display the blob of text or don't display it. That's it.

If the content is separated neatly and stored as chunks, and if that content is also marked up with the appropriate metadata—using the techniques we talked about earlier in the chapter—then you have a bit more power and flexibility. Now, manipulating the content order isn't quite as difficult. Structured content gives you options. You're able to make decisions about how content should behave on a much more granular level.

HELP IS JUST AROUND THE CORNER

Unfortunately at the moment there isn't much to be done to solve the problem of content order without using some server-side negotiation or JavaScript hackery (see the sidebar, "Shifting Content" for more information). There are, however, a few CSS layout methods being worked on that should help reduce the issue of source order: the Flexible Box Layout Module (Flexbox for short) and Grid Layout.

Flexbox would allow you to style containers so that they can be arranged in any direction and can "flex" their size to accomodate the space available to them. Among the many useful features is the ability to define an order that your content should display in. So, for example, you could have your navigation element come first in your source, but display last on the page.

Shifting content

If you just want to shuffle a few pieces of content around on a page, say an ad for example, then appendAround (found on GitHub at https://github.com/filamentgroup/AppendAround) from Scott Jehl and the rest of the Filament Group may be just the ticket.

His clever solution involves inserting empty div elements into the page to serve as containers for the content to slide into. Each div is given the same data-set attribute value to designate that they are all related. For example:

```
1.   <div class="foo" data-set="foobarbaz"></div>
2.   <ul>
3.        ...
4.   </ul>
5.   <div class="bar" data-set="foobarbaz">
6.        <img src="ad.png" />
7.   </div>
```

In the case of the above, both div's have the same data-set value. One is empty and one contains the ad. Using CSS, you make sure that only one of the two div's is ever visible. For example, you might hide the div with the class "bar" for small screens and hide the div with the class "foo" for larger screens.

When the page loads, the appendAround script looks to see which element is displayed and ensures that the ad is placed within it.

It's a clever solution, though it's probably not advisable to make substantial changes to the order of your content using the script. For simple shuffling of an ad or specific chunk of content, however, it's a very handy tool.

Grid layouts also offer a way to re-order how your content is displayed. Using CSS Grid layouts you would be able to create columns and rows, and then assign an element to display within a specified cell.

Unfortunately, at the time of writing both specifications are still in a state of flux and therefore, support is scarce. Still, you should take some time to become familiar with them. Once they're here you're going to want to use them.

Where we need to go

Here's the thing: The issue of platform and device fragmentation isn't getting better anytime soon. In fact, it's going to get worse. To survive in this increasingly complex ecosystem, the way content is stored and accessed has to change.

Code soup

Today, many sites are powered by content management systems (CMSs). These systems are intended to make it easier to maintain and update content by allowing a simple method of input. This ease of input is made possible in no small part thanks to WYSIWYG editors.

WYSIWYG editors give the content creator controls similar to what they'd have in a document editing application, such as Microsoft Word (**Figure 7.5**). Using them requires no knowledge of HTML—just select some text, click a button, and it's magically 18px, hot pink, and Comic Sans!

This abstraction comes at a very steep cost. The markup generated by these editors is a muddled mess of content and markup—often markup that is both unnecessary and misused. We then store this muddled mess of content and markup into the database.

Let's ignore the storage issue for a minute. If you're considering your content in the very limited perspective of how it appears on that specific page on a specific kind of device, then a WYSIWYG sort of works. The problem is that content on the Web is not constrained to a single page—it can go anywhere.

Figure 7.5 WYSIWYG editors try to provide content creators with the same kind of controls they have in a document editing application.

In Rachel Lovinger's excellent "Nimble Report," she discussed the need for content to transcend the single page:

> This is what content needs in order to survive. It must be free to go where and when people want it most.
>
> It must be free to be read or viewed on a wide range of portable and networked devices. It must be free to mix and mingle with services, social networks, apps, and content from other sources. In a highly connected world, content that's trapped in a silo is basically invisible. And invisible content might as well not exist.

Content today has to be able to go anywhere—different contexts, different devices, even different styling. Being able to control content to the level a WYSIWYG might imply is just not realistic anymore.

Going back to the muddled mess of markup, it should now be obvious why this can't work. By storing code soup in the database, we chain the content to a very specific display format. If we need to alter the display, the markup, or the hierarchy, we've just made things very difficult for ourselves.

This issue transcends responsive design. Database-driven content has the potential to go anywhere. In theory, you should be able to use that single database of content to serve all your initiatives—your site, your applications, e-book collections, even print. That mess of markup and content, though, limits that potential. It makes the cost of reuse much, much higher.

▶ **Note**
Rachel Lovinger's "Nimble Report" is essential reading for anyone who cares about content in the current digital age—that should be everyone by the way. Go to http://nimble. razorfish.com/ publication/?m= 11968&l=1 to find it.

Baby steps

Unfortunately, we can't just take away everyone's WYSIWYGs overnight (though I admit, I wish we could). We need to get past the existing mental models that are now well engrained into content producers.

WYSIWYGs bring comfort and familiarity to many content producers today; moving from a WYSIWYG model is going to be quite painful for many of them.

Yet, it has to happen. If we're going to capitalize on the unique characteristics of the Web and survive the ever-increasing diversity of Internet-enabled devices, we need to start taking our content seriously.

We need to understand that this familiarity exists and take the time to communicate with content creators. Take the time to show how WYSIWYG actually reduces the amount of control they have.

If you must provide WYSIWYG controls, opt for an editor that's as stripped-down as possible. For example, instead of offering color, size, and font choices, only include basic formatting controls such as making text bold or italicized. Doing this eliminates many of the most serious pain points when it comes to WYSIWYG-generated code.

In the end, content creators want to make quality content. If you take the time to show them how to do it, you'll get a lot further along.

Building an API

One way to ensure that your content can go anywhere is to build an internal API. First, build an API to your content. Then, use that API to power your digital initiatives.

That's exactly what NPR (National Public Radio) did. They set a lofty goal of achieving what they termed COPE (Create Once Publish Everywhere). Instead of needlessly duplicating time and effort, they wanted their database of content to power all their initiatives.

So, they rolled their own CMS. All the content is separated into different fields to ensure that the structure is solid. Before storing the content in a database, they filter out the markup. The location and type of markup is stored in one table, while the raw content is stored in another. They then use an API to pull this content from the database and bring it to their applications, their site—everywhere.

The future of content relies on this kind of structure and consideration. It must have three basic layers: storage, translation, and view layers.

STORAGE LAYER

Content must be stored in chunks, with meaningful metadata, so it can be requested and utilized however and whenever it's needed.

TRANSLATION OR API LAYER

However you stored your content, this layer then translates it into something usable. It's the translation layer that requests the specific chunks of content that are needed for any specific device, site, application, or platform.

VIEW LAYER

Now that you've got that content translated into something usable, the view layer determines how it's displayed: order, interactions, and so on.

Viewing content in this way gives you incredible flexibility. You can request only the content that you need and format it in any number of ways. This is content that is truly adaptive.

It also lets people focus on the part of the task they do best. Writers can focus on what the content means, while people who are more familiar with the site or the device that will be accessing that content can focus on how that content should look to best convey meaning.

Wrapping it up

While content must be considered from the very beginning of a project, don't expect final content before you start designing. Instead, know first what the site needs to communicate—the key messages—then what types of content will be displayed, how it will be created, what each type of content's purpose is and how it is structured. Some sample content can be very helpful for guiding design decisions.

Sometimes it makes sense to truncate content on smaller screens. However, don't assume that just because you have a View Desktop link on your site that you can start stripping content on smaller screens. People use many devices to access your content and if the experience isn't familiar, they'll lose trust in the site.

Instead of hiding content, enhance it. Design how the content will change for each environment and then choose the right technique to make it happen. Some clever coding and planning will let you create a solid base to build on as the screen size allows.

Content order, too, needs to change. Consider your content's metadata, and plan carefully to make sure the hierarchy is consistent across devices.

Moving forward, content needs to be taken more seriously. Continued use of WYSIWYGs will only add to the problem. Instead, use structured content served up by an API. Even if you're not using an API, thinking about how your content would need to be structured to go through an API can help guide your decisions about how that content should be created and stored.

Now it's time to start looking at how detection can augment our responsive site. The content, and the experience in general, will benefit from a bit more customization from device to device.

In the next chapter, we'll discuss how feature detection and server-side detection can both play a part in creating a more optimized experience for visitors.

CHAPTER 8
RESS

It is a bad carpenter who quarrels with his tools.

—MOHANDAS GANDHI

I'm no carpenter. Give me a hammer, some nails, and a pile of boards and you'll get a bunch of bent nails, a pile of boards (with hammer indents), and some cheap comic relief. That doesn't mean the tools were bad. Give those same materials to a carpenter and you'll get a sturdy bench built to last a long time.

There's a lot of debate surrounding server-side detection and responsive design. Many developers claim that server-side detection is inherently wrong. Of course, many of those on the other side of the fence say the same thing about client-side responsive design.

Neither approach is a solution in and of itself, but they are valuable tools. We've spent a great deal of time talking about client-side responsive design and what it can do. Let's highlight a few things it *doesn't* do well:

- **Content adaptation.** Content adaptation, optimizing markup on devices to target their unique capabilities, is not something responsive design does particularly well. Client-side solutions can only work with what's being sent down the pipe.

- **Performance considerations.** We already discussed just how difficult it is to serve appropriately sized images using client-side adaptation. Responsive design is also incapable of optimizing the markup, JavaScript, and CSS to ensure that no unnecessary data is downloaded.

- **Targeting low-end devices.** If built carefully, it's remarkable how many devices you can reach with a responsive site. However, if you need to target older, low-end mobile devices you may need a bit more. Many of them support only a subset of the HTML standard, called XHTML-MP.

- **Targeting TVs.** TVs are still picking up momentum, but you can rest assured that they will soon be wreaking chaos for web developers everywhere. Client-side detection is useless for TVs. The resolutions are similar to many desktop monitors and TVs don't support the "tv" media type (discussed in Chapter 3, "Media Queries").

These are issues that are difficult, if not impossible, to resolve using client-side responsive design alone. For these kinds of improvements, some sort of server-side detection is necessary as well. That's where Responsive Design and Server-Side (RESS) components—a concept developed by Luke Wroblewski—come in.[1]

---

1   "RESS: Responsive Design + Server-Side Components" at www.lukew.com/ff/entry.asp?1392

In this chapter, you'll learn

- How to use user agent detection

- How to use feature detection

- How to combine user agent detection and feature detection

- How to implement an RESS approach

- How to install and configure a WURFL library

- How to use WURFL to optimize for small-screen phones and devices with touch screens

Let's start by looking at the two basic detection methods: user agent detection and feature detection.

User agent detection

User agent detection is the practice of looking at the user agent string of the browser and using that to make decisions about how to serve your site. This is done at the server.

User agent detection has a bad reputation, and deservedly so. For a long time, it was misused and abused. User agent detection was used to serve up one version of a site for, say, Internet Explorer and another for Netscape. Because the two browsers had different levels of support, developers resorted to user agent detection to fork the experience, and in many cases, exclude some browsers from an experience entirely.

As a result, most user agent detection implementations ended up excluding people (**Figure 8.1**). Fundamental decisions were made about who got to see what content based on this little string, often with no good reason. So, the browsers that weren't getting any love decided to lie. They started manipulating their user agent strings so they would be recognized as the more popular browsers.

This is why using too basic of a method of detection can be dangerous and unreliable. User agent strings are often purposefully trying to present themselves something they're not.

Now before you go blaming the browsers for this mess, remember it was the developers who forced their hand. Had the technology been handled appropriately from the beginning, the situation would not have become nearly so muddled.

That's not to say there isn't value in user agent strings—there is. Device databases have been carefully curated by developers to ensure a fairly high degree of accuracy. You just need to be careful about how you use them. Don't make the mistake of using user agent detection to exclude, like so many have done in the past. Instead, use user agent detection to enhance the experience where it makes sense.

Anatomy of a user agent string

A user agent string is one of several HTTP headers that get sent by the browser whenever a page or resource is requested. Its purpose is to identify the client (browser) in use. Unfortunately there's no standard convention for how user agent strings should be written and there's a lot of useless information. Consider the following example taken from a Samsung Acclaim:

> Mozilla/5.0 (Linux; U; Android 2.2.1; en-us; SCH-R880 Build/FROYO) AppleWebKit/533.1 (KHTML, like Gecko) Version/4.0 Mobile Safari/533.1

All that matters out of that string is the following information:

- **Android 2.2.1:** This phone is running the Android OS, version 2.2.1.

- **AppleWebKit/533.1:** This is the layout engine and build number.

That's about it. The SCH-R880 part tells us that this is a Samsung Acclaim, and that's potentially of value as well, depending on what you want to do.

If you're uncomfortable dissecting user agent strings manually, don't worry: there are a lot of services out there that will do it for you. Still, it's good to be aware of the general structure of user agent strings in order to understand how these services gather information based on them.

What can you do with user agent detection?

You can use user agent detection in a variety of ways. There are simple scripts that will parse the string and tell you if the device is "mobile" or something else.

At the other end of the spectrum, device detection repositories (DDR) like *WURFL* and DeviceAtlas bring back an incredibly detailed list of information about the device, the browser, the operating system, and what is supported.

Take WURFL, for example. If you were to pass the Samsung Acclaim's user agent string to WURFL, you'd get a list of 500 different capabilities in return. These capabilities range from checking to see if CSS gradients are supported to determining whether or not the device can place a phone call.

● **WURFL**
WURFL is one of the oldest and most widely implemented device detection repositories.

Once you have this kind of information, you can customize the experience and tailor the markup, CSS, and JavaScript to ensure that only what is needed is sent down to the device.

PROS OF USER AGENT DETECTION

- It provides detailed information.

- Since it's server-side, it lets you eliminate unnecessary resources from being sent down to the device.

CONS OF USER AGENT DETECTION

- If not carefully applied, it can be unreliable, due to a long history of spoofing.

- Getting detailed information requires use of a third-party service, which adds expense to a project.

Feature detection

The other popular detection approach is feature detection, which is typically a client-side approach. With feature detection, you don't bother with the user agent string. Instead, using JavaScript, you test whether or not a specific feature is supported. For example, you might check to see if the browser in use supports JSON (JavaScript Object Notation) natively by using the following:

```
return !!window.JSON;
```

Then, armed with information about whether native JSON is supported, you could use JavaScript to fork the behavior of the page.

One caveat: Browsers behave a little like fishermen—they tend to exaggerate a bit. Support is not binary; it's a gradient of levels. While a browser may claim to support a specific feature, the quality of that support may vary dramatically. As with user agent detection, using feature detection correctly requires careful consideration.

Modernizr

Many scripts that help with feature detection have popped up, the most popular of which is Modernizr. Modernizr tests over 40 different features and provides three things to help with development:

▶ **Note**
You can download the latest version of Modernizr from http·//modernizr. com.

- It creates a JavaScript object containing the results of the tests.

- It adds classes to the HTML element indicating which features are and are not supported.

- It provides a script loader so you can conditionally load polyfills.

Forty tests is a lot, and probably overkill for most sites. As a result, Modernizr lets you create a custom build of the script containing only the tests you need for your specific project.

Once you have the build in place, drop the script into the head of your document. It's also a good idea to add a class of nojs to the html element of your page:

```
<html lang="en" class="nojs">
```

When the user requests the page, if Modernizr is able to run successfully, it will replace nojs with js, indicating that JavaScript is supported. By adding nojs by default, you provide a way to style elements on the page if no JavaScript is supported. For example, the following declaration would allow you to apply overflow:hidden to the body element if JavaScript is unsupported.

```
body.nojs {
    overflow:hidden;
}
```

The other thing Modernizr does is add a series of classes to the html element indicating what features are supported. For example, if your build tests only for canvas support, geolocation support, RGBA support, and touch support, your HTML element might look like this:

```
<html lang="en" class="js canvas gelocation rgba touch">
```

In addition to the classes to aid in styling, you have access to the results of the tests in JavaScript through the Modernizr object.

A great example of when you might want access to this information is for a device that is touch enabled. Touch-screen devices convert click events to touch events to ensure that the behavior of a site remains consistent. However, this conversion results in a 300–500ms delay that is consistent across devices. Using the results of the Modernizr.touch test, you could replace the click events with touch events:

```
1. if (Modernizr.touch) {
2.     //use touch events
3. } else {
4.     //use click events
5. }
```

Going to the server

Feature detection can be useful, but since it's typically done on the client side, your ability to reduce the amount of data being downloaded and to customize the experience of your site is limited. To make any sort of structural changes, the server needs to know that information *before* the page is sent to the browser.

Understanding this, James Pearce created modernizr-server, a library that lets you bring Modernizr results to your server-side code so you can make structural changes and stop unnecessary resources from being downloaded.

▶ **Note**
Visit GitHub at https://github.com/jamesgpearce/modernizr-server to download modernizr-server.

Using modernizr-server will be familiar to you if you've already used the client-side library. To kick things off, download both modernizr-server and the latest version of the JavaScript library. Place the JavaScript into a file called modernizr.js, located in the folder at modernizr-server/modernizr.js/. Then, include the PHP file in your page:

```
<?php
include('modernizr-server.php');
?>
```

From there on, you can access Modernizr test results just as you would with the JavaScript:

```
1.    if ($modernizr-touch) {
2.        //touch is supported
3.    } else {
4.        //no touch
5.    }
```

The first time a visitor accesses the page, the library executes the JavaScript file and grabs the test results. Those results are then added to a cookie and the page is reloaded immediately.

On the next page load, the library uses the information in the cookie and, if it can, places it in a session variable for quick retrieval going forward.

Understanding how it works is important, because there's a catch here: to run the test the first time, the page is loaded twice. You're causing one extra HTTP request. This is true even though the content isn't loaded the first time because the JavaScript is executed immediately. Depending on the network your users are on, that can be either a minor inconvenience or a fairly large annoyance.

PROS OF FEATURE DETECTION

- It doesn't rely on the user agent string.
- It allows you to tailor functionality in JavaScript based on feature support.

CONS OF FEATURE DETECTION

- JavaScript may be disabled or not supported.
- Browsers exaggerate their capabilities. Support is often not as simple as true or false.
- If done on the client side, you can't perform significant content adaptation. If done the sever side, it requires an extra page load.

Combining user agent detection and feature detection

User agent detection and feature detection offer different information and have their own limitations. By themselves, they're probably good enough for most sites. But there might be times where you need something a little more powerful. In those cases, you can combine the two.

In a combo approach, you accumulate device profiles over time. You can do this by storing the results of your tests and associating them with the user agent string in use.

Let's say that same Samsung Acclaim is used to access your site. You grab the user agent string and send a request to WURFL to get the lowdown. You then take those results and store them in a database.

When the page loads, you run your feature tests. Again, the results of these are pushed back to the server and stored in the same database.

Bridging the gap with Detector

One helpful tool for bridging the gap between client-side feature detection and server-side detection is Dave Olsen's Detector, which can be found at http://detector.dmolsen.com.

Detector is a browser- and feature-detection library based on modernizr-server and the popular ua-parser.php, a browser-detection script that collects general information about the device such as the operating system or device name. Using this information, Detector can dynamically create profiles for each user-agent string that accesses a page.

While it doesn't come with the power of WURFL or DeviceAtlas, it also doesn't have to rely on a hefty database of device information. In that way, it's a much more nimble solution. For many projects you may find you don't need the kind of detail that WURFL supplies. If that is true, Detector is an excellent solution.

The next time anyone uses a Samsung Acclaim, you check the database and find the results associated with that user agent string. It's a good idea to double-check this data once again by running some more feature tests the next time that UA string appears. The first time someone came with that UA string, it could very well have been someone on a desktop browser who was just spoofing the UA string. It never hurts to double-check.

RESS: The best of both worlds

Server-side detection has some fundamental flaws as well. If you try to use it independently of responsive design, it's unscalable. As the landscape of devices becomes more and more diverse, it will become increasingly difficult for server-side detection (at least the most common implementation, which is based on user agent detection) to keep up. You can already see the stretch marks.

The most robust approach is to combine server-side detection with responsive design. This approach, dubbed RESS, marries the best of both worlds: It provides one core site (a single set of base templates) to all devices, while allowing individual components to be rendered server side and tailored to a specific class of devices.

For example, if an article contained a photo gallery, the article page itself could be one template served to all devices. The gallery, on the other hand, could be a component that would be served differently for different devices (say, a touch-enabled device).

Combining responsive design and server side detection effectively eliminates most of the of concerns with either approach:

- Thanks to responsive design, the layout is device agnostic. This enables the site to support a broader range of devices than simply building a separate site would.

- The use of server-side detection lets you reduce the amount of data being downloaded, saving the user from unnecessarily long download times.

- Swapping out components allows you to tailor the experience so that it best suits the device being used.

Troubled waters

So far, we've been playing in safe waters by testing on iOS, Android, and desktop browsers. We've been avoiding an unfortunate reality: Not everyone uses these devices and browsers.

On mobile devices, the most popular browsers in terms of worldwide market share are Opera Mini and Opera Mobile. The traffic is far from insignificant. According to an Opera report, 168 million people used Opera Mini in March 2012 to browse 117 billion pages.[2] Those are numbers that shouldn't be ignored.

If you have an iPhone or Android, you can install Opera Mini and test on your device. Otherwise, navigate to http://implementingresponsivedesign.com/ex/ch8/ch8-1.html and use the online simulator.

Opera Mobile plays along nicely with the *Yet Another Sports Site* page, but Opera Mini is another story entirely. That's because Opera Mini is a browser whose goal is to reduce data use and speed things up at all costs. As a result, it uses some server compression to compress the page before it's even passed along to the device.

Opera Mini does support JavaScript, but it runs on the server, not on the device. As a result, the amount of JavaScript interaction that will work with your page is a bit more limited.

Let's fire it up and see just how bad it is.

Thankfully, as a result of the progressive enhancement approach taken with the page, the site actually looks pretty good.

---

2 "State of the Mobile Web, March 2012" at http://fr.opera.com/smw/2012/03/

Erik Runyon

RESS IN THE WILD

Erik Runyon lives in Michigan and has been building websites since 1995. He is a staunch advocate for web standards, semantic markup, the mobile experience, and data portability. He can be found talking geek on Twitter (@erunyon) and at his personal blog (weedygarden.net).

We knew early in the ND.edu design process that we would be employing RESS with the intent of keeping the mobile experience as fast and lightweight as possible. The goal of the redesign was to allow the visitor to experience the University of Notre Dame through imagery and in-depth content. For desktops and tablets, this involved large feature images that took up the majority of the screen, as well as pulling several top-level pages onto the homepage. We had used this long-form style of content on a series of feature stories that appeared on the previous iteration of ND.edu.

However, the sheer volume of content and resources required would have resulted in a less-than-ideal mobile experience. That's where the "server side" of RESS came in.

We used a simple user-agent library to classify devices into two categories: "mobile" and "not mobile" (like I said, simple). This let us compile the correct content on the server and supply only what was necessary. We determined what to include by the experience we were trying to convey. First, since the long form of the tablet/desktop version was a combination of top-level pages, we could safely omit that content and instead rely on the top-level navigation to provide it to mobile users. This greatly reduced the page size, but still provided easy access to the content for those users who wanted it.

Next we considered drop-down navigation, which consisted of large, apron-style drop-downs with links to internal and external resources. This functionality did not translate well to our mobile layout, and since all the links were available through other navigation, we decided to not load them for mobiles.

Last, and most troubling from a content parity standpoint, were the feature images and related content. The goal was to show the beauty of Notre Dame's campus and provide pertinent information for each image in a slide-out wing. Our decision to not include this feature came down to two things. First, the experience of large imagery doesn't translate to small mobile screens, and second, each location required a great deal of content that would be detrimental to the overall mobile experience. So in the end, we did not include this feature, but instead sought a way to provide similar content that played to the strengths of mobile devices: We presented tour locations with mobile-friendly content pulled directly from our map API. The advantage of this was that if we determined a user's device was capable of geolocation, we could ask the user to share

her location and, if she was on campus, show her the nearby tour locations. We could even provide features such as walking directions.

We learned from this experience to consider the strengths and weaknesses of each device classification, and to then use RESS to branch the content and experience to provide the best possible result to each. We were able to present a rich, immersive experience for large screens weighing in at 136 requests and 3MB, and a mobile version that made only 23 requests and downloaded a mere 292KB. This was accomplished with nearly complete content parity. The advantages of an RESS approach to web design and development are pretty obvious.

Figure 8.2 On Opera Mini, the navigation is expanded, leaving little room for content.

As a result of Opera Mini's limited JavaScript interaction, the navigation is expanded by default. It's ugly, but functional (**Figure 8.2**).

Honestly, this issue isn't a deal-breaker. It's certainly less than ideal, but the content is accessible and everything is functional. Here's where you need to decide how far you're willing to go. The project requirements, site traffic, and budget will help you arrive at the correct answer.

For demonstration purposes, let's fix the issue. We need only watch the resolution of the device. In the next section we'll grab that information from WURFL and adjust the experience accordingly.

Alternatively, you could easily test the resolution using an approach similar to modernizr-server. We'll build on this example in a moment though, so you'll see the reasoning behind using WURFL.

Installing WURFL

First, you'll need to install the WURFL PHP library. You can find it either on the companion site for this book or at SourceForge (http://wurfl.sourceforge.net).

Once you have the library downloaded and unzipped, the main folder should be named wurfl-php-version-number. Move that folder into your working directory for these examples.

If you open the wurfl-php-version-number folder, you'll find an examples/resources directory. Copy that resources folder into your main working directory. You can then safely delete the examples folder.

Inside the resources directory, there are two folders: cache and persistence. Both of these folders need to be writeable by your server.

Also inside the resources directory is a wurfl.zip. This is where the magic happens. The zip file contains the wurfl.xml file that houses all the device information. You can also download this file by itself, in case you want to update the XML file periodically to keep up to date with all the changes.

◆ **Tip**
WURFL also offers a cloud service (www. scientiamobile.com/ cloud), which is simpler to get up and running with. We won't use it in the book because to play along you would need to register for a paid account, but it's worth checking out.

Licensing WURFL

The WURFL API is available under the Affero General Public License v3 (AGPL). This means that if you comply with the AGPL restrictions, you can use the WURFL APIs free of charge.

The AGPL license is a little tricky. For example, running the WURFL APIs on a server counts as distribution. This, in turn, means that anything you create using the APIs would need to be licensed as open-source as well. If the AGPL license is too restrictive for your project, you can buy a commercial license for WURFL.

The WURFL XML database is licensed separately and can only be used in conjunction with the WURFL API.

Configuration

Now back in the main working directory, create a file named wurfl_config.php and place the following code inside:

```php
<?php
// Enable all error logging while in development
ini_set('display_errors', 'on');
error_reporting(E_ALL);

$wurflDir = dirname(__FILE__) . '/wurfl-php-1.4.1/WURFL';
$resourcesDir = dirname(__FILE__) . '/wurfl-php-1.4.1/resources';

require_once $wurflDir.'/Application.php';

$persistenceDir = $resourcesDir.'/storage/persistence';
$cacheDir = $resourcesDir.'/storage/cache';

// Create WURFL Configuration
$wurflConfig = new WURFL_Configuration_InMemoryConfig();

// Set location of the WURFL File
$wurflConfig->wurflFile($resourcesDir.'/wurfl.zip');

// Set the match mode for the API ('performance' or 'accuracy')
$wurflConfig->matchMode('performance');

// Setup WURFL Persistence
$wurflConfig->persistence('file', array('dir' => $persistenceDir));

// Setup Caching
$wurflConfig->cache('file', array('dir' => $cacheDir, 'expiration' =>
36000));

// Create a WURFL Manager Factory from the WURFL Configuration
$wurflManagerFactory = new WURFL_WURFLManagerFactory($wurflConfig);

// Create a WURFL Manager
/* @var $wurflManager WURFL_WURFLManager */
$wurflManager = $wurflManagerFactory->create();
```

Meet DeviceAtlas

WURFL isn't the only game in town. There are several other options, with DeviceAtlas being the most noteworthy.

DeviceAtlas, started in 2008, is a commercial device database. DeviceAtlas aggregrates information from carriers, manufacturers, and even from WURFL. DeviceAtlas tends to be a little more focused on mobile web-specific concerns than WURFL, so while there's some overlap in capabilities, there are some notable differences as well.

For example, WURFL has a whole category of capabilities dealing with downloadable objects like wallpaper, ringtones, and screensavers. DeviceAtlas does not. On the other hand, DeviceAtlas has an entire category devoted to HTML5-related features such as canvas and application cache, whereas WURFL does not.

WURFL and DeviceAtlas both have a high level of quality and are frequently updated, so your decision will ultimately come to down to a combination of project requirements and personal preference.

Let's walk through that config file.

Lines 3–4 enable PHP error reporting. This setting isn't required for WURFL to run, but error reporting can be helpful when working on your development site. Make sure to pull those lines on your production site.

Lines 6–7 point to the WURFL directory and the resources directory you just set up.

Line 9 includes the primary WURFL application file. Lines 11–12 point to the persistence and cache directories. The cache directory stores the user agents that have been detected in order to speed up repeat requests.

Line 15 instantiates the configuration object so we can tell it where everything resides. Line 18 tells the configuration object where the main WURFL database lives.

Line 21 sets the `matchMode`. There are two options: performance and accuracy. In performance mode, desktop browsers are simply returned as generic web browsers instead of attempting to identify them in any greater detail. Most of the time that's sufficient.

Lines 24 and 27 set the persistence and cache methods. In this case, they tell WURFL to use file storage, where the directory resides, and, in the case of the cache folder, how long the cache remains valid.

On lines 30 and 34, the configuration file creates the WURFL manager object that will allow you to identify devices and return their capabilities.

Detecting capabilities

With these variables in place, you're ready to include WURFL into the *Yet Another Sports Site* page.

Add the following lines to the top of the page:

```
1.   <?php
2.   // Include the configuration file
3.   include_once './wurfl_config.php';
4.   // This line detects the visiting device by looking at its HTTP Request
     ($_SERVER)
6.   $device = $wurflManager->getDeviceForHttpRequest($_SERVER);
7.   ?>
```

The code snippet includes the configuration file and then passes the *server variables* to WURFL. WURFL then identifies the device and returns the capabilities information.

● **Server variables** PHP stores information about headers (including the user agent string), paths and locations in a $_SERVER array.

You can now query WURFL to see if it's a small screen device using the resolution_width capability:

```
1.   if ($device->getCapability('resolution_width') <= 480) {
2.       $smallScreen = true;
3.   } else {
4.       $smallScreen = false;
5.   }
```

The example above checks the resolution width of the device to see if it's below 480px. The first line uses the getCapability method, which allows you to get the value of a specific capability from WURFL. In this case, WURFL returns the resolution width of the device. If it's less than or equal to 480px, the $smallScreen variable you've created will be set to true. If not, it will be set to false.

Armed with the $smallScreen variable, you can now adjust what gets passed to the browser for the navigation:

```
1.   <?php if ($smallScreen) { ?>
2.       <a href="#bottom" class="nav-collapse active"
         id="nav-collapse">Menu</a>
3.   <?php } else { ?>
4.       <a href="#nav" class="nav-collapse" id="nav-collapse">Menu</a>
5.       <ul class="nav" id="nav">
6.           <li class="active"><a href="#">Football</a></li>
7.           <li><a href="#">Baseball</a></li>
8.           <li><a href="#">Soccer</a></li>
9.           <li><a href="#">Tennis</a></li>
10.          <li><a href="#">Ice Soccer</a></li>
11.          <li><a href="#">Basketball</a></li>
12.      </ul>
13.  <?php } ?>
```

If the $smallScreen variable is true, a Menu link that links directly to the footer navigation will be provided to the device. If not, the full navigation will be passed along.

This eliminates the navigation issue with Opera Mini. Now, on a small-screen device, the Menu button will simply bring the user directly to the bottom of the screen for navigation (**Figure 8.3**).

Figure 8.3 Thanks to some very simple server-side detection, the navigation is left for the bottom of the screen, leaving plenty of room for the content.

Here, user agent detection is used to enhance, not to exclude. If the device is below 480px wide, everything still functions, just in a slightly different way. The user experience isn't negatively affected. Since we built the page using progressive enhancement, it will still function even if a larger screen device doesn't collapse the menu. No matter the situation, the navigation will be useful and small screens won't be filled up entirely with navigation.

This is a great example of why you may want to use server-side detection from time to time. A better experience will be provided to devices that don't support the drop-down navigation and more importantly, this optimization doesn't exclude anyone from enjoying the site. Using server-side detection doesn't have to mean exclusion.

ADDING FEATURE DETECTION

You can make this approach more foolproof by adding some feature detection. While the screen resolution provided by WURFL is helpful as a base, it may not tell the full story. For a desktop browser, WURFL can't tell you the actual width the user has the browser set to: it could be very narrow.

As we discussed in Chapter 5, "Planning," some new devices can project their display. Likewise, it's possible to hook up an Android smartphone to an external display using an OS provided by Ubuntu. For these situations, WURFL's reported resolution will be less accurate than detecting the width via JavaScript. Server-side detection makes sense for the first page load, but after that you should grab the width using JavaScript and use that value on subsequent page loads.

▶ **Note**
These functions were originally created by Peter-Paul Koch and can be found on his site (http://www.quirksmode.org/js/cookies.html).

Start by creating functions to read and write cookies in JavaScript and add them to the `Utils` object.

```
1.   var Utils = {
2.       createCookie : function(name, value, days) {
3.           if (days) {
4.               var date = new Date();
5.               date.setTime(date.getTime() + (days*24*60*60*1000));
6.               var expires = "; expires="+date.toGMTString();
7.           }
8.           else var expires = "";
9.           document.cookie = name + "=" + value + expires + "; path=/";
10.      },
11.      readCookie : function(name) {
12.          var nameEQ = name + "+";
13.          var ca = document.cookie.split(';');
```

```
14.            for (var i = 0; i < ca.length; i++) {
15.                var c = ca[i];
16.                while (c.charAt(0)==' ') c = c.substring(1, c.length);
17.                if (c.indexOf(nameEQ) == 0) {
18.                    return c.substring(nameEQ.length, c.length);
19.                }
20.            };
21.        return null;
22.        },
23.        ...
24.    }
```

With those utility functions in place, it's time to create a Utils.tests object, which will contain any feature tests you create. For now, you need only test the width, but building it this way allows for easy scaling as more features get tested.

```
1.    var Utils = {
2.        ...
3.        tests : {
4.            getWidth: function(){
5.                return (window.innerWidth > 0) ? window.innerWidth :
                   screen.width;
6.            }
7.        }
8.    }
```

In the above snippet, the getWidth function is created and added to the Utils. test object. On line 5, the function returns either the window.innerWidth property, or if that's not a valid value, it returns the screen.width property.

With these functions in place, you can add some code to the window.onload function to run the test and store it in a cookie for later use:

```
1.    var features = {};
2.    //check for cookie
3.    if (Utils.readCookie('features')) {
4.        features = Utils.readCookie('features');
5.        features = JSON.parse(features);
6.    } else {
7.        //test width
8.        features['width'] = Utils.tests.getWidth();
9.        //save features
10.       Utils.createCookie('features', JSON.stringify(features));
11.   }
```

Line 1 creates the features object where the results of any feature tests are stored.

Line 3 checks to see if the features cookie exists. If it does, then the value is stored in the features object and JavaScript's JSON.parse() function turns the value into an object.

If the features cookie doesn't exist, line 8 tests the width and then stores the value as a string in a cookie named 'features'.

Finally, you have to tell the server-side code to look for the features cookie and get the width from there if it can:

```
1.    if (isset($_COOKIE['features'])) {
2.        $feature = json_decode($_COOKIE['features']);
3.    }
4.    if ($feature->width) {
5.        $width = $feature->width;
6.    } else {
7.        $width = $device->getCapability('resolution_width');
8.    }
```

Line 1 checks to see if the cookie has been set. If it has, the value is stored in the $feature variable (line 2). Then, on line 4, the $width variable is either passed the value of the feature width test, if it exists, or the WURFL width test.

Now you can tell the code to use the $width value to determine if the device has a small screen:

```
1.    if ($width <= 480) {
2.        $smallScreen = true;
3.    } else {
4.        $smallScreen = false;
5.    }
```

With that code in place, the first time a page loads, the WURFL screen resolution will be used to determine the width. For subsequent loads, assuming JavaScript is supported, the feature test will be used instead.

Making calls

The folks at *Yet Another Sports Site* have decided to start a talk show where their loyal listeners and readers can call in with questions and comments. They want to add an 800 number to the sidebar for people to call.

Being the clever developer that you are, you think, hey, if someone accesses this with a phone, they should be able to make a call just by clicking on that number. (Really, it's true. These mini-computers actually have a phone in them! Who knew?)

Many devices will try to recognize a phone number via pattern recognition, but it's not always perfect. There's actually a special tel: link that many devices support that lets you tell the device that the link is for a phone number:

```
<a href="tel:+18005555555">1-800-555-5555</a>
```

This works great on mobile devices that support the format, but as usual, things aren't that easy. As it turns out, desktop browsers are pretty stupid about these sorts of things. Some make the text look like a link, but the link won't actually *do* anything. Others, like Safari, try to open the link as if it were a URL. Some mobile browsers don't support the format and instead support the older Wireless Telephony Applications Interface (WTAI) format:

```
<a href="wtai://wp/mc;+18005555555">1-800-555-5555</a>
```

Once again, a little server-side detection can help solve the problem.

First, include the talk show blurb, just above the "Related Headlines" section.

```
1.    <aside>
2.        <section class="talkshow">
3.            <h2>We're talking sports!</h2>
4.            <p><a href="tel:+18005555555">1-800-555-5555</a></p>
5.        </section>
6.        <section class="related">
7.            ....
```

Then, add a few styles to make the phone number easy to see and touch. (The call class will be used later on the paragraph if no link is included.)

```
1.    .talkshow a, .call{
2.        font-size: 1.5em; /* 24px/16px */
3.        padding: .416666667em 0 .416666667em 50px; /* 10px/24px */
4.        background: url(../images/phone.png) left center no-repeat;
5.    }
```

Now, you'll need to tap into WURFL to decide whether it should be a link or simply state the number. Two capabilities in particular are useful here: has_cellular_radio and xhtml_make_phone_call_string.

The has_cellular_radio capability reports whether the device has cellular technology. It's important to note that this doesn't guarantee that the device is a phone. A Kindle, for example, has a data-only cellular connection. The has_cellular_radio capability gets close though. The xhtml_make_phone_call_string capability returns the method that can be used for initiating voice calls.

By combining these two properties, you can detect whether or not a device is capable of making a phone call by adding the following lines to the PHP code at the top of the page:

```
1.    if ($device->getCapability('has_cellular_radio') === 'true') {
2.        if ($device->getCapability('xhtml_make_phone_call_string')
          !== 'none') {
3.            $wireless = true;
4.            $method = $device->getCapability('xhtml_make_phone_call_
              string');
5.        } else {
6.            $wireless = false;
7.        }
8.    } else {
9.        $wireless = false;
10.   }
```

The first line checks to see if the device has cellular technology. If it doesn't, $wireless is set to false and nothing further happens. If it is wireless, it next checks to see if the xhtml_make_phone_call_string is none. If it is, there's no reason to include the link to make a call, so you can safely set $wireless to false. Otherwise, $wireless is set to true and the xhtml_make_phone_call_string string is passed to the $method variable so you can use it later in the page.

Next, wrap the link that's currently in your HTML inside a PHP if/else statement, like so:

```
1.    <?php if ($wireless) { ?>
2.        <p><a href="<?php echo $method; ?>+18005555555">1-800-555-5555
          </a></p>
3.    <?php } else { ?>
4.        <p class="call">1-800-555-5555</p>
5.    <?php } ?>
```

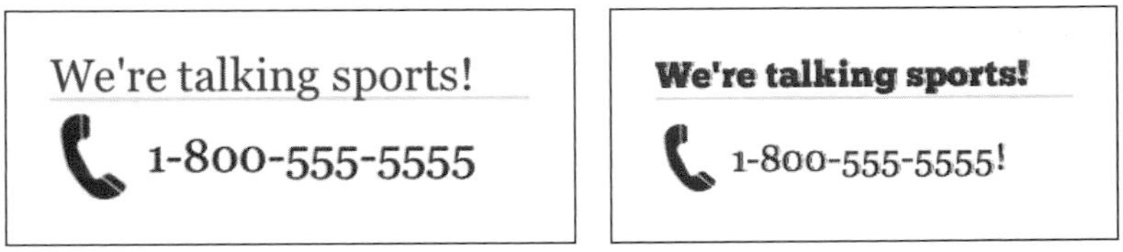

Figure 8.4
On devices that can make phone calls, the phone number will be a link making it easy to place a call (left). On others, such as desktop browsers, the phone number will display as text (right).

If $wireless is true, the link is included. The $method is echoed out to ensure that the proper syntax is being used. If $wireless is false, the number is still displayed but the link is removed so you won't have to worry about any of the odd issues that tend to arise with tel: links in desktop browsers (**Figure 8.4**).

Optimizing for touch

By using carefully applied server-side detection, we've enhanced the experience for even more devices. Let's take it a step further and enhance the experience for touch-enabled devices. In particular, the links in the sidebar for the related headlines are far too small for a touch display. Apple suggests a touch target of at least 44px in height, so those links could use a bit more padding.

While feature detection for touch is quite popular, there's an important caveat: touch feature detects are checking for touch event support, not necessarily whether or not the device has a touch screen. For example, WebOS phones have touch-enabled screens, but they don't support touch events. Using feature detection, the test would fail and those devices would receive none of the special styling for touch devices.

WURFL has a pointing_method capability that will return touchscreen if the device has a touch-enabled display. Unfortunately, there's a caveat here as well: a touch-enabled display does not mean touch events are supported.

The point is that you need to use the right tool for the job. If you want to alter the styles that are served for a touch-enabled device, use server-side detection. If you want to alter the JavaScript, use feature detection.

To get a hook to alter the styles for touch screen devices, just echo the pointing_method capability as a class on the body element:

```
<body id="top" class="<?php echo $device->getCapability
('pointing_method'); ?>">
```

Now, if the device has a touchscreen, the body will have a class of touchscreen.

To make sure the related headline links are touch-screen friendly, they need to be at least 44px tall. Currently, the font size is 16px and the line height is 24px so we need another 20px. We can get this by adding 10px padding to the top and bottom of the links. The target/context = result formula from Chapter 2, "Fluid Layouts," gives us the appropriate em values to use:

```
1.    .touchscreen .related a{
2.        display:block;
3.        padding: .625em 0;
4.    }
```

▶ **Note**
display:block is needed here to make sure the link receives the padding.

Let's apply the same styles to the "More in Football" links.

```
1.    .touchscreen .more-stories a{
2.        display:block;
3.        padding: .625em 0;
4.        border-bottom: 1px dotted #999;
5.    }
```

For the "More Stories" section, the images are loaded in at the 37.5em breakpoint (600px) so at that point the bottom border is unnecessary and looks a little out of place (**Figure 8.5**). You can easily override that property by adding the following styles inside the media query:

```
.touchscreen .more-stories a{
    border-bottom: 0;
}
```

Figure 8.5 On touch screen devices (right) the links are given a little extra padding.

Now if you load your page on a touch-enabled device, you'll see those links have much friendlier touch points. On a device that doesn't have a touch display, the sizes remain as they were.

TOUCH-FRIENDLY JAVASCRIPT

Visually, the site is now ready to go for touch-enabled devices. But there's still one more adjustment to make.

Currently, if a device with a resolution of greater than 480px has a touch-enabled display, the navigation drop-down is triggered by a click event. Touch devices are smart enough to make use of the click event, but not without a penalty of about 300–500ms. That might not sound like much but it can have a considerable impact on how visitors perceive your site.

In multiple studies done since the 1960s, 100ms was found to be the limit at which the user feels that the system is acting instantaneously to their input.[3] Anything over that and it starts to feel disconnected.

If the device supports touch events, it's much better to use those and provide that instantaneous feedback. Remember: You can't rely on WURFL here. The pointing_method capability tells you if the screen is touch-enabled, but not if touch events are supported. You need to use feature detection for that.

Detecting whether or not the device has touch event support is fairly simple:

```
hasTouch = 'ontouchstart' in window || 'createTouch' in document;
```

The above line of code checks for two different touch-event related properties. If either one exists, the device likely has touch support enabled and you can safely use the touch events.

Unfortunately, because touch events allow for complex gestures, there's no simple, native replacement for the onclick event we're currently using. Thankfully, others have already tackled this.

For the *Yet Another Sports Site* page, you can use Alex Gibson's Tap.js plug-in, which is freely available at https://github.com/alexgibson/tap.js on GitHub. To save an extra HTTP request, grab the code from tap.js and place it in the top of yass.js.

Tap.js uses feature detection to determine if touch events are supported. If they are, it will use the touch events; if not, it falls back to the click event.

---

3 "Response Times: The 3 Important Limits" at www.useit.com/papers/responsetime.html

To use it, replace the collapse.onclick function:

```
1.   collapse.onclick = function() {
2.       Utils.classToggle(nav, 'hide');
3.       return false;
4.   };
```

with the following code:

```
1.   myTap = new Tap(collapse);
2.   collapse.addEventListener('tap', function(){
3.       Utils.classToggle(nav, 'hide');
4.       return false;
5.   }, false);
```

Line 1 creates a new Tap object named myTap. Lines 2–5 tell the browser to listen for a tap event on the collapse button. When a tap event fires, the classToggle function (lines 3–4) fires.

Wrapping it up

There's a lot of discussion that pits responsive design and server-side detection against each other, but in reality, neither solution is complete by itself. The best opportunities for supporting many devices come with the careful application of both.

User agent detection is incredibly powerful, but you have to apply it with care. Enhance the experience for visitors, don't exclude them.

Feature detection is a popular choice for developers and can be done on the client side or, with the help of a clever hack, on the server side. It's not a foolproof approach, however. False positives do occur and if you want to run it on the server, an extra page load is required.

WURFL is an incredibly helpful library for performing device detection. With over 500 capabilities at your disposal, it gives you incredible power over the user experience.

Carefully consider the capabilities of devices and how the experience can be tailored for them. By swapping out components and styles, you can easily optimize for touch screen devices, low-end devices, and devices with phone capabilities.

In the next chapter, we'll build on this discussion and start to push beyond responsive layouts to build responsive experiences.

CHAPTER 9
RESPONSIVE EXPERIENCES

Always in motion is the future.
—YODA, STAR WARS EPISODE V:
THE EMPIRE STRIKES BACK

We humans are good at many things, but anticipating the future is not one of them. Our vision of what is to come is clouded by our past experiences. It can be hard to let go of the constraints of mediums we've worked in before when a new medium presents itself.

Evidence of this behavior is easy to find. When we got television, the first shows were radio shows put on a screen. They featured essentially the same content a radio show might—with people reading into microphones from a script. It took awhile before people started creating new kinds of content to watch.

Even our naming conventions tell us just how hard it is for us to separate ourselves from the past. The cinema used to be commonly referred to as the "moving pictures." It was a comfortable, but inaccurate, description.

You see the same thing with the Web. Much of web design was transitioned from print. We even use the terminology, words like "page" and "the fold." But our obsession with layout is causing us to miss out on much of the potential that the Web offers. The Web is an interactive medium. If we're going to capitalize on its potential, we have to look beyond its visual appearance.

In this chapter, we'll consider what it means to build a responsive experience:

- How to think of responsive design as a series of sensors
- How to adjust a site for different network speeds and data limitations
- Why context is important in design
- How device APIs can help you create immersive, personalized experiences

A system of sensors

Ethan Marcotte cited a movement called "responsive architecture" as the inspiration for responsive web design.[1] In responsive architecture, walls can bend and flex as people draw near. That's layout.

---

1   Ethan Marcotte, *Responsive Web Design* (A Book Apart: 2011)

But responsive architecture wouldn't be very exciting if it stopped there. Rooms can also be adjusted for lighting and temperature. Glass can become more opaque to provide privacy. It's not just the layout of the room that responds to its occupants; the environment and experience adapt as well.

If being responsive is truly about embracing the potential of the Web, then the discussion is much broader than layout. Instead, being responsive is about creating a personal, responsive experience that adapts to the needs and environment of the user as well as the capabilities and constraints of the device.

Yes, sites should respond to the screen size of the device, but that may be the least interesting aspect of what we can do.

In a blog post, Mark Boulton talks about responsive design comprising three distinct things:[2]

Sensors

Things that sense the environment (not the weather, but the stuff around it—whatever it is).

Systems

A system that takes the information from the sensors and tells the actuators what to do.

Actuators

The things that actually do the moving. The motors, the CSS, the cables.

If we view responsive design in this way, then it becomes a matter of understanding what "sensors" are available. Suddenly, it's easy to see that the discussion must go beyond adapting to screen size. A truly responsive experience also takes these elements into account:

- Network
- Context
- Capabilities

---

2 "A Responsive Experience" at www.markboulton.co.uk/journal/comments/a-responsive-experience

Device experiences

Another way of looking at the topic of different experiences for different devices was discussed by Luke Wroblewski in his blog post "Device Experiences & Responsive Design."[3]

In Luke's post, he talks about the need to create appropriate interfaces for each classification of devices: to create different device experiences. He mentions three categories in particular to consider:

- Usage/posture
- Input methods
- Output/screen

These three categories line up well with the three (network, context and capabilities) discussed in the following section. However you choose to categorize these different devices, the takeaway is the same: these different devices will have different requirements for layout, interactions and content hierarchy. Media queries, fluid layouts and fluid images are a start, but they're not enough.

Network

The quality and speed of a network can have a tremendous impact on the quality of the user experience. As we discussed in Chapter 4, "Responsive Media," a site's performance seriously affects how the user interacts with it.

Unfortunately, not all networks are created equal. There's a big difference between a high-speed wired connection and a slow cellular network. But the type of network is just the start: network performance can be affected by location, the number of people using the network, the weather, the carrier—there isn't much in the way of consistency.

---

3   Device Experiences & Responsive Design at https://developers.facebook.com/html5/blog/post/6/

There may also be data limitations. As the amount of data traffic increases on mobile networks, more and more carriers are putting data caps on plans and penalizing people who exceed certain limitations.

To be clear, you can't make assumptions about the performance of a network based on the device. It's true that mobile devices are more likely to be connected to a slow connection and that these devices are also often less powerful than their desktop brethren. It is also true, however, that mobile devices could be connected to a high-speed wireless connection while a laptop could be connected to a slow mobile network via tethering. The type of device is not enough.

A site that is truly responsive adjusts itself to accommodate for slower networks or data caps.

What can we do?

Start by always striving for the best performance you can provide, regardless of the connection type or the device in question. Users have spoken: performance is not an option, nor is it a feature; it's a *requirement*.

You can try to further optimize the experience by gathering a little information about the network. Let's look at a couple of ways to do this.

TEST LOAD AN IMAGE

One method to test the speed of the network is to send a request for a small image and measure the time it takes for the request to be completed.

A rudimentary version of this kind of test is shown below:

```
1.   var testImg = document.createElement('img');
2.   testImg.onload = function() {
3.       endTime = ( new Date() ).getTime();
4.       var duration = (endTime - startTime) / 1000;
5.       //if duration is over a certain amount, then load small images
6.       //else load large images
7.   }
8.   startTime = ( new Date() ).getTime();
9.   testImg.src = 'http://mysite.com/myimage.gif';
```

The above snippet is simplified, but you get the point. You create an image using JavaScript and, before setting the src, record the starting time. When the src is set, the image automatically starts downloading.

Once the image is loaded, the `onload` function is called. An end time is recorded and a duration is determined. Based on this duration, you can decide if the network is fast enough to provide heavier resources, such as high-resolution images. This method is not particularly accurate, though it might suffice for a quick Boolean test of "is it high speed or is it not." For many sites, you'll need to use a test that is a bit more reliable.

NETWORK INFORMATION API

Another method of testing connection type is to use the Network Information API, which lets you query the browser to determine the type of connection the device is on. Android currently supports an older, limited version of the specification that only allows you to determine the kind of network in use. Accessing this information is simple:

```
var connection = navigator.connection;
```

The connection object, as implemented by Android since version 2.2, now contains the following properties:

```
1.    {
2.            "type": "1",
3.            "UNKNOWN": "0",
4.            "ETHERNET" : "1",
5.            "WIFI": "2",
7.            "CELL_2G": "3",
8.            "CELL_3G": "4"
9.    }
```

The `type` property tells you which type of connection the device is currently using. In this case, the type is 1 (line 2). Looking at the rest of the properties, you can see that 1 means the device is connected via an Ethernet connection (line 4).

With this information, you could decide to serve up a lower-resolution image when, say, the network is a `CELL_2G` or `CELL_3G` network.

This implementation does leave a lot of room for error. A 3G network could be fast and a Wi-Fi network could be slow. It would be much better to have access to the actual bandwidth.

Thankfully, there's an updated version of the specification that allows for more information. The only currently running browser that implements the new specification is Firefox 12+. However, the nightly builds of WebKit also support the specification, so it's safe to expect that some version of it will make its way into Safari, Chrome, iOS, and Android before too long.

To account for these different levels of support, we have to check a few more prefixed values. Other than that, the use is again straightforward:

```
1.  var connection = navigator.connection || navigator.mozConnection ||
    navigator.webkitConnection;
2.  //check the bandwidth
3.  alert(navigator.connection.bandwidth);
4.  //is it metered
5.  alert(navigator.connection.metered);
```

The new version of the specification removes the type property and adds the much more useful bandwidth and metered properties.

The bandwidth property returns one of three values:

- 0 if the device is offline
- 'Infinity' if the bandwidth is unknown
- An estimation of the current bandwidth in megabytes per seconds (MB/s)

The metered property returns true if the connection is metered (limited by the provider) and false otherwise.

This information is significantly more useful. The bandwidth approximation is a far better judge of network speed than the type. Knowing whether the connection is capped, or metered, can help guide decisions about implementing potentially data-heavy operations.

The new specification also lets you set a function to watch for when the network information changes.

```
1.  function changed(){
2.      alert('The bandwidth is now: ' + navigator.connection.bandwidth);
3.  }
4.  navigator.connection.addEventListener('change', changed, false);
```

In the above code, when the connection information changes (line 4), the changed() function is called, alerting the new bandwidth information.

As support for this API improves, developers will be able to make decisions about loading images appropriately and performing data-heavy operations such as polling only when the user's connection can support it.

Context

● *Context*
The circumstances (physical, environmental, behavioral, social, or otherwise) in which a device is used.

Context, particularly as it relates to mobile users, is a murky topic that has been the subject of much debate. Unfortunately, many people are tempted to define "context" narrowly, using it to refer only to technology.

In no area is that more apparent than with mobile devices. "Mobile" is a terribly loaded word. It brings with it years of historical assumptions that are no longer true. When we think of the context of mobile use, often the first thing that comes to mind is a user on the go. He isn't doing recreational browsing; his search is driven by a specific task. He doesn't have much time to get the information, so he wants it quickly.

For a little while, it seemed that this interpretation of mobile worked. One word encompassed both the context of use and the context of the technology. We assumed the context of the environment and the task based on the device that the user had in hand.

We got away with this because, well, at first mobile web use was painful. Agonizingly, bite-your-fingernails painful. Networks were slow, methods of input were clunky and extremely limited, and devices could only display a monochromatic textual representation of a site.

That's simply no longer the case. The rise of smartphones—in particular the iPhone and Android devices—have shown that mobile web browsing can actually be enjoyable. These devices are capable of delivering a full experience. As such, the context is much more variable.

People use them at home, relaxing in their favorite La-Z-Boy (**Figure 9.1**). They use them while traveling, over slow mobile networks. The context of use is fuzzy.

A quarterly report for Compete in 2010 showed just how much the context of use varied for smartphones:[4]

- 84 percent use their phones at home

- 80 percent use their phones during miscellaneous downtime

- 76 percent use their phones while waiting in line for appointments

---

4 "Smartphone Owners: A Ready and Willing Audience" at http://blog.compete.com/2010/03/12/smartphone-owners-a-ready-and-willing-audience

Figure 9.1 Phones are no longer just being used when "on the go." The "mobile" context isn't as easily defined as it once was.

- 69 percent use their phones while shopping
- 64 percent use their phones at work
- 62 percent use their phones while watching TV
- 47 percent use their phones during their commute to work

Another study, performed by Google in 2011, demonstrated that stats can go too far by revealing that 39 percent of people use their mobile devices in the bathroom![5] This means two things: firstly, 61 percent of people lie and secondly, these devices can, and will, be used everywhere.

The problem with most "contextually" optimized experiences today is that we don't have enough information to accurately infer a user's intent. Context is difficult, intent is ridiculously hard. To accurately infer intent, a number of different criteria could come into play:

---

5 "The Mobile Movement" at www.thinkwithgoogle.com/insights/library/studies/the-mobile-movement/

- Behavioral history
- Location
- Time
- Weather
- Nearby locations
- Proximity of friends, crowds, or enemies
- User movement

Mark Kirby of Ribot wrote, "Mind reading is no way to base fundamental content decisions."[6] He's exactly right. We need to be careful how much we try to tailor the experience based on our current limited knowledge of context. Remember, we're not in control: the user is. As Giles Colborne says, "You can't control the environments where people use your software. You have to design it to fit."[7]

Despite all this murkiness, context is still relevant and can be very powerful if you have reliable information. Consider the classic example of a website for a museum. If you can accurately determine that a person is accessing your site from within the museum, use that information to provide a more optimized experience. Focus more on the information a visitor would need on-site, such as maps and tours, and less on information such as tickets and planning a trip.

As someone who reads quite a bit of science fiction, I find context to be an incredibly important conversation. In those books, a common refrain is a piece of technology that is ubiquitous. It adapts based on the determined context to provide an experience that is truly responsive to the users' needs—no matter the situation. Portable devices, in particular mobile phones, have this kind of potential. If we don't continue to experiment with context, we sell the technology short.

Classifying context

Start by expanding the way you think of context. Rather than defining it as "mobile" (which isn't really helpful to anyone), try thinking of it as a composite picture or in terms of user posture.

---

6 "The Mobile context" at http://mark-kirby.co.uk/2011/the-mobile-context/

7 Giles Colborne, *Simple and Usable Web, Mobile, and Interaction Design* (New Riders, 2010)

COMPOSITE PICTURE

In a 2007 presentation, Nick Finck suggested viewing context as a combination of four different aspects:[8]

- **User**

  Who is your user? What are his needs?

- **Task**

  What task is the user trying to accomplish?

- **Environment**

  What is the user's environment like, in both physical and social terms?

- **Technology**

  What technology does the user have and what is that technology capable of?

Considering context in terms of these four different aspects creates a more accurate *composite* picture of the ways in which your site will be used. It also shows just how complicated context can be: there is no neat "mobile" context just as there is no "desktop" context. The context is not defined by any one criterion, but by a combination of several.

USER POSTURE

Another helpful consideration is to think in terms of posture. For example, to guide decisions about how the user experience should be optimized, Netflix considers whether the user is stationary, on the go, leaning back, or sharing the experience with others.

Again, thinking of the context of use in this way helps you to more clearly design different user experiences. You may not be able to predict a user's posture, but you can certainly keep each possibility in mind when designing.

Observe and research

When talking about context, people tend to focus on all the little bits of data that are floating around and try to determine context programmatically. That's all fine and good: there is value in gathering contextual clues through sensors

---

8 "Contextual Web" at www.slideshare.net/nickf/contextual-web

and the like. But at the end of the day, there's no replacement for observation. As Adam Greenfield stated in his book, *Everyware*:

> If nothing else, it would be wise for us all to remember that, while our information technology may be digital in nature, the human beings interacting with it will always be infuriatingly and delightfully analog. [9]

Research should combine quantitative methods (such as analytics) and qualitative methods (such as interviews) to be as complete and accurate as possible.

Comb through your analytics to see how people are behaving. What pages are they visiting and on which devices? Are some pages noticeably more popular for a specific type of device (say, tablets versus desktop)? Does the number of pages visited and time spent on the site vary dramatically based on the device or location? All of these things are clues to how users are currently interacting with your site.

Conduct interviews with users to determine what their goals are and how that varies depending on the context in which they access your site. Just beware of inaccuracies: when self-reporting, people tend to exaggerate in one way or another.

It's worth observing behavior as well. This can range from giving a user a specific task to achieve and then watching how he goes about accomplishing it to merely going to the nearest store and watching how people interact with their devices.

Capabilities

Different devices have different capabilities. Using progressive enhancement, you can take advantage of advanced features to create a more powerful user experience.

HTML5 input types

Perhaps the simplest optimization is to make use of HTML5 input types where appropriate. Historically, options for input fields have been limited, with the most common type of input field being plain text.

---

9   Adam Greenfield, *Everyware: The Dawning Age of Ubiquitous Computing* (New Riders, 2006)

Storing articles on a device

A great example of taking advantage of the capabilities of a device is the Boston Globe responsive site. Understanding that their readers may want to come back to an article to read later, they implemented a "My Saved" feature. The "My Saved" does pretty much what it sounds like: it allows you to save an article to read later by storing it in your saved items. Now, regardless of device you have access to it.

They then took it one step further. Many devices are able to store content locally, on the device itself. So, using this functionality for devices that support it, they store these saved articles directly on the visitor's device. Once on the device, a visitor can later read that article regardless of whether or not they have an active internet connection.

It's an excellent way to capitalize on the unique functionality provided by modern devices. Simply by applying some careful thought, the experience for users can be dramatically enhanced.

HTML5 came along and added a bunch of new options with additional meaning. Four in particular are useful for mobile devices:

- **email:** for email addresses
- **tel:** for phone numbers
- **number:** for numeric input
- **url:** for urls

What's so great about these input types is that they help the browser understand what type of input the field is expecting and optimize the experience accordingly. Using them is simple, and if a device doesn't support them, it will simply fall back to the plain old text input field.

For example, consider the following field in a form, used to collect an email address:

```
<input type="text" name="email" id="email" />
```

When you view that page on your mobile device, you'll see the typical qwerty layout. Now, switch the type to email.

```
<input type="email" name="email" id="email" />
```

Figure 9.2 When iOS sees the "email" input type, it subtly adjusts the layout of the keyboard (right).

Figure 9.3 HTML5 input types, such as "url" (left) and "tel" (right) provide additional information to the device so that it can optimize the keyboard for users.

Now if you view the form on an iOS device, you'll see that the @ sign has been moved to where the space bar was to make it easier to access (**Figure 9.2**). It's a small, but helpful, optimization.

While Android doesn't do anything for email fields, both Android and iOS optimize the keyboard layout for other field types. See **Figure 9.3** for examples of how the screen becomes more user-friendly depending on the input type.

APIs

Form input fields are just the beginning. One of the most exciting ways to capitalize on the unique characteristics of devices is by making use of emerging device APIs. Devices are being increasingly filled with different sensors that can determine location, orientation, and a host of other conditions in which the devices are being used.

This information provides an incredible opportunity to create a truly personalized and optimized experience for your users. Take advantage of it whenever possible.

Luke Wroblewski

BEYOND LAYOUT

Luke Wroblewski is a digital product leader who has designed or contributed to software used by more than 700 million people worldwide. Luke is also the author of three popular Web design books (Mobile First, Web Form Design, and Site-Seeing: A Visual Approach to Web Usability).

Login screens are broken. Almost 82 percent of people have forgotten the password they used on a website and password recovery is the number one request to intranet help desks.[10] That adds up to a lot of lost business, increased costs, and upset customers.

Yet when considering how an important interaction like login will work across different devices, most teams focus on layout. They make sure the login experience "looks right" on small, medium, and large screen devices (see image of Windows Live Sign in). Though they may look great, these solutions carry over all the existing problems of login screens and leave a lot of opportunities to do better lying on the table.

By stepping back and considering how the unique capabilities of different devices could allow people to log in to a website, we can go well beyond adaptive layout solutions. Consider the ability to send and receive text messages on a mobile device.

The Windows Live Sign in screen on a desktop and mobile web browser.

A log in screen design that uses SMS messaging in the background to authenticate users.

10 Data Monday: Login & Passwords at www.lukew.com/ff/entry.asp?1487

Microsoft's Windows 8 uses personal pictures and touch gestures for login.

Instead of relying on people to type a username/e-mail and password in a set of form fields using a tiny keyboard, we can simply have them press a button that sends an SMS text message in the background to verify their account and let them into the site (image on facing page). No typing required!

Of course, SMS isn't the only capability we can turn to. A device that supports touch could instead require a unique combination of gestures to log people in. Microsoft's Windows 8 system does just that: people can either snap or find a picture of their liking, then set up a "picture password" by making a series of lines, circles, or taps on the image (see image). To log in, they need only recreate these gestures on the image.

At this point, we're well past adaptive layout solutions. In fact, Microsoft's re-thinking of login might even be (gasp) a much more humane form of authentication. After all, what feels more human: drawing some marks on a picture of your family or entering a required length of lowercase and uppercase letters and numbers (but not symbols!) into a small form field that only displays •••••• in return?

Without thinking beyond layout and making use of the new capabilities our devices have, we might be stuck with •••••• for a long time—which seems like a big missed opportunity to do better for our customers and for ourselves.

GEOLOCATION API

Consider a page that helps you locate a store. The most common implementation is to force you to drill down by location. You pick a state or a zip code and the site returns the locations nearest to you. There's a much better way.

The Geolocation API is one of the best supported device APIs around. Using it allows you to create much better defaults for your site's users.

To get familiar with the API, let's whip together a quick demo that will tell you how far away you are from historic Lambeau Field in Green Bay, Wisconsin. The HTML structure is simple:

```
1.    <html>
2.    <head>
3.        <title>Geolocation</title>
4.        <meta name="viewport" content="width=device-width" />
5.    </head>
6.    <body>
7.        <p>Testing the Geolocation API.</p>
8.        <div id="results"></div>
9.    </body>
10.   </html>
```

You'll insert your JavaScript before the closing body tag.

The first thing to do is make sure the device supports the Geolocation API. In a real-world example, you would want to provide a graceful fallback (such as letting the user input a zip code). The proper fallback depends entirely on the specific use case for your site. Since this is just a demo, let's output some generic text if the API is unsupported:

```
1.    <script type="text/javascript">
2.    var results = document.getElementById('results');
3.    //check for support
4.    if (navigator.geolocation) {
5.        // yay! we have geolocation support
6.    } else {
7.        results.innerHTML = 'Bummer—looks like there is no geolocation
      support. Good luck!';
8.    }
9.    </script>
```

Line 1 grabs the element where you can insert the results of your geolocation tests.

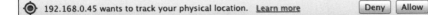

Figure 9.4 When you try to access the Geolocation API, the visitor will see a prompt asking them for permission.

On line 4, the script checks to see if the geolocation property exists. If it does, the devices supports geolocation and you're good to go. Otherwise, you can display your unhelpful generic text.

If geolocation support is available, you can access the user's current location by using the getCurrentPosition method:

```
1.  if (navigator.geolocation) {
2.      navigator.geolocation.getCurrentPosition(function(pos) {
3.          alert(pos.coords.latitude);
4.          alert(pos.coords.longitude);
5.      }, function(error) {
6.          //ruh roh!
7.          alert('Whoops! Error code: ' + error.code);
8.      });
9.  }
```

Lines 2–5 check the user's current position and tell him his current latitude and longitude coordinates (lines 3 and 4).

Lines 5–8 define a function to throw an error in case there's a problem accessing the users current location for any reason.

If you open this page on a browser, you should be greeted with a prompt asking if you're willing to share your location with this site (**Figure 9.4**). This is an important step for security, and you don't have to answer it every single time the page loads.

Let's make this a little more interesting. To determine how far away the user is from Lambeau Field, we'll need the location of the field. We'll also need a function to determine the distance between two pairs of latitude/longitude coordinates.

You can store the coordinates for Lambeau Field in a variable:

```
var lambeau = {
    'lat' : 44.5013805,
    'long' : -88.062325
}
```

The function for calculating distance is a little complicated and full of math. The logic is available under a Creative Commons thanks to Movable Type (www.movable-type.co.uk/scripts/latlong.html):

```
1.   //creative commons distance function
2.   function calculateDistance(lat1, lon1, lat2, lon2) {
3.       var R = 3959; // miles
4.       var dLat = (lat2 - lat1).toRad();
5.       var dLon = (lon2 - lon1).toRad();
6.       var a = Math.sin(dLat / 2) * Math.sin(dLat / 2) +
         Math.cos(lat1.toRad()) * Math.cos(lat2.toRad()) *
         Math.sin(dLon / 2) * Math.sin(dLon / 2);
7.       var c = 2 * Math.atan2(Math.sqrt(a), Math.sqrt(1 - a));
8.       var d = R * c;
9.       return d;
10.  }
11.  Number.prototype.toRad = function() {
12.      return this * Math.PI / 180;
13.  }
```

The end result of the above function is the distance in miles between the two locations passed to the function. I won't get into the details about how it's calculated, because again, it's kind of complicated. If you're interested, it's the "haversine" formula and you can find a decent explanation on Wikipedia.

Armed with the location of Lambeau Field and the haversine formula, finding the distance between the two points can be accomplished in just a few lines of code:

```
1.   //check for support
2.   if (navigator.geolocation) {
3.       navigator.geolocation.getCurrentPosition(function(pos) {
4.           results.innerHTML += "<p>Only " + calculateDistance
             (pos.coords.latitude, pos.coords.longitude, lambeau.lat,
             lambeau.long) + " miles from hallowed Lambeau Field.</p>";
5.       }, function(error) {
6.           alert('Whoops! Error code: ' + error.code);
7.       });
8.   }
```

On line 3, the coordinates for the current position, as well as those for Lambeau Field, are passed to the calculateDistance function. The resulting mileage is then returned and added to the results element (**Figure 9.5**).

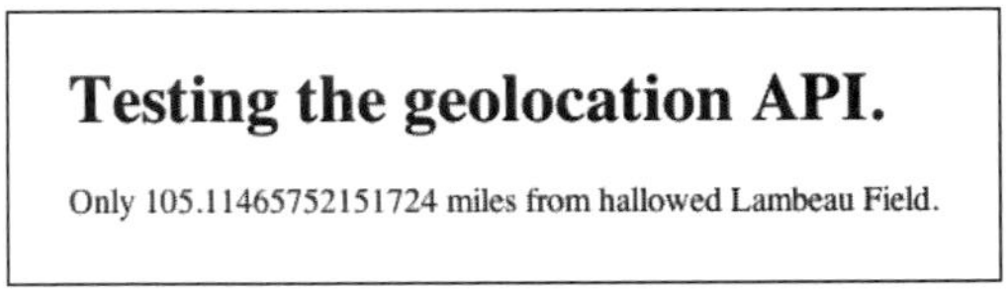

<table>
<tr><td>

Testing the geolocation API.

Only 105.11465752151724 miles from hallowed Lambeau Field.

</td></tr>
</table>

Figure 9.5 With the help of the haversine formula, the Geolocation API lets you show how far the visitor is from their destination.

This is a simple example, but now the user knows just how far he is from the football field.

We can make this example a bit more powerful.

Particularly with a device being used on the go, it would be nice to see in what general direction you need to go to get to your destination. With the latitude and longitude coordinates, it's possible to calculate a bearing. Using that bearing, you can then rotate an arrow so that it points in the direction of the field.

```
<span id="arrow">&#8593;</span>
```

The calculateBearing function again comes from the Movable Type page mentioned previously:

```
1.   function calculateBearing(lat1, lon1, lat2, lon2) {
2.       return Math.atan2(
3.           Math.sin(lon2 - lon1) * Math.cos(lat2),
4.           Math.cos(lat1) * Math.sin(lat2) -
5.           Math.sin(lat1) * Math.cos(lat2) *
6.           Math.cos(lon2 - lon1)
7.       ) * 180 / Math.PI;
8.   }
```

Now, you can update the code to include the bearing check when the current position is calculated:

```
1.   if (navigator.geolocation) {
2.       navigator.geolocation.getCurrentPosition(function(pos) {
3.           results.innerHTML += "<p>Only " + calculateDistance
             (pos.coords.latitude, pos.coords.longitude, lambeau.lat,
             lambeau.long) + " miles from hallowed Lambeau Field.</p>";
4.           var bearing = calculateBearing(pos.coords.latitude,
             pos.coords.longitude, lambeau.lat, lambeau.long);
5.           var arrow = document.getElementById('arrow');
6.           arrow.style.transform = 'rotateZ(' + bearing + 'deg)';
7.           arrow.style.msTransform = 'rotateZ(' + bearing + 'deg)';
8.           arrow.style.mozTransform = 'rotateZ(' + bearing + 'deg)';
9.           arrow.style.webkitTransform = 'rotateZ(' + bearing + 'deg)';
```

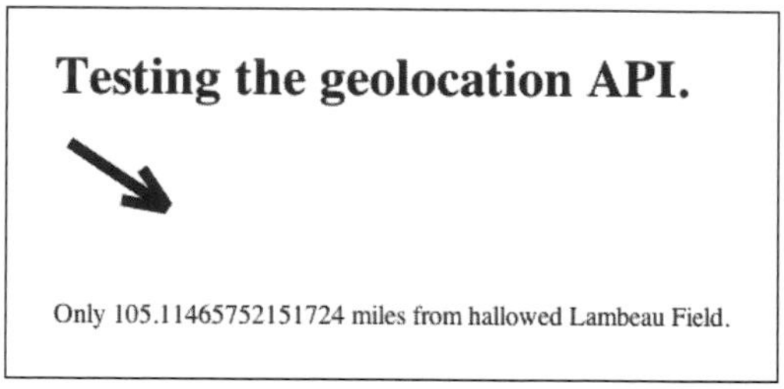

Figure 9.6 With a little extra consideration and effort, the user sees an arrow pointing in the direction they need to head.

Testing the geolocation API.

Only 105.11465752151724 miles from hallowed Lambeau Field.

```
10.        }, function(error) {
11.            //ruh roh!
12.            alert('Whoops! Error code: ' + error.code);
13.        });
14.    }
```

Everything is the same as before, but with a few additions. Line 4 now calculates the bearing in degrees. Line 5 grabs the arrow and lines 6–10 rotate the arrow using the CSS3 rotateZ transform. Now if you load the site on a browser that supports geolocation, you'll see the arrow pointing in the direction of Lambeau Field (**Figure 9.6**).

On a desktop computer, you might question the value of having an arrow in place, and that's fair. It's unlikely that anyone is going to be walking around with a laptop trying to pinpoint a nearby location.

But on a device such as a smartphone or tablet, the arrow could be incredibly useful. You could query the user's location every few seconds and update the direction the arrow points (as well as the distance), ultimately guiding the user right to the destination. It's a simple, but effective, enhancement of the user experience.

For fun, let's look at some of the more cutting-edge uses of device APIs to get a glimpse of their potential.

MEDIA CAPTURE API

Another API, the Media Capture API, provides programmatic access to the device's camera and microphone through the getUserMedia method. This is actually already supported by Opera Mobile as well as in special builds of Chrome Canary. Mozilla also hopes to have the Media Capture API fully supported by Firefox 17. As with many of the device APIs, it's amazing what you can accomplish with a little code.

Building a compass

Many web-enabled devices are now able to report their orientation thanks to a built-in accelerometer. Many phones, for example, use this information to rotate the display when the device is rotated. When the device orientation changes, the deviceorientation event fires.

The latest builds of WebKit, implemented in iOS5, added two new, experimental properties to the event: webkitCompassHeading and webkitCompassAccuracy. webkitCompassHeading returns, in degrees, the direction relative to magnetic north. For example, true north is 0 degrees and east is 90 degrees. webkitCompassAccuracy provides information about the accuracy of the heading. If the value of webkitCompassAccuracy is 5, for example, the heading could be off by plus or minus 5 degrees.

Using this API, James Pearce, Head of Mobile Developer Relations at Facebook, built a compass entirely in HTML, CSS, and JavaScript. If you have an iPhone, head over to http://jamesgpearce.github.com/compios5 and check out the demo. Move your phone around, and the compass needle adjusts to point in the correct direction.

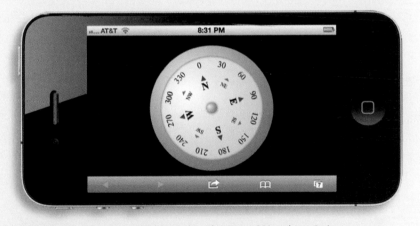

A fully functional compass built entirely with HTML, CSS and JavaScript.

Again, for demonstration purposes, let's keep the HTML simple.

```
1.    <html>
2.    <head>
3.        <meta name="viewport" content="width=device-width" />
4.        <style type="text/css">
5.            #canvas{
6.                background: #eee;
7.                border: 1px solid #333;
8.            }
9.        </style>
10.   </head>
11.   <body>
12.       <video id="myVid" width="300" height="375" autoplay></video>
13.       <input id="camera" type="button" disabled="true"
          value="Take Photo"></input>
14.       <canvas id="still" width="300" height="375"></canvas>
15.   </body>
16.   </html>
```

There's not much going on here, but if you aren't that familiar with HTML5 yet, there might be a few foreign elements in use.

The <video> element lets you embed videos without the use of Flash. Typically, there's a source applied, but in the example above, you'll be dynamically setting it to use the camera so for now an empty element works fine.

The <canvas> element lets you draw graphics on it through the use of JavaScript. You can render text, photos, animations, graphs—you name it. For this example, the canvas will display a photo once it's been taken.

Now you need only a few lines of JavaScript to make a camera. Add the following to the page, just after the closing body tag:

```
1.    <script>
2.        navigator.getUserMedia({video: true}, function(stream) {
3.            var video = document.getElementById("video");
4.            var canvas = document.getElementById("still");
5.            var button = document.getElementById("camera");
6.            video.src = stream;
```

```
7.                  button.disabled = false;
8.                  button.onclick = function() {
9.                      canvas.getContext("2d").drawImage(video, 0, 0);
10.                 };
11.         }, function(err) { alert("there was an error " + err)});
12.     </script>
```

Line 2 calls the getUserMedia method. The method accepts three arguments. The first argument tells the device what media you want access to. The argument must be passed as a JavaScript object. Here, we're passing {video: true} to tell the device we need access only to the video. If you wanted access to both video and audio, you would pass {audio: true, video: true}.

When you try to access the camera, the user is prompted to allow or deny access, similar to how they were prompted for the Geolocation API. The second argument is the function to run if you're granted access. If the success callback is called, the stream is passed back for use. The third argument is the function to run if you're not granted access. This third argument is optional.

Lines 3–5 grab the video, the button we'll use to take the photo, and the canvas where the photo will be displayed.

Line 6 sets the src property of the video to equal the stream the device has passed back to the code. Line 7 enables the button. You don't have to have it disabled by default, but it's a good idea to do so. Given the security concerns a user may have with granting a site camera access, keeping the button disabled by default is a nice visual reassurance.

Finally, the function on lines 8–10 watch for the button to be clicked. When it is, it draws the image on the canvas using the canvas drawImage method. The first parameter (video in the example above) that is passed to the drawImage method refers to the picture to draw on the canvas.

The next two parameters are the x, y coordinates of the position where the image should be placed. In the example above, passing "0, 0" tells the browser to display the image in the top left corner of the canvas.

Figure 9.7 When the page loads in Opera Mobile, you'll see real-time video from the camera of your device (left). When you click Take Picture a still shot of the video will appear below the button (right).

When you load the page in Opera Mobile (which you should be able to install on any Android device), you'll be prompted to allow the site access to the camera. If you accept, you'll see the real-time video feed from your camera showing up on the screen. When you click Take Picture, the photo appears as a still shot on the canvas below the button (**Figure 9.7**).

In addition to the initial "wow" factor, this could be incredibly useful. Imagine any site that has user profiles. You could let the user snap a photo using his device and immediately set it as his avatar.

MORE APIS ON THE HORIZON

As more and more device APIs become available, developers will be able to create websites and applications that rival the technology in today's science fiction stories—responsive technology that until now we've only dreamed of.

It's my hope that using these APIs will become second nature, not an afterthought. The ability to interact with a device on this level is something we've never before had the ability to do. We can't just stop at layout or else we sell the potential of this unique medium short.

The Geolocation and Media Capture APIs are just the start. Here are a few other APIs that are in development:

Table 9.1 Device APIs

API	PURPOSE
Contacts API	Lets you read, add, and edit contacts stored on the device
Messaging API	Lets you send, receive, and manage SMS messages
Calendar API	Lets you read, add, and edit the device calendar
Battery Status API	Indicates the battery charge level and whether or not the device is plugged in
Vibration API	Controls device vibration for tactile feedback
Sensor API	Lets you access sensors such as accelerometer, ambient light, magnetic field, and proximity
HTML Media Capture	Lets you interact with the device's camera/microphone through HTML forms
Web Intents	Allows integration between web applications through client-side service discovery

Wrapping it up

It's difficult to transition to a new medium. We tend to stick with what is familiar and comfortable, but over time we slowly shed the restraints of past mediums and embrace the new one.

The Web is an interactive medium, not just a series of documents. We need to move past our obsession with layout and start building responsive experiences. Thinking of responsive design as a series of sensors can help to expand the way we build for the Web.

Networks vary dramatically and can significantly alter the user experience. A truly responsive experience takes this into consideration and adjusts the experience accordingly. Our tools are limited at the moment, but the Network Information API offers tremendous opportunity.

The context of use also varies. We need to be careful not to use misleading references such as "mobile." Context is a complex thing made up of the user, the task, the technology, and the environment. It's far more complex than any one word implies. Consider these different aspects when designing your sites.

Different devices have different capabilities. These can range from simple things such as using different field types in forms, to more complex examples involving device APIs. Some of these APIs, such as geolocation, can be used today to make experiences more personalized. As more and more APIs are implemented, we'll be able to create the kind of responsive experiences we've only dreamed of.

AFTERWORD
LOOKING FORWARD

It's clear that technology is not the limiting factor, it's just our desire to imagine a different future. —SCOTT JENSON

The 2013 Ford Fusion features an 8-inch touch display and the company's SYNC® technology.

The challenge of working in a medium as dynamic as the Web is its incredible diversity and its rapid evolution. That's also the exciting part.

Responsive design is just a start. It's a step toward fulfilling the Web's potential, but only a step. Thinking about the Web in terms of its present diversity will help you prepare for the diversity to come.

In this book, we focused mainly on the desktop, mobile devices, and tablets. There's a flood coming soon, though. Smart TVs are on the horizon, bringing with them a whole set of new concerns. Many of them share the same resolution as the monitors you use at work. Adjusting layout will not be enough to cater to both the user who's two feet away from his screen and the user sitting on a couch 12 feet away.

Connected cars are also rapidly increasing in popularity. Mercedes-Benz, Ford, and Audi are already pushing cars with Internet connections. You can question the safety of having applications built into a car's dashboard, but they're on their way regardless.

Cars and TVs are just the start. Connected devices such as vacuum cleaners, windowpanes, and yes, refrigerators are all being worked on.

One Swedish TV company lets you sync your phone to your browser, allowing you to use it as a remote control for the video playing on your desktop.

In the introduction, I mentioned Scott Jenson's article about the upcoming zombie apocalypse of devices.[1] As technology becomes more affordable, the number of web-enabled devices is rapidly increasing. The Web is not a platform constrained by a single device.

People are already making rudimentary use of content shifting. Services like Instapaper and Readability let you find something on your desktop, save it, and then read it later on your phone or tablet.

In October 2011, the W3C announced it would be working on a specification for discovering nearby devices.[2] This opens the potential for content shifting to be taken to an entirely different level. One use case could be to use a phone to discover content and then control the playback of that content on a nearby TV.

1 "The Coming Zombie Apocalypse" at http://designmind.frogdesign.com/blog/the-coming-zombie-apocalypse-small-cheap-devices-will-disrupt-our-old-school-ux-assumptions.htm

2 "Web applications: discovering and binding to services" at www.w3.org/QA/2011/10/web_applications_discovering_a.html

The jsdo.it Controller allows you to control a spaceship in your desktop browser from your phone.

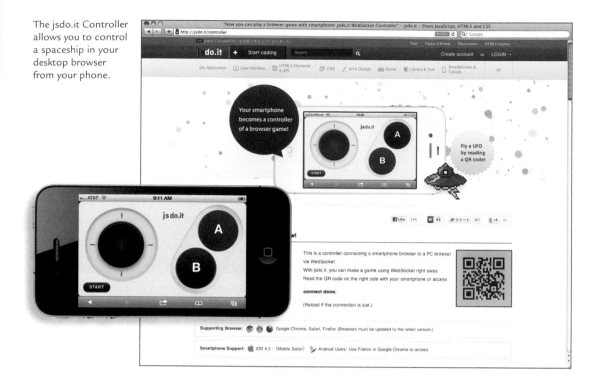

Technologies like WebSockets—which is already supported in Internet Explorer 10, Chrome 17+, and Firefox 11+, and partially supported in Safari, Opera, iOS, and Opera Mobile—allow you to open a session between a browser and server for interacting between the two. This opens the door for multi-user interaction, as well as multi-device interaction.

The space between devices is rapidly diminishing, and with it, so should our singular focus on layout. As more devices become connected, the interactive nature of the Web becomes much harder to ignore. We must start looking beyond the device in hand and instead consider the constellation of experiences.

The Web is an incredibly powerful medium, one that can respond to any number of sensors and go beyond the physical walls of a device. Let's challenge ourselves not to settle for merely responding to layout.

Photo Credits

EXAMPLE SITE
Photo by Jayel Aheram at www.flickr.com/photos/aheram/440478825
Photo by Jack Rydquist at www.flickr.com/photos/chaos123115/2994577362
Photo by Ed Yourdon at www.flickr.com/photos/yourdon/3890007962
Photo by Trevor Manternach at www.flickr.com/photos/trvr3307/2352092039

CHAPTER 1
Page 11: Photo by Chris Harrison, Carnegie Mellon University. Used by permission.
Page 16: Photo from *Adaptive Web Design: Crafting Rich Experiences with Progressive Enhancement* by Aaron Gustafson (Easy Readers, 2011). Photo used by permission.

CHAPTER 4
Page 109: Photo by John Martinez Pavliga at www.flickr.com/photos/virtualsugar/2972610947
Page 117: Copyright The Royal Observatory, Greenwich

CHAPTER 5
Page 133: Photo by Luke Wroblewski at www.flickr.com/photos/lukew/7382743430/in/set-72157630151452558. Used by permission.
Page 149: Photo by Jeremy Vandel at www.flickr.com/photos/jeremy_vandel/4279024627

CHAPTER 6
Page 167: Photo by Jeremy Keith at www.flickr.com/photos/adactio/2888167827
Page 172: Photo by David Fulmer at www.flickr.com/photos/daveynin/6027218091

CHAPTER 9
Page 235: Photo by Eelke Dekker at www.flickr.com/photos/eelkedekker/5339017351

Index

About the Author

Tim Kadlec is a web developer working in northern Wisconsin. His diverse background working with small companies, large publishers, and industrial corporations has allowed him to see how the careful application of web technologies can impact businesses of all sizes.

Tim is the co-founder of Breaking Development, one of the first conferences dedicated to web design and development for mobile devices. He is very passionate about the Web and can frequently be found speaking about what he's learned at a variety of web conferences.

He was a contributing author to *Web Performance Daybook Volume 2* and blogs at http://timkadlec.com. He can also be found sharing his thoughts in a briefer format on Twitter at @tkadlec.

Tim lives in the small town of Three Lakes, Wisconsin, with his wife and their three daughters.

About the Technical Editor

In 2000, Jason Grigsby got his first mobile phone. He became obsessed with how the world could be a better place if everyone had access to the world's information in their pockets. Those mobile dreams hit the hard wall of reality—WAP was crap. So Jason went to work on the Web until 2007, when the iPhone made it clear the time was right. He joined forces with the three smartest people he knew and started Cloud Four.

Since cofounding Cloud Four, he has had the good fortune to work on many fantastic projects, including the Obama '08 iPhone app. He is founder and president of Mobile Portland, a local nonprofit dedicated to promoting the mobile community in Portland, Oregon.

Jason is co-author of *Head First Mobile Web* and is a sought-after speaker and consultant on mobile. If anything, he is more mobile obsessed now than he was in 2000. You can find him blogging at http://cloudfour.com; on his personal site, http://userfirstweb.com; and on Twitter as @grigs.